Praise for *Voices of the Faithful*:

"With sophisticated sociological research and scholarly theological interpretation, William D'Antonio and Anthony Pogorelc have brought together the beginnings of the story of the Voice of the Faithful. It will leave no doubt that this is a movement of the Holy Spirit for the reform of the U.S. Catholic community. Like VOTF itself, *Voices of the Faithful* does a great service to the Church, helping it to move beyond crisis to renewal."

— **Dr. Thomas H. Groome,** Director of Boston College's
Institute of Religious Education and Pastoral Ministry,
author, *What Makes Us Catholic*

"D'Antonio and Pogorelc have given us a new understanding of the spiritual energies active in American Catholicism today. They analyze Voice of the Faithful, the fastest-growing of the new movements, in a way which shows us why it arose, who supports it, and what its future prospects are. Voice of the Faithful has its supporters and its detractors. The book combines new research with historical and ecclesiological reflections by six commentators, thus producing the best diagnosis of present-day American Catholic culture available today."

— **Dean Hoge,** author of
The First Five Years of Priesthood

"Voice of the Faithful is the most important popular initiative to emerge from the sexual abuse crisis in the American Catholic Church. Since the storm broke in 2002, reforms of the church's personnel practices have been minimal but Bishops act as if the crisis has been resolved. Priests and religious orders have lost numbers and power, large new cadres of deacons, lay educators, and pastoral ministers are unorganized, older reform advocates have been marginalized, and small groups of conservative Catholics exercise disproportionate influence in Rome and the United States. Almost alone for five years VOTF has stood against the tide. Its members have made the case for justice for survivors of sexual abuse by priests and for reasonable reforms that will ensure truthfulness and accountability in ecclesiastical affairs. Now we have a serious sociological study of this remarkable movement, together with a set of thoughtful analytical essays on the problems confronting VOTF and other Catholic reformers. The data is fascinating and the arguments compelling. Catholics and their church are very important in American life, so VOTF is important. And so is this excellent book."

— **David O'Brien,** Loyola Professor of
Roman Catholic Studies, College of the Holy Cross

"No one interested in the future of the American Catholic Church can afford to miss this admirable book. Here one finds excellent research on a social movement in progress along with astute analysis of what it all means in historical context. The results of the study are commented upon by six noted scholars and theologians as well as by the authors. I found the work instructive, insightful and fascinating."

— **Sidney Callahan,** author of *Created for Joy*

"*Voices of the Faithful* details one of the most interesting new social movements in the Catholic Church in the United States. The book is a valuable resource for understanding the movement, its membership, and its moment in history."

— **Mary L. Gautier,** Senior Research Associate, Center for
Applied Research in the Apostolate, Georgetown University

"The editors' deep grasp of Catholic doctrine and history makes *Voices of the Faithful* a fascinating, stimulating, and provocative book. With new insights, and a great flair for narrative, here is the compelling story of those courageous Catholics who with love in their hearts demanded justice for sexual abuse and launched a reform movement. Most importantly *Voices of the Faithful* sketches a road map for the future which includes addressing questions of faith and morals as well as collaboration with other institutional players. *Voices of the Faithful* is a must read for those who seek to save the Catholic Church." — **Kathleen Kennedy Townsend,** former Lieutenant Governor of Maryland

VOICES
OF THE
FAITHFUL

The Boston College Church in the 21st Century Series

Patricia De Leeuw and James F. Keenan, S.J.,
General Editors

Titles in this series include:

The Church in the 21st Century Center at Boston College seeks to be a catalyst and resource for the renewal of the Catholic Church in the United States by engaging critical issues facing the Catholic community. Drawing from both the Boston College community and others, its activities currently are focused on four challenges: handing on and sharing the Catholic faith, especially with younger Catholics; fostering relationships built on mutual trust and support among lay men and women, vowed religious, deacons, priests, and bishops; developing an approach to sexuality mindful of human experience and reflective of Catholic tradition; and advancing contemporary reflection on the Catholic intellectual tradition.

VOICES OF THE FAITHFUL

*Loyal Catholics
Striving for Change*

WILLIAM D'ANTONIO
AND
ANTHONY POGORELC

WITH ESSAYS BY

NANCY T. AMMERMAN
MICHELE DILLON
MARY E. HINES
ROBERT P. IMPELLI
WILLIAM A GAMSON
JOHN D. MCCARTHY

A Herder & Herder Book
The Crossroad Publishing Company
New York

The Crossroad Publishing Company
16 Penn Plaza – 481 Eighth Avenue, Suite 1550
New York, NY 10001

Printed in the United States of America

The text of this book is set in 11/14.5 Sabon.

Cataloging-in-Publication Data is available from the Library of Congress.

ISBN-13: 978-0-8245-2460-9 (alk. paper)
ISBN-10: 0-8245-2460-8 (alk. paper)

1   2   3   4   5   6   7   8   9   10   12   11   10   09   08   07

Contents

List of Tables

Foreword

There are three broad ways to begin thinking about social change—fatalism, reform, or revolution. The first is a do-nothing, wait-and-see approach. The second presupposes the possibility, and then focuses on the reality of new ways of doing things as well as on steps that will lead to significant change. The third is simply an overthrow or demolition approach to the problem.

Voice of the Faithful (VOTF) is a reform movement. This book is not only a sociological study of the origins of VOTF viewed as an incipient social movement in the church in response to the clerical sex-abuse scandal that became public in 2002, but it also offers, through reflective chapters written by six scholar-commentators on the sociological data, an analytical critique of the early stages of this movement.

There is a well-known American penchant to substitute blame for analysis. Blame is employed sparingly in the pages that follow. Analysis is offered in a way that will be valuable to VOTF chapters around the country as they face up to the question of, once organized, what will members do?

As one of the many active VOTF members interviewed by the authors said, "I think many of the local chapters have had a hard time figuring out their function. Once they get together, express discontent, make ties with the survivors groups, and try to help, what else do you do? This is their question, and they haven't had good guidance on that."

Some of the necessary guidance can be found in this book.

The demographic data presented here are instructive—the movement is 60 percent female; it lacks youth and Hispanic participation, and it is well above the national Catholic average in Mass attendance and educational attainment. These facts can be ignored by friends of the movement only at the risk of jeopardizing its future. Enemies of the movement would do well to heed the data if they are serious about meeting the pastoral needs of Catholics in all parts of the United States.

Faithful Catholic people want to have a voice in the selection of their parish priests and local bishops; they want a voice in deciding how parish and diocesan income is spent.

In chapter 9, William A. Gamson, one of the scholar-commentators, draws on a 1970 book by economist Alfred Hirschman titled *Exit, Voice, and Loyalty* (Harvard University Press). As is so often the case, a study of the threat of exit over against the pull of loyalty to an organization in one area — Hirschman studied business firms, voluntary associations, and political organizations — is applicable to another; in this case, the Catholic Church. Note the fulcrum position of "voice" in that triad of "exit, voice, and loyalty."

"Hirschman is looking at the interplay between two options that members have when an organization to which they belong is experiencing difficulty," writes Gamson. "They can leave and put their energy into some other organization or into other pursuits; or they can try to change the organization — that is what Hirschman means by exercising voice."

And that is why voice — well informed, incisive, articulate, respectful, and, it must be said, appropriately modulated — is so critically important to whatever VOTF proposes to do in the years ahead.

In acknowledging the welcome contribution William D'Antonio and Anthony Pogorelc have made in producing this book, I want to note that structural change never happens suddenly, but structural adjustments are happening all the time. Enlightened criticism from VOTF will bring about structural adjustments, which eventually will lead to noticeable change. For this to happen, however, the movement needs staying power.

Former Health, Education, and Welfare Secretary John Gardner's wise words are worth recalling here. He spoke at Cornell toward the end of the troubled decade of the 1960s and said that when historians look back at that time they will see it as a period when institutions of higher education "were caught in a savage crossfire between unloving critics and uncritical lovers." The uncritical lovers wanted "to smother their institutions in the embrace of death, loving their rigidities more than their promise, shielding them from life-giving criticism." The unloving critics wanted to tear the institutions apart; they were "skilled in demolition but untutored in the arts by which human institutions are nurtured and strengthened and made to flourish."

Criticism without cool reason will not help the church today. The tendency to substitute blame for analysis must be resisted. At the same time those in authority must resist a tendency to identify influence with control. They must also be willing to listen, ease up on control, and, in an atmosphere of integrity, transparency, and collegiality, work with other faithful Catholics to heal a church that was wounded in 2002 by the events that launched the movement that is analyzed in the pages that follow.

William J. Byron, S.J.

Acknowledgments

We owe many people and organizations our deepest gratitude for making this study possible. We are most indebted to the Louisville Institute and its executive director, Dr. James W. Lewis, for their faith in our ability to carry this study to a successful conclusion. Without their grant this study would not have been possible. We also received grants from the Religious Research Association and from the Life Cycle Institute at Catholic University, which enabled us to hire graduate and undergraduate assistants and cover other costs.

Several colleagues encouraged us to pursue this study of VOTF; they include an early supporter of the project, Dr. Michele Dillon of the University of New Hampshire, as well as Dr. James Davidson of Purdue University, Dr. Dean Hoge, Dr. James Youniss, Dr. Stephen Schneck, and all our colleagues at the Life Cycle Institute who provided ongoing support and critical commentary on our work.

Crucial to our progress was the advisory committee, which provided encouragement as well as helpful commentary on our research instruments and our findings. Perhaps most importantly they saw the value of holding a symposium in Boston to present our findings, and made key suggestions regarding the composition of a panel that would represent diverse perspectives and effectively analyze our findings. We are deeply grateful to them for their generous commitment of time and talent and extend a warm and heartfelt thanks to The Most Reverend William B. Friend, D.D., Shreveport, Louisiana; Reverend Ted Keating, S.M., Washington, DC; Reverend James Coriden, Washington, DC; Dr. Ruth Wallace, Washington, DC; Dr. Kathleen Maas Weigert, Washington, DC; Dr. Dean Hoge, Washington, DC; Reverend Raymond B. Kemp, Washington, DC; Reverend William

Byron, S.J., Baltimore, Maryland; Mr. Hector Rodriguez, Columbia, Maryland.

While the grant from the Louisville Institute laid the financial foundations for this study, it was the willingness of the founders and early leaders of Voice of the Faithful to be studied that enabled us to realize our research hopes. It is not possible to list all the people we talked to in the greater Boston, Connecticut, New York, and Washington, DC, areas. However, we hope you will read our account with interest, and find that we have done an adequate job of telling your story. Still, it is important for us to mention several people who helped make this project successful. We begin with Dr. James Post, president of VOTF during the time of our study; Steve Krueger, executive director whose help was invaluable as we conducted our interviews and the national survey; Suzanne Morse, director of communications, who assisted us in posting our questionnaire online for the national survey; Rose Walsh, office manager during 2003 and 2004; Bill and Cathy Fallon, who made available to us their collection of valuable news clippings documenting the period of the scandal, and Paul Baier, who first put VOTF on the Web, and encouragingly responded to our earliest inquiries about VOTF. To these and to all the other VOTF founders and leaders who so generously welcomed us and gave of their time, we say, thank you. We also thank those outside of VOTF in the academic and Catholic communities who also shared their insights on the movement and contributed to giving us an important contextual perspective. In a special way we remember the late Fr. Robert Bulloch, first president of the Boston Priests' Forum, who graciously received and shared his thoughts with us.

As we were completing our data analysis and thinking about how to reach a broad audience in the Boston area with the results of our study, our advisory committee urged us to approach the Church in the 21st Century Center at Boston College (C 21). Their projects had attracted a wide audience and were addressing crucial issues for the Catholic Church. Rev. Joseph Appleyard, S.J., vice president for university mission and ministry, one of several Boston College faculty we had interviewed, expressed interest in our project, and was quick to encourage us to make a formal proposal to the C 21 board for a symposium. It received their unanimous support and was to be held on Sunday, October 23, 2005, with Fr. Appleyard as moderator. Unfortunately an accident prevented him from participating. We thank him for his support, as well as Dr. Tim Muldoon, director of the C 21 Center, who stood in his place; Dr. Dawn Overstreet; and the C 21 staff for attending to the preparations, and creating a warm and inviting atmosphere for the symposium.

To the six symposium participants, Dr. Nancy Ammerman, Dr. Michele Dillon, Dr. Mary Hines, Rev. Dr. Robert Imbelli, Dr. William Gamson, and Dr. John McCarthy, we offer special thanks for their outstanding papers, which greatly enhanced this study.

Fr. John Ardis, C.S.P., director of the Paulist Center, and his confreres hosted us during our visits to Boston, and we thank them for their gracious hospitality, for their thoughtful reflections, and for sharing their wonderful view of Boston Commons.

Thanks to Ann Kasprzyk and Mary Anne Eley of the Life Cycle Institute who provided technical and moral support throughout this project, producing written materials, organizing luncheon meetings, facilitating communication, and taking care of the thousands of little things that a good staff does that all too often go unnoticed. Dr. J. C. Smith, a visiting scholar at LCI during 2004–5, helped us solve some difficult coding problems.

An array of students worked on various phases of the project, transcribing interviews, entering data, and developing a codebook to analyze qualitative data. Our thanks go to Florence Cole, Kara Erickson, Mallori Merandino, John Rudolf, Sarina Ward, Jackie Wenger, and Lele Yang. We were fortunate to have Azeb Berhane, with her newly minted M.A. in sociology, to help us through the last year of the project. Her ability to handle complex statistical problems, organize qualitative data, and help us disseminate the information was crucial to our readiness for the symposium.

We thank Dr. Dean Hoge, Fr. Ray Kemp, Fr. Ted Keating, and Robert Stewart for their critical readings of the text and suggestions for revision. In the last analysis, we are responsible for what we wrote.

We thank Dr. Patricia Deleeuw and Rev. James F. Keenan, S.J., for accepting our book for inclusion in the C 21 Book Series, published by the Crossroad Publishing Co. We appreciate the assistance of John Jones, the editor, for his strong support of and early commitment to our manuscript; and we add our thanks to John Eagleson (edisetter), Piper Wallace (cover designer), and Nancy Neal (editorial assistant) for their technical help in transforming the manuscript into this book.

Rev. William Byron, S.J., was kind enough to write the foreword for the book, and we deeply appreciate his support throughout the three years of its gestation. His thoughtful words are a reflection not only of his support for us but of his contribution to the growth of laity in the church.

Finally, thanks to Lorraine D'Antonio, who sustained us with delicious meals and listened to our travails as she wondered if we would ever get a final draft to the publisher. We leave the evaluation of our efforts to you the reader.

William V. D'Antonio
and Anthony J. Pogorelc

April 9, 2007

Introduction

Voice of the Faithful
A Sociological Study

How the Authors Became Involved

In January 2002, the Catholic Church in Boston was in a state of crisis. The *Boston Globe* published a series of articles that detailed the abuse of minors by priests and its systematic cover-up by the bishops of Boston. The outrage this scandal provoked in members of the Catholic community led to the emergence of a social movement of Catholics in Boston: Voice of the Faithful (VOTF). Eventually this movement spread throughout the United States and even to other countries.

The news about the Boston scandal reached Washington, DC, through newspapers, such as the *Washington Post* and the *National Catholic Reporter,* as well as by network television and radio. The Internet also became an important resource, quickly disseminating news of these horrendous events and facilitating communications and networking among concerned parties as they processed their reactions. VOTF founders like Paul Baier helped the fledgling group to raise consciousness about the scandal and to bring into the public sphere an almost daily account of the group's activities and efforts to engage Cardinal Law and other church officials. As Baier said: "We used many Internet tools (emails, message boards, etc.) which have redefined how nonprofits deliver their message and organize." The Internet played a key role in the rapid establishment of VOTF and its growth beyond Boston.

This plethora of information led me (Bill D'Antonio) to become more and more interested in this new movement. For years I had been

1

a student of American Catholicism. With fellow sociologists I had published three books on the American Catholic people, the latest of which had just been published in 2001: *American Catholics: Gender, Generation, and Commitment.* Between February and May of 2002, I appeared on CNN several times and was quoted extensively in the *Boston Globe,* the *New York Times, USA Today,* and a host of other newspapers, as the media tried to relate our research on American Catholics to the scandal and cover-up.

From the Internet I learned about a convention that VOTF was sponsoring on July 20, 2002, at the Hines Civic Auditorium in downtown Boston. As I spotted the names of many well-known Catholics on the program, I decided that I wanted to be there to hear what they had to say. I registered online and flew to Boston early on the morning of July 20, arriving at Hines just after the meeting got under way. I was indeed impressed to find that the predicted four thousand people were there. I had to struggle to find a seat, and as I looked around at the crowd I became immediately aware that its hue from the top was gray and silver. A much younger speaker, Professor Tom Beaudoin of Boston College, made a direct reference to this fact. He asked the gathering to raise their hands in turn if they were pre-Vatican II (in their sixties or older), Vatican II (ages forty-one to sixty-one), or post-Vatican II (ages eighteen to forty). Less than a fifth identified themselves as members of the youngest generation, those born after Vatican II.

I saw a few familiar faces there and chatted with many attendees; but mostly, I heard person after person speak up about the need of the laity to realize their responsibility to become active participants in a movement to "Keep the Faith, and Change the Church."

I returned to Washington filled with admiration for the people who had organized the gathering, which was clearly no small task, one requiring significant organizational skills. The convention had a real dynamic to it; the movement to bring about important changes in the church seemed very much alive! Supporters inclined to view the world from a theological perspective would see this meeting of concerned Catholics in Boston as a gathering inspired by the Holy Spirit, for all were speaking with a unified voice in calling for action. There seemed reason to believe that VOTF was about to take off. For several days following, I found myself talking about VOTF, who said what, and who electrified the audience. I pondered what the movement's future might be.

By August of 2002, however, I was seriously engaged in trying to improve my golf game, while giving some thought to applying for a grant to carry out a study of the religious factor within the two political parties in the U.S. Congress. I had been working on this project off and on for a couple of years with a colleague from George Washington University. Essentially, for me, VOTF was a movement occurring in Boston. While I continued to be interested in the Catholic laity's efforts to address the scandal in a meaningful way, it did not loom large on my academic horizon.

Then in August 2002, a new colleague, the Rev. Dr. Anthony J. Pogorelc, arrived at Catholic University to commence work at Theological College and as an adjunct in the Department of Sociology. Tony Pogorelc and I had mutual friends. Jim Davidson, who had directed Tony's dissertation in the sociology of religion at Purdue, had been one of my most productive graduate students during the 1960s, when I was at Notre Dame collaborating on a major research project that yielded several important publications. More recently, since 1987, he had become a vital member of the research team that had completed three volumes about American Catholics.

Over the next few weeks Tony and I talked about a variety of things. We even talked about VOTF and discovered we had both been following its emergence and development. We also talked about our ideas for future research and about his hopes to publish his dissertation about another social movement in the Catholic Church: Call to Action. I asked to read it and made suggestions to help him rework it for publication. As I read the dissertation and realized how conversant Tony was with the social movement literature, it became clear to me that his study of Call to Action as a social movement could provide a helpful background for a study of Voice of the Faithful.

Suddenly I found myself intrigued by the thought of being able to study a social movement within the Catholic Church, almost from its very beginnings. The next national survey of American Catholics was not due until 2005, and the study of the religious factor influencing Congress seemed less pressing, especially with Tony available and as interested in the study of VOTF as I was. We proceeded to discuss the idea with colleagues. Then followed a period of planning and writing a proposal.

The Research Proposal

In early 2003 we submitted a proposal to the Louisville Institute requesting funding for this study; it was returned with a request to revise and resubmit. In their commentary, the Institute board suggested that we form an advisory committee that would bring together scholars capable of providing input from the perspectives of theology and canon law, as well as wider church and sociological viewpoints related to this study. We assembled the committee and found it to be extremely helpful in all phases of the project (a list of the advisory committee members is found in Appendix A, page 190). In the late summer of 2003, the Louisville Institute gave us a grant to carry out a two-year study of Voice of the Faithful as a social movement within the Catholic Church.

The purpose of the study was to document the emergence of VOTF as a social movement by interviewing as many of its founders and leaders as possible and then carrying out a survey of its members (presumably to be limited to the Boston area). The purpose of the survey was:

• to ascertain whether the members and leaders of VOTF shared similar socio-religious characteristics as well as a common vision of VOTF and its goals;

• to complete a demographic portrait of VOTF's founders and leaders, including their religious backgrounds, beliefs, and practices;

• to conduct open-ended interviews designed to allow the founders and leaders of VOTF to explain its emergence, development, and long-term goals as they saw them;

◆ to complete a comparative description and analysis of VOTF members' religious beliefs, attitudes, and practices, and knowledge of Catholic documents;

◆ to complete a descriptive summary of the extent of the VOTF members' participation in church life, in parish life, and in VOTF activities;

◆ to complete a descriptive summary of VOTF members' attitudes and behavior toward church policies in relationship to VOTF goals;

◆ to compare VOTF members and leaders, and also where possible the national population of American Catholics as found in the 2005 survey.*

To accomplish these goals, we developed and tested a questionnaire that would provide basic demographic information about the founders and leaders; it also included questions about religious background, beliefs, and practices (see the questionnaire in Appendix B, page 192). In addition, we developed a set of open-ended interview questions that allowed the interviewees to tell the story of their awareness of and involvement in efforts to confront the scandal and its cover-up, culminating in their participation in VOTF (see the Interview Schedule for Founders and Leaders, Appendix C, page 199).

To obtain data from the members, we adapted the leader's questionnaire and interview questions and constructed an eighty-five-item questionnaire with twelve open-ended questions (see Appendix E, page 210).

Gaining Support and Acceptance from VOTF Leaders

We wanted to study VOTF. Now an even more important question loomed: Did they want to be studied by us? We knew that many

---

*In the spring of 2005 a national survey of American Catholics was carried out by the Gallup Organization using a questionnaire provided by William D'Antonio, James Davidson, Dean Hoge, and Mary Gautier. Table A summarizes the comparison between VOTF leaders, VOTF members, and Catholics in the 2005 National Survey on selected issues. See Table A, Appendix F, page 226.

social movements fail almost immediately, but we hoped that VOTF would survive at least as long as the duration of our study. Social movements in their beginning phases are vulnerable and can be hurt as well as helped by the kind of study we sought to carry out.

Even while we were preparing a proposal to the Louisville Institute asking for funding, we felt it would be bolstered if we could assure the institute that VOTF leaders were willing to allow us to study the movement. Since we did not know the leaders personally, we sent an email to Paul Baier, a founder of VOTF who had set up the original website. He replied with an enthusiastic note in support of our study, but he did not commit any of the other founders or officers. (A copy of Paul Baier's supportive email note is found in Appendix D, page 202.)

Baier also informed us that the founding president, Dr. James Muller, was writing a book about VOTF in collaboration with a professional writer; he provided us with contact information for both. By the time we began our interviews in December of 2003, the book, *Keep the Faith, Change the Church,* was on its way to press, and Dr. Muller, a renowned cardiologist, had retired from the VOTF presidency to return to his medical practice. Dr. Muller's book provides a rich personal account of the events culminating in the July 20, 2002, convention at the Hines Civic Auditorium in downtown Boston.[1]

At this point the people in charge were Dr. James Post, the president, and Steve Krueger, the executive director. In late August we contacted Post and Krueger to inform them that the Louisville Institute had given us a grant to conduct a two-year study of VOTF, and we spelled out in some detail the purpose and goals for our study. We also provided our academic resumes to give them a sense of who we were.

By good fortune, Dr. Post was scheduled to make a presentation at the Northern Virginia gathering of VOTF members on October 1, 2003; I was able to attend the gathering. There I met the two leaders of the Northern Virginia VOTF Affiliate, who introduced him to Dr. Post. They exchanged business cards and continued contact through email and telephone. We also entered into communication with Steve Krueger, who in June 2002 became the executive director and opened the national office.

Beginning with $12,000 and one full-time employee, Krueger himself, this office, based in Newton, Massachusetts, became the center of the VOTF organization. It grew to twelve paid staff and over thirty volunteers. Staff members and volunteers communicated with supporters, received donations, and set the agenda for VOTF's organizational growth and mission. Because of the work done in the national office the profile of VOTF increased, and it moved beyond its beginnings as a local group to national stature.

Krueger encouraged other VOTF leaders to respond positively to the survey as an opportunity to learn more about the membership. Post and Krueger consulted with the VOTF board of trustees, and VOTF leadership approved our study. (Relevant correspondence leading to VOTF's decision to cooperate is found in Appendix D, page 202).

Studying VOTF Founders and Leaders (2003–4)

We were provided the names of founders and current leaders in the Boston area. Space was made available within the national office for interviews; in other cases we conducted interviews in homes or offices or a mutually convenient location. Over the course of the next several months, we carried out sixty interviews: thirty-five were with founders and leaders (to simplify matters we will henceforth refer to this group as the leaders). We also interviewed area clergy and academics who had been involved with VOTF or the Boston Priests' Forum, or who had perspectives that would provide us with a more comprehensive range of views. We also interviewed three regional VOTF leaders from outside Boston, to provide a sense of how they might compare with the Boston group. All interviews were taped and later transcribed. Most interviews ran about an hour in length. To augment our portrait of the leaders, we also asked them to complete a questionnaire providing demographic and other background information.

As we look back at this phase of the study, we realize that we were interviewing people in the process of stabilizing a national office while at the same time responding to both enthusiastic support from around the country, as well as attacks from those questioning their motives. We continue to appreciate their cooperation and assistance.

Surveying the National Membership of VOTF (2004)

When the VOTF national office was established, an enhanced website was developed. Since 95 percent of VOTF supporters have Internet access, it has played an essential role in organizing VOTF. In preparation for the survey the national office sent an email, composed by us, that detailed the purpose of the study and its method of sampling.

The survey was conducted on the Internet at modest cost, using the program Survey Monkey to send the survey questionnaire and to receive and to collate the returns from the members. (The American Sociological Association has used Survey Monkey to conduct some of its own surveys and has found it very reliable.)

The national office provided access to its email list for purposes of drawing the sample. Using a table of random numbers we drew an extra large national representative sample of 4,542 members, approximately one in every six (we deleted from the sample members outside the United States). We were aware that many of the members might not be willing to take the time to fill out a lengthy eighty-five-question survey, and that many would put it off and then forget about it. For these reasons we used a large sample. The survey was set up in Survey Monkey, and VOTF sent an email to the sample with a link to the survey. We received a 28 percent return, that is, 1,273 completed surveys, which included twelve open-ended questions. (A copy of the eighty-five-item member questionnaire is in Appendix E, page 210.)

We divided the VOTF national membership into five regions, and found that the proportions drawn in the sample closely reflected the populations in four of the five regions. Only one region was slightly underrepresented. There were no biases in gender, age, or ethnicity, the three variables on which the VOTF national office had adequate comparable data. We did not attempt to survey the members without Internet access, so our findings and generalizations are restricted to the 95 percent of the members on the Internet.

Telling the VOTF Story

This book is the final product of the two-year project funded by the Louisville Institute. The survey's findings on which this book is based were first presented at a symposium sponsored by the Boston College Church in the 21st Century Center, on October 23, 2005. At the symposium we presented a summary overview of our findings, followed by the presentations of four sociologists with expertise in the areas of identity and social movements, and two theologians with expertise in the theology of the church. To enable the six scholars to prepare their papers, we provided them with summaries of all the basic findings as well as copies of all the tables and samples of direct quotations from the leaders and members. The reader will note that the scholars had varying degrees of knowledge about VOTF prior to their agreement to participate in the Boston College symposium. The book is divided into two major parts. Part 1, chapter 1 begins in January 2002 and tells the story of the emergence of VOTF from the responses of Boston Catholics to the scandal and cover-up. The story is told through the eyes of the leaders using their own words.

Chapter 2 includes a demographic portrait of the leaders, followed by a comparative analysis of their beliefs, practices, and attitudes as Catholics. We use gender as a key variable for comparing the leaders.

The focus of chapters 3 and 4 is the national survey of VOTF members. The survey is concerned with examining Catholic attitudes and practices, knowledge of Catholicism, and ideological and political beliefs. Chapter 3 provides an overview of the main findings, followed by an examination of the differences among members when controlling for Catholic education and Mass attendance. The chapter concludes with a discussion of the tensions experienced by VOTF members who perceive themselves as loyal to the church yet also feel a responsibility to speak out and challenge it, or possibly even leave.

Chapter 4 further sharpens the strains of loyalty and voice as it examines the effects of gender, generation, and region on members' responses to questions about their religious practices and beliefs.

The second part of the book comprises six chapters, each prepared by a scholar known for his or her specialization in a particular field of sociology or theology. Professors Nancy Ammerman and Michele Dillon, who are nationally known as sociologists of religion, were asked to write about the Catholic identity of VOTF leaders and members. Some critics have charged that VOTF members are disgruntled Catholics at the fringe of the church. Professors Ammerman and Dillon reviewed the findings and spoke to this question.

Rev. Dr. Robert Imbelli and Dr. Mary Hines are distinguished theologians, with particular expertise in ecclesiology. We invited them to reflect on the ecclesiological implications of Voice of the Faithful as a social movement within the Catholic Church.

Professors John McCarthy and William Gamson are two of the most distinguished sociologists of social movements. They were invited to examine the data to reflect on the social movement character of VOTF and its future possibilities.

The final chapter summarizes the main findings of this study and reflects on both the problems and prospects facing Voice of the Faithful as it entered its fifth year.

Chapter One

VOTF as a Social Movement in the Catholic Church

Interviews with the founding leaders of VOTF were a rich source of data on how they were affected by revelations of the sexual abuse of minors by Boston priests and its cover-up by the hierarchy. This chapter draws on the actual words of the founders to depict how VOTF came into being. It begins by tracing how Catholics in Boston became aware of the scandal, mainly through the reports published in the *Boston Globe*. It continues with the strong emotional responses provoked by these revelations and how local Catholics dealt with them. We look at their personal action responses and how they gave way to collective action. Starting with family and friends these Catholics shared their grief and anger, finally moving their conversations into the larger community of the parish. In this context we see the importance of pastoral leadership and how it was a factor in nurturing the collective action. Finally we consider the specific resources possessed by this particular group of Catholics and how these resources contributed to the origins, growth, and potential for the persistence of VOTF.

The *Boston Globe*'s Spotlight on Clerical Sexual Abuse: Becoming Aware

A Sunday headline in the *Boston Globe* on January 6, 2002, read: "Church allowed abuse by priest for years"; Monday headline: "Since 1985, Law had reports on repeat abusers"; Thursday headline: "A 'grieving' Law apologizes for assignment of Geoghan." Day after day during the first weeks of January 2002, Boston Catholics were pummeled by the revelations published in the *Globe* of sexual abuse by priests and cover-ups by the hierarchy. This was not the story of something far off: it was personal, in their own backyards. They knew these priests; they were in their parishes. One of Geoghan's parishioners commented:

I'll never forget the morning of January 6; that's the very day that the news broke. We brought the paper in and were sipping our coffee, there it was, this front-page headline, John Geoghan was accused of multiple acts of pedophilia. He had been in our parish, most recently, for nine years. We were outraged.

As the coverage continued and headlines about the abuse and cover-up appeared consistently throughout January, Catholics thought the revelations couldn't get worse, yet they did. A parishioner lamented:

The news got worse every day. When you thought you heard the worst there was more. I think many Catholics thought it was really awful, but we'll deal with this and move on, but it just kept hurting, for weeks and months.

A woman more familiar with the underside of the church reflected:

From hindsight, I don't think I was surprised; upset, horrified, but not surprised. After a while it became worrisome. It was relentless, the volume of it in the *Globe* day after day after day. I'm familiar with the church as an institution, so I don't think I was ever surprised.

Even Catholics who did not want to believe what the *Globe* was saying reluctantly became convinced by the portrayals of case after case where consistent denial and maneuvering were the church's response to tragedy.

I did not want to accept what the papers were saying. I've been interviewed, and what I said didn't always come out how I said it. But as I read about the scandal it became pretty clear that the church was involved in a dilemma, and I accepted that there was a problem, a big problem.

Emotional Reactions

It is likely that anyone remotely associated with the Catholic Church would be ashamed of the sexual abuse allegations profiled in the *Boston Globe,* revealing, at best, the Boston's hierarchy's incompetence and, at worst, its indifference, if not malice, in responding to clerical sexual abuse. For those who were active Catholics, such as those who founded VOTF, the scandal provoked shock, anger, betrayal, and a range of visceral reactions. One woman parishioner described her feelings provoked by a realization that the church she trusted had betrayed her:

> First I was shocked because I absolutely couldn't believe that a bishop would do this. Then I was really angry, and I felt much betrayed. I was also sad and ashamed for the church.

Another woman expanded upon the first woman's sentiments:

> Shock. I think shock describes it. My first reaction was a cumulative reaction, over a couple of days, over a couple of months. I had thought these were isolated cases, I didn't think of it as something systemic. I was embarrassed, embarrassed to be a Catholic. Wondering what my friends were thinking because I was still going to a Catholic church every Sunday. This was so over the top, it upsets acceptable moralities in terms of the damage it's done to our own people and families. There were stories about how the cardinal and other bishops totally ignored heartfelt letters from parents and children who had been abused, multiple children and families, just blown off, just brushed off, just arrogant, arrogant behavior.

One man had a similar reaction and was especially galled by Cardinal Law's response:

Reading the *Globe*'s articles on January 6 and 7, I was shocked with everyone else. What was even more shocking was the lack of appropriate response from Cardinal Law. He was lying to the media; he was hedging. There were a lot of denials and that was insulting. It got me more suspicious. He was trying to hide something, not actively trying to correct problems in his institution.

The role of the cardinal and key archdiocesan administrators in perpetuating the abuse was the focus of many as they tried to analyze what had occurred in Boston:

I was shocked that they [the Boston hierarchy] had known so much about some of these guys, and had been so totally ineffective in terms of stopping the abuse. That was the shocking thing, not that sexual abuse occurs; it's a very widespread thing in society. The problem was that because they dealt with it so poorly they had essentially made membership in the priesthood a safe haven. That will always draw pedophiles who will feel they have a safe operating range.

Another commented in a similar vein:

A lot of things were shocking. The extent of the scandal was shocking, but most shocking, as more documents were published over the course of the month, were the implications for the hierarchy. There was clear evidence that they knew about it and covered it up. That was the most shocking and distressing thing of all.

As time went on the numbness of disbelief and shock made way for other, stronger emotional reactions. Parents felt a particular vulnerability, identifying with parents of the abused:

I was horrified. I was angry. I still am angry. I think I was just so disappointed; I was devastated; I was sad. As a parent who experienced the highs and lows of children growing up, I was so sad for the families.

Some parents also experienced new concerns about children they had known and their own children:

> I was horrified, and the other sick feeling that I got in the pit of my stomach was thinking back, to when I was working at a Catholic school in Philadelphia, where I had older children that were in third and fourth grade, and I knew that they would leave to be altar servers when there were funerals or events that were taking place, and I never questioned it. And they would come up from the office and the children would leave, and it was part of the practice at that time. And then I thought about my own children, who had been very active, and I had never before ever had any question about this in my mind.

For Catholics the church is both divine and human; culturally and ecclesiologically it has historically provided an important connection to God. Headlines detailing the abuse of power in the Catholic Church paralleled abuses of power in corporate and government life. Many believed that the conduct of church leaders revealed levels of integrity even below that of secular leaders:

> Like everybody else I was stunned, and toward the end of the month there was simultaneous coverage of the scandals at Enron and in the Catholic Church. I wrote a letter to the *Globe* saying I think responsible executives resign when they find themselves in this kind of situation. And the Catholic Church should behave at least as well as Enron.

For boomer Catholics this scandal evoked memories of Watergate:

> It was a sickening feeling, like being punched in the stomach. I remember saying to myself, "Oh, no, you're not going to believe this; it is just like Watergate." It reminded me so much of the feeling I had as a young lawyer in 1972 when I learned about the Watergate break-in. It was a very sickening feeling.

For others it indicated that the church had not learned lessons from earlier cases of abuse:

I reverted back to thinking about the [Father James] Porter case. [He molested children in the Fall River Diocese in the 1960s.] I remember when I read about that I believed it was an isolated incident of someone who had a problem, but I didn't think it was systemic at that point. So my emotions ran the gamut, of feeling like I was betrayed, and also not understanding how this could happen, when children were in the charge of adults.

There was disappointment that the church they expected to respond in a helpful way did not:

The anger was building up and there was no place to put it; in the Catholic Church there still isn't. It was clear that there was no paradigm for dialogue; the church didn't bring us together.

Toward Personal Action

Jim Muller, a member of St. John's parish in Wellesley, Massachusetts, is a Nobel laureate and a distinguished physician. He was born into a family that steeped him in the Catholic tradition. More than any other person he was responsible for taking the actions that led to the formation of VOTF. Like other Catholics on that January day, Jim and his wife, Kathleen, struggled to make sense of what was happening and to channel their strong emotions into actions that would address this crisis in the church. This is seen in a conversation between Jim and his wife:

January 6, 2002, is the day when Kathleen and I read the paper and were shocked by the story. Kathleen said she didn't know what to make of it. And I said, "It looks like a cover-up or some-thing." And she said, "No, that's ridiculous; it will be Porter all over again. We don't want that." And I agreed, saying, "You know I don't want that." And then she went to visit her sick mother. When she came back she said, "Jim, I can't stand it." She said, "As Catholics we need to do something; Jim, you should try and do something."

Others were talking as well. In fact St. John's church was abuzz with conversation about the scandal and what was to be done. One woman parishioner described the scene in this way:

> There was a lot of conversation and we were very interested, talking it through with our friends from church. We immediately talked about it ourselves; we still had some children at home. We talked to our friends; those who were not Catholic were very hesitant to step over the line into something that was very embarrassing until they heard us being very open with our disappointment. It was very nice, within a week, to be able to talk about it in church.

Another woman had a similar experience:

> I talked with my children about it; we were just astounded, and my husband went to a wake that afternoon with people he had gone to school with many years before and he said to them: "Have you seen the story? It's going to be a very big story." And they did not believe it, which was surprising. So we had a lot of discussion about it.

This St. John's parishioner was especially affected because of her role as a campus minister:

> I was a chaplain, so I'm representing the institution. I was very conscious of the fact that it was the front-page news and the students were always bringing to me those things happening in the church. It bothered me enough that I felt it viscerally and went and saw a priest-friend. I told him it troubled me a lot, and I asked how I can be part of this institution when we are discovering these terrible things. The abuse is one thing, but it's the cover-up that I just found so hard. And I said what I do as I am representing the church at this campus where there are these young, intelligent, bright students. I said, "I don't know if I can stay there with integrity," and he looked at me and he said, "You're telling the truth." And at that point I just started crying.

In other Boston area churches, conversation was also people's first response to the scandal. One man said:

> I usually worship on Sunday at 5:30 p.m., and that's a very good liturgy at my parish. As I was in the midst of my Sunday morning routine, between all the news programs and my big mug of coffee, I called some friends that participate in the 10:00 a.m. Mass. They were both spiritual friends and people I would have discussions with, not only about our spiritual life but also about the life of the church. So I was immediately swept up in it [discussion of the scandal].

The Movement to Collective Action

As time went on, Catholics moved beyond the more private conversations with family, friends, and priests, and gravitated toward the larger parish community. Parishioners shared their recollections of the beginnings of parish meetings:

> I talked to my children within a couple of days, and there was nothing encouraging to say. I was so shocked, and I couldn't deny that it was true. I didn't know what to think and I needed more information. Monday I had talked with some friends at church as soon as I got home from work, and I was told there was going to be a meeting in the church. So I went to church. And I think I probably would have gone there anyway, just to be there, because the church really means a lot to me. When devastating things happen, you go where you get comfort. So I was going to go to church anyway, and then I heard about this meeting and went to it.

Jim Muller recalled how he moved toward initiation of collective action:

> And I said [to my wife] I don't know what to do. Maybe I should write an article for the newspaper; I've written them before but I'm not scholarly about the church. And I said maybe we should start a discussion group and talk to some other intelligent people

to find out what this all means. Kathleen said go ahead; go to St. John's and see what you can do. So I saw Father Powers [the pastor] in the back of the church and asked if he would mind starting a discussion group. I told him that I thought the laity should lead it. He said he'd think it over and check with the staff, and he called me back a couple of days later and it was okay. So Father Powers started that, and once it got into place it broke the silence in the pews. This very educated congregation started talking.

The pastor's willingness to address the effect of the scandal in a public forum is seen by many of the St. John's parishioners as an important element in VOTF's foundation. A couple recounted a meeting with Father Powers:

Father asked right then and there, "What does everyone want to do?" And we all agreed, "Let's get together, let's talk after Mass about it." He didn't say yes or no right then but, "Let me think about this. Let me talk to people to see who would be running it. I feel I should be there, but not in charge." So that is how it started, and on the following Sunday we had our first listening session.

One woman recalled first finding out about the meetings:

The key part was walking into church that Saturday evening and seeing in the bulletin that Father [Powers] was going to have a listening session. I made sure that everyone I knew was aware that they should set some time aside for it. For that weekend, they were organized after every Mass and then Monday night in case people were not able to stay on Sunday. When Monday night came along I was curious to see what other people were thinking, so my husband and I went again. There were a lot of people there on Monday night who had been there over the weekend.

She described how the meetings continued:

Immediately at the end of the first Monday night, people spoke up and said, "I'd like to meet again." Many people were interested in doing that, so we met again the next Monday night. That happened two or three times, and it became pretty clear that there was a need for this. It also coincided with an annual archdiocesan meeting the parishes have with the cardinal [in March]. So we very quickly jumped at the opportunity to make that more significant than it would normally be. We spent a lot of time preparing positions. We knew people would have an opportunity to speak, so certain people were prepared. That happened very quickly.

Another woman shared her recollections:

Father [Powers] and about twenty people were there, and we met in the hall beneath the church. We all got in a circle, and we weren't saying much, and I think Jim [Muller] said something to the effect that, "This is such a surprise, such a devastating thing; maybe we should just go around the room and talk about it." Each week the meeting was bigger; I think the next one had about fifty people then sixty people. It was encouraging to see so many people, because it was a very lonely feeling to think that the church had acted like this, and we wondered what we could do. When we got together with other Catholics, I realized, "Yeah, there are other people who are this angry." And so there was solidarity among us.

This woman echoed the value of the meetings for those who attended and how the group developed:

I just was devastated and thought, "We need to continue to meet," and we did. There were forty-five of us who were committed to that. We just poured our hearts out and then it got to be okay. And that's when the word spread; we began the mission statement and the goals and then the word got out that something was going on at St. John's and the press wanted to hear something.

Some of the participants wanted to avoid the limelight. "We kept saying, No, and no." I guess the Catholic way was to just say, "Absolutely no." It was Jim Muller's leadership that led them to cross a significant threshold. "But Jim Muller knew that we really needed the press to spread the word." As the parishioners met, a more formal organization developed:

It got pretty organized and we were having regular meetings. An interesting phenomenon occurred early, early on, people who were interested in survivors' issues in the parish, and people who were interested in changing the church began to separate into those kinds of groups. What happened to me was that I was going to central meetings and I realized that I was very interested in helping to build VOTF, and I shifted to the central committee.

This woman was not surprised at the level of activity at St. John's:

VOTF is independent, and most people are from St. John's, so we already had a good habit of talking. We are independent. So we talk about the scandal and what was going on. It was very interesting to hear. What I heard is just a total outrage. I wasn't surprised because I have a professional background; other people are just shocked at the cover-up.

St. John's was not the only parish where there was activity. This man recalled what was going on in his own parish when parishioners chose to meet:

I knew about half of the people there. There definitely were some new faces there. It was similar to what happened at St. John's first meeting; people were just given an opportunity to express what was on their minds. At the end of it, there was the question, What do we do now? What do we do next?

Eventually some of the parish groups affiliated with the larger organization of VOTF.

Our Lady's [Newton, Massachusetts] group continued as independent for a while, and then openly affiliated with VOTF.

Most affiliates are the VOTF creations, but that affiliate actually had an independent existence before VOTF.

Others met in their homes before joining VOTF:

I went to a meeting at someone's house in February; she was trying to pull together the people who were agitated in various ways. And I think I went to probably two meetings there, and then by that point different things were kind of going on. Jim Muller was getting Voice of the Faithful started.

Yet the role of St. John's was central in the formation of VOTF as a social movement. This can be seen by how St. John's parishioners participated in the annual diocesan convocation. Two Catholics from another parish shared their recollections of watching St. John's parishioners at the convocation:

We went to this convocation in March, and the whole thing focused on the scandal. There were five ballrooms, each with an open mike, each filled with several hundred people. You had three minutes to say your piece. We all began to notice that the people who had the most to say all had red jackets. They did that on purpose, so they could be remembered. They also came up with a statement and each person presented a part. [We thought] this gang in red knows what they're doing. They're not just passionate; they see what has to be done, the next steps. We've got to get to know some of them better. As we were walking out we recognized a friend among them who said, "Here," and handed us probably two hundred flyers to put in our own church. And two days later we were there, and standing up to introduce ourselves and what we could bring to this fledgling organization. There were probably thirty people in the room, and we were some of the first from outside that parish.

Throughout the previous narratives we have referred to the movement by its name, Voice of the Faithful. However, the naming of the movement was a significant moment. One of the founding leaders recalled this dialogue that occurred among some of the founding leaders:

> Somebody introduced the idea of Voice, and we talked about that and about the sense of the faithful, *sensus fidelium,* or some version of it in Greek. Someone else said that was too old church. We then took these ideas to the larger group that following Monday. Some said that people wouldn't understand the foreign phrases, so someone said let's call it Voice of the Faithful, and that seemed right. It just clicked. The mission statement and the goals were much more carefully worked out over the next two- or three-week period.

Motivations for Action

From our surveys we know that VOTF members participate in the church more actively than Catholics in general. Their levels of Mass attendance, personal prayer, involvement in parish life, and service to the poor exceed that of the general Catholic populace. These characteristics will be examined in greater detail in chapter 3. Members view their participation in VOTF as part of their Catholic vocation. This is reflected in their responses to questions about why they are invested in the mission of the movement. One woman expressed it this way:

> Sometimes it [VOTF membership] almost feels like a calling. What we're doing is definitely the right thing to do relative to the survivors, the type of care and attention they will need for the rest of their lives. So, at a minimum, there is an injustice that needs to be brought to justice. But, in addition, it's also clear that the church cannot continue on its trajectory; it will start to fade out. And I think that has become our motivation and something that will keep me active; that's why I almost describe it as a calling.

Many used the images of transformation, such as from being blind to being able to see, from being passive to becoming active. One woman reflected on her newfound sense of responsibility for the church and how it led her to participate:

> I thought that this [participation in VOTF] would be expected of me as a Catholic. And I had a lot of criticism and wondered how people I trusted could allow this to happen. Now you could just keep saying this over and over again, like a mantra, or you could say okay, I'm a part of this church, I wasn't awake, and I had visors on. I don't anymore. Now I can take some responsibility and initiative to work out a solution.

Responsibility and wanting to be part of the solution also motivated another woman:

> The only way I could deal with it is if I became involved some-how, and so when I went to the meetings, the initial meetings, I went because I was looking for some kind of direction and consolation, and that's what I found at VOTF.

For another woman it was a movement from passivity and frustration to embracing her sense of responsibility:

> I think there was an awareness that we all had a common con-cern and a responsibility to do something. New people came every week; it got bigger. We faced the consequences of leaving things in someone else's hands and allowing ourselves to be led [astray]. But we weren't going to do that anymore.

Moving beyond anger to shaping structural change motivated this woman:

> I guess I thought anger could be a motivating spark, but it can't be the engine for change. It was good to give people a chance to vent, but it seemed to me that what we were about is trying to change the church. We had to start focusing on how to do that. I wanted to make sure that that was our focus. When they formed the executive council before the July 2002 convention

they asked each group about affiliation. I was very strong for affiliation because I was very impressed with the larger group. There were plenty of people within the group who weren't happy with that and most of them are now doing other things. They have a mortal fear of restructuring the hierarchy.

A desire for structural change and solidarity also moved this woman:

I guess that I just feel so deeply that I do not want to leave the church in the shape that it's in for my children and grand-children, number one. And I can't imagine not being incensed and upset and sad as I see fewer and fewer people at Mass. I just know that I have to continue doing what I'm doing. I'm not about to give up on my church, but the structure is a problem.

The same was true for a man who attended Mass weekly, but was not active in the organizations of his parish:

I'm watching the church, watching priests get older, priests dis-appearing, nobody coming in, and then I started observing that there seemed to be less young people, and I said, "Geez, we've got ceremonies, but we don't have community." So when this thing busted in the *Globe,* I started going to VOTF. I was appalled with the sexual abuse and the clerical system try-ing to avoid doing something. The second thing I found was that VOTF people were very religious people and trying to do something for the church.

Another woman's concern for children and young people was the result of her being a parent:

My mother said, "Why are you doing this?" She comes from Boca Raton and she's eighty-two and she thought I was going to go to hell. Tearfully, I said, "Because I wanted to." She asked me: "Why are you even bothering to do this?" And I said, "Because I am protecting my son." She said, "Your son is twenty!" I didn't care. That's where it's coming from. That's where it came from. And it's getting hard to tell you this. It could have been my baby. It was somebody else's baby. It was other people's babies.

For this man it was his concern for victims:

> I would say connection to the victims continues to be a powerful
> motivator. I would say by and large most still remain Catholics,
> maybe with the exceptions of a few. But outrage and a sense
> for justice and to do what's right by them was one of the prime
> motivators of the group.

Another man expressed his drive with humor: "What keeps us hopeful? I don't want to let the bastards get away with it." Another woman
saw the confluence of factors as a work of the Spirit:

> It was a coalescing of the right people, the right time, and the
> right motivation, and we wanted to work together. It was a
> moment that was touched by the Spirit.

The threefold mission of VOTF has engaged some people who have
a history of social movement activity.

> VOTF moves in three directions at the same time: first helping
> those abused in the cover-up by the church. But supporting our
> priests and above all creating a mechanism for change is equally
> important. I remember being involved in the '60s, when I was
> in college, and we thought changes in the church were going to
> happen overnight like married clergy and female clergy. So when
> I became aware of what was going on in the spring of 2002, it
> was, oh, my goodness, here's an opportunity for change, some-
> thing I've been looking for for thirty-five years, and I wondered
> if this was going to be an opportunity to go forward with that.
> So there's excitement in that.

This man realized that the parishioners of St. John's of Wellesley were
able to mount a challenge because they had resources over and above
those possessed by most Catholics:

> My son-in-law asked, "Isn't it funny it started at Wellesley?
> If it started down river in Roxbury the hierarchy would have
> dismissed the people as crazy, but in Wellesley they were profes-
> sionals who had to be dealt with." As Catholics we have been

the abused, not sexually, but by being treated like children. I think a lot of us felt this; it was bottled up and then all of a sudden it came flying out, and there was no way to stuff it back.

Organizational Resources

VOTF members are highly educated. They are used to being leaders in their professions and communities, and this has impacted the way they function as Catholics. This is reflected in the comments of this leader:

> I think we are a faith-based community. We are very strongly committed to our faith and we are prayerful people. We have some very, very intelligent, diligent, compassionate, and well-educated people. I think the leadership is very, very good.

VOTF leaders view the people in the movement and the experience they bring as valuable human resources. As Vatican II Catholics who accent the primacy of conscience, they are highly educated, prizing openness and diversity, and they find it difficult to understand why these qualities are not always appreciated in the church today:

> The door has to be open enough to respect different visions. You get twenty people in a room, or twenty thousand, not everybody's going to think alike. God gave you free will and a conscience; you have to pray and form your own conscience. I've done it all my life because I was taught to do that.

Another leader concurs:

> I think the church needs to hear the voices of an independent, loving, caring, compassionate group of people like us. We're in the church; we're not throwing stones from the outside. We are trying to build up the church.

Material resources are also something that VOTF members possess. As one leader says: "Money gives you leverage."

Yet VOTF members are wise enough to realize that their material resources are only one type of resource and that they must reach out to the wider body of Catholics. As one leader states:

I think for Voice of the Faithful to fulfill its mission, to encourage the laity to have an active role in the church, it needs a wide group of affiliates. So I very much see laity to be vital.

Yet this has been an effort:

We need to mobilize more Catholics to support the need for change in the church. We have a strategy right now built around parish voice that will not produce huge numbers of Catholics. We are not trying to recruit large numbers of Catholics; we are trying to recruit affiliate groups across the country. Think of it like cells, relatively small cells. Thinking about it from an organizational perspective we need more resources to supply parish voice with a structure to mobilize large numbers of Catholics to become members or supporters of VOTF. That will take money. That will also take some cultural change within VOTF.

Some see the ecclesial climate in which VOTF is trying to grow as less fertile than that of the earlier post-Vatican II period. Their educational and professional backgrounds at American institutions have not prepared them for the distinctiveness of the organization of the Catholic Church. One academic informant made these comments:

I think many local groups don't have much background; they don't know that there's a history to these things. They don't have any of that information or education, and once again I'm struck by how VOTF nationally and locally has not drawn to it people who are professionals in the church, people who could give them the resources, the history, and a more strategic way of proceeding. My image of that, is that if it were ten or fifteen years ago, on the third meeting of VOTF in Wellesley, [Msgr.] Jack Egan would've flown in from Chicago. He would've been over in the corner, and when the meeting was over, he would've said to Jim Post and Dr. Muller, "Come on over here for a minute.

Let's go talk." And he would've begun to mentor them as to how the church works, and what are the things you have to move on, who you have to know, and how you have to move. I think they've had to learn all that on their own almost, and there still is a level of amateurishness about their church reform work.

Who Participates?

VOTF leaders are concerned that their movement has emerged only among people of their own profile, but not very far beyond it. They are mainly Vatican II or pre-Vatican II Catholics, of Western European ancestry from the middle and upper classes.

One leader talked about her quandary regarding the absence of the young:

> I am concerned that young people are not interested in VOTF and the church. I have two children and raised them Catholic; neither attends church, and this is very difficult for me. I don't know the answer.

Others believe that though they are not active participants, young people are watching to see if VOTF members can actually shape structural change in the church:

> We think that many young adults, even if they haven't committed to getting involved in a hands-on way, are watching to see whether their middle-aged parents and grandparents are really going to make a difference. Many of them are at odds with the church, and they are not sure that it should be repaired. So they are watching and waiting.

Another reflected on VOTF members in the wider context of the church, saying that the young and minorities today are absorbed with the task of survival:

> The world church is obviously changing, and not in ways we would like. We just have our own little piece of responsibility to nurture what we've gotten from the past, and pass it on to the

next generation so they can decide what to do with it. We do have some responsibility — but we're not the whole ballgame by any means. You meet blacks and Hispanics — it's like I said about young people. They have other tasks to do.

Another leader echoed this:

It's hard. We want to [have more diversity]. I've tried a couple of things. I tried to give ten free tickets to our convocation to an inner-city pastor I know, but they had to give names, for the security badges, and nobody did. I think they felt threatened by [Cardinal] Law and didn't send anybody.

This leader more pointedly discussed the issue of ethnic and class diversity:

Many would like to extend the message of VOTF into ethnic communities in eastern Massachusetts. Most of the leadership feels they do not have the skills to do that. I'm part of Jim Post's executive committee; we always begin and end our meetings with prayer. At one of our meetings, Jim asked me to say a prayer and instinctively, I said the Our Father — in Spanish. I then realized I was the only one saying the words; others were saying it in English to themselves. Everybody looked at me, and Steve Krueger said, "Marvelous." That was the only word that could come out of his mouth. He was pleased that I was bringing the issue of ethnicity to the table. They all know that we need to do something more than we are doing right now.

VOTF has chapters in some central city parishes. It is very difficult for people who come from abroad to come to this country and, number one, have the resources to get involved in VOTF. They're concerned about putting heat in the room and food on the table for their children. Many of the people I deal with in the ethnic community work two or three menial jobs. So having the resources to do what I do, like driving down to Wellesley, is not common. The other is the linguistic and cultural sensitivity to be able to talk to people from other cultures and raise the issue. Abuse is huge in the Philippines, and we have a lot of people from the Philippines in our area. We have to learn to communicate with them in a language they understand.

One leader thought the ethnic segregation in VOTF was reflective of the wider segregation in American society:

> We recognize we do not have substantial numbers of people of color in our membership, and it's a function of where we started. We have been doing a serious amount of outreach into the urban parishes of Boston, and I think we've made some progress in developing an awareness of and interest in the idea of a renewed church. But in general, the demographics of VOTF are pretty much a white, middle-age, middle-class people, suburban and urban. It is not as diverse as the church.

One leader thought that as immigrant groups gain more education and become part of the mainstream, they would become more critical of church structure:

> I would be surprised if the experiences of Haitians, of other immigrant Americans, and Asians, are going to be any different from the experience of the Irish Americans. People with the experience of time [when they] are educated are going to be more at odds with the church. It's just a matter of time.

Growth

Even in the face of challenges, VOTF leaders have hopes for the growth of their movement. A major question concerns how the success of such a movement is measured. Leaders had varying ideas about this. Some tie success to the mission of the movement:

> People ask about numbers, but I see our evolution in a different way. In our first year we were tested by fire to see if we could come together and become a Voice of the Faithful. I think we have. In our second year the bishops and our critics tested us to see if we could keep going. I think we have, despite some strong opposition. And in our third year, starting in 2004, the

challenge will be to put forward ideas for constructive change in the church that will get a fair chance to be tried and become part of the work of the ongoing living church.

Another leader echoes similar thoughts:

I think whether VOTF is here five years from now is less important than whether our church embraces the need for change, and the reforms that we see. I think the extent to which the church reclaims its integrity by doing what is necessary to incorporate the lessons of the twenty-first century is what is important.

Consolidating a mission has been difficult:

I think many of the local chapters have had a hard time figuring out their function. Once they get together, express discontent, make ties with survivors' groups, and try to be of help, what else do you do? This is their question, and they haven't had good guidance on that.

Some see the passivity of the "pay, pray, and obey" Catholics as an obstacle to growth:

The rapid growth that we had in the first six months has leveled off, yet it is spreading in other regions of the country. We still have a lot of the couch potatoes just sitting there observing what we're doing.

Another echoed this thought:

I ask people in the pews and priests to be courageous. We're no longer allowed to lead [affiliates] from parishes. I don't believe that every Catholic has to be a member of VOTF, but I would like them to be actively involved in being part of the solution. They need to be part of the conversation.

Some see the kind of training that mobilizes members as a way to overcome passivity and fear:

I feel that training is essential, for our leadership, and so my hope is that we will have regional conferences. What I would love to do is tag on to any of the conferences a day set aside for leadership training.

In spite of the challenges and obstacles, some leaders are ready to stay the course:

> Oh, I'm not putting any limits on this. I think there is a need for a lay organization in the church. I would love for it to be VOTF. So I think my hope is that Voice will always be around, and I'll be around as long as I can, as long as I have a contribution.

Conclusion

Voice of the Faithful emerged because a group of Boston Catholics with extraordinary resources mobilized to confront the hierarchy of the archdiocese of Boston, which had systematically covered up the abuse of children by predatory priests. The Catholics of St. John's of Wellesley who founded VOTF were strongly connected to the church through their parish and acutely felt the pain that resulted from this scandal. They were also a community that was particularly blessed with resources such as education, organizational skills, visionary pastoral leadership, and material wealth. These factors laid the foundation for them to be critical members of the church; they had the capacity to see, analyze, and choose their course of action. They are also loyal Catholics who choose to raise their voices in calling for reform of the institution. In the chapter that follows, we will examine in greater detail the profile of the Catholics who served as the first leaders of Voice of the Faithful.

Chapter Two

VOTF's Founding Leaders

Our first major research question concerned the leaders of VOTF, their backgrounds, religious beliefs, attitudes, and practices. To answer these questions we conducted interviews and a survey. The survey concentrated on basic demographic data. Thirty-six people identified as founders and current leaders (2002–4) were interviewed, and thirty-five questionnaires were completed and returned.[1] This chapter discusses what we found and summarizes findings we wish to highlight in a series of five tables.

The Leaders: Gender and Generation

Women constituted 60 percent of the leaders; we later found this same ratio in the general membership. Most of the leaders were born in the East or in the Midwest. Most of the women leaders (71 percent) were Vatican II Catholics, that is, born between 1941 and 1960; and the men were equally split (43 percent each) between the two older generations. The most notable finding was that very few leaders were post-Vatican II Catholics, i.e., born after 1960. VOTF leaders are most conscious of this fact and regularly reflected on it in our interviews. One woman in the minority of younger leaders proposed this explanation for this absence:

> We are looking for younger adults and have a group focused on recruiting them. Many of them are pretty much at odds with the church, and they are not sure that it should be repaired. Yet we believe many young adults are watching to see if their middle-aged parents and grandparents can make a difference. On the

other hand we are also struck by the presence of strong traditional movements on college campuses; some of the Newman societies have become very conservative.

A Vatican II Catholic explained the generational imbalance as a difference of cultures and life demands:

> Those of us now in our fifties came of age in the 1960s. We have a cultural affinity for protest and justice. Every time you turned around there was a movement — it was the environment, or women, or civil rights, or anti–Vietnam War. People in their thirties and forties are part of the self-actualization bubble. They may still go to church and raise their children with Christian values, and write checks. And they are busy. They are working, most in two-income households, and have children. Their priorities are appropriate for them. We now have more time.

Ethnic Roots

Since Boston was the locus of this early stage of VOTF's development, we would expect Irish Catholics to be among the early leaders of VOTF. They still constituted the largest single white ethnic group in the city, with the U.S. census for the year 2000 reporting the number of Irish Catholics as 93,360. This was almost twice as many as the second largest group, Italian Catholics, who were numbered at 49,017.[2] Overall, Boston Irish in the year 2000 comprised 15 percent of the entire Boston population. It may not be surprising then to learn that three out of four of the women and almost half the men (six of fourteen) VOTF leaders claimed their ancestry as totally Irish. Almost all the women (99 percent) and more than half of the men (57 percent) reported being at least part Irish. German heritage trails at 20 percent. The Irish have traditionally dominated the numbers of the clergy and hierarchy in the U.S. church, but their prevalence in the leadership of VOTF also indicates their prominence in the educational, professional, and intellectual leadership of the Catholic laity. We found a similar pattern among VOTF members nationally, which we will comment on in the next chapter.

Education, Occupation, Income

VOTF leaders are highly educated, with two out of three having at least one advanced degree, and almost half having a professional or doctoral degree. This high level of education is reflected in the annual household incomes of the leaders, with a majority of the men and half the women reporting annual household incomes in excess of $100,000 (Table 2.1).

Sociologist Max Weber discussed stratification in terms of economic class, status, and party — that is, power relationships. VOTF leaders score high on all three dimensions, and the latter is evident

Table 2.1. A Demographic Portrait of VOTF Leaders, by Gender (percentages)

	Total N=35	Male N=14	Female N=21
Gender	100%	40%	60%
Age Cohorts			
Pre-Vatican II (born 1900–1940)	31	43	24
Vatican II (born 1941–60)	60	43	71
Post-Vatican II (born after 1960)	9	14	5
Ethnicity*			
Irish only	60	43	75
Irish plus	26	14	24
German	20	36	5
Italian	11	10	14
English	11	21	5
Other	23	21	24
Education level			
B.A./B.S.	34	36	33
M.A./M.S.	31	29	33
Ph.D.	14	14	14
Professional	20	21	19
Annual household income			
$30,000–$49,000	20	14	24
$50,000–$99,999	14	21	9
$100,000 and higher	51	57	48
No response	14	7	19

*Percentages shown exceed 100%; some leaders listed two or more ethnicities.

in the leadership they have exercised in professional, civic, and voluntary associations. Four of the leaders were academics, seven were doctors, lawyers, or other professional workers; most of the others were in business. One leader described her background in this way:

> I have an honors B.A. in English, and a master's and Ph.D. in engineering. I've been involved in technical groups and know how to organize; I'm interested in politics. I could see that this [my work with VOTF] was similar to other things I had done. To see the Church and VOTF as human institutions is not a trivial task. I love the Catholic Church; I have both emotional and intangible ties to the church.

The founding president of VOTF and by all accounts the single most important person in the earliest stages of the development of Voice of the Faithful was Dr. James Muller, a renowned cardiologist. Of Irish, German, and Swiss ancestry, he is one of seven children from a very devout Catholic family from Indianapolis. His family heritage was one of achievements. From his father through his aunt to his siblings, he described the family's actions to be built on the realization that "if you can make the world better you should try, because you're stuck in it."

Throughout his life Jim Muller was involved in the founding or leadership of organizations, beginning with the presidency of his college dorm at Notre Dame, followed by establishing the first medical society for students at Johns Hopkins and then a sojourn to Moscow in the 1970s that paved the way for the formation of International Physicians against Nuclear War, which won the Nobel Peace Prize in 1985. Voice of the Faithful was the latest of these endeavors.

Though he agreed to be the founding president of VOTF, Muller realized that he could not serve in this position indefinitely. In May 2002, he approached Dr. James Post, a professor of business management at Boston University and a fellow parishioner at St. John the Evangelist, and asked him to be a candidate to succeed him in the presidency of VOTF.

Jim Post was a very accomplished man in his own right. Not only did he have academic experience in business management, which helped him appreciate the task ahead, but he also had some practical experience that proved to be crucial. In the late 1970s, Post became active in what was then called the "infant formula scandal." As he described it:

> This was the promotion of powdered formula for mothers to use instead of breast-feeding. Because of the lack of clean water, babies who were fed the formula were dying. It's a long story, but I came at it from the perspective of an industry regulating itself. I worked with the World Health Organization (WHO) and was very active because I could see the need for some kind of an international code. My work with WHO and later with the Nestlé Infant Formula Product Commission to monitor Nestlé's compliance with the international code taught me some valuable lessons. The chair of that commission was former Senator Edmund Muskie, so I learned in the shadow of a very great American how to deal with difficult issues. It led me to have a keen sense of the critical questions.

Jim Post was elected president of VOTF in the spring of 2002 and served until 2006.

Catholic Roots

VOTF leaders have deep Catholic roots (Table 2.2). Many were cradle Catholics raised in families that were active in the parish. The great majority of VOTF leaders attended Catholic grade school and high school; two out of three women and a third of the men attended Catholic colleges.

One of the women leaders recounted that her entire education occurred in Catholic schools. "I was born and raised Catholic in the Midwest. My education began with a parish school, and then a regional Catholic high school. My brother went to a Jesuit high school, and I was impressed with Jesuit education so I went to the University of Detroit. Then after all that I got my Ph.D. in a Catholic university."

One Boston-reared leader reflected that in his neighborhood there was no question about where young Catholics went to school.

Table 2.2. Catholic Roots of VOTF Leaders, by Gender (in percentages)

	Total	Male	Female
Catholic roots			
Baptized as infants	94%	93%	95%
Father Catholic	91	86	95
Mother Catholic	91	93	91
Catholic school education			
Grade school	74	79	70
High school	59	57	60
College	52	31	65
Marriage			
Married	82	93	75
by Catholic Church	86	85	87
Spouse Catholic	79	78	80
Have children	94	93	94
1–3	80	86	76
4 or more	20	14	24

When I was growing up, it was not an option to go to public schools. If you were Catholic you went to Catholic schools. Elementary school — absolutely. That was your obligation. If you graduated from a Catholic high school, you couldn't get a letter of recommendation if it wasn't to a Catholic college. A friend of mine wanted to go to Princeton. He went to a guidance counselor for a letter of recommendation and they said, "See you later."

The strong Catholic roots of VOTF leaders are reflected in their marriage and family commitments (Table 2.2). Eight in ten VOTF leaders have Catholic spouses and are in marriages blessed by the church. Almost all of these have children, the great majority having one to three, and a minority with four or more. As with many Vatican II Catholics, VOTF leaders revealed that their grown children have not adopted their own religious practices or their involvement in VOTF. One leader noted, "My involvement in VOTF has been on my own. Neither of my children is involved. My son is a practicing Catholic; my daughter probably does not consider herself Catholic now."

Another leader reflected on her conversations with her two children about their views of the scandal and the church:

> My daughter graduated from a Catholic college, but my son never was in Catholic school until now; he's in a Catholic law school. I asked them if either had been abused. My son told me he looked at the church as an institution and at his faith as separate from the institution. He said the purpose of the institution was to facilitate the growth of faith in a community. But he never had a commitment to the institution. And I thought, okay, I understand.

Religious Beliefs, Attitudes, and Practices

On the most commonly used indicators of beliefs, attitudes, and practices, the leaders of VOTF score high (Table 2.3). Two out of three VOTF leaders attend Mass at least once a week. This high attendance rate was not only the result of growing up in the highly Catholic culture of Boston and its environs. Other leaders grew up in different sections of the country, some of which were more religiously heterogeneous. One leader, who said she had many Protestant and Jewish friends growing up in an Iowa town, reflected on her family's Catholicism in this social context: "We had a strong Catholic faith — Mass on Sunday, prayed the rosary, May altar processions." Another non–Boston native, an older male, reflected on his strong faith in the Eucharist: "What defines me as a Catholic is Scripture and the Eucharist, which is central to the Catholic faith. It is one of the central features of my life. It is one of the reasons I go to daily Mass." He went on to describe the difficulties he perceived in the way Catholics understand the Eucharist.

> It's hard for a human mind to look at a piece of bread and say, "That's the body of Christ." It's not intuitive. It takes faith. Some Catholics don't have a sense of the real presence. They'll accept it, but don't think about it, but Christ is really present

Table 2.3. VOTF Leaders:
Measures of Commitment to the Catholic Church,
by Gender (in percentages)

	Total	Male	Female
Attend Mass			
Daily/weekly	63%	71%	57%
Monthly or less	26	21	29
Seldom/never	11	7	14
Pray			
At least once a day	69	50	80
Importance of church			
Most or among most important	58	36	74
Quite important	42	64	26
Probability of leaving the church			
Never	48	36	59
Probably not	19	21	17
Might leave	32	43	24

in the Eucharist, and that's an important part of my belief and my life.

The regular practice of prayer is also an important part of the lives of VOTF leaders, with most of the women (80 percent) and half of the men reporting the habit of daily prayer. Women (74 percent) were twice as likely as the men to declare the Catholic Church to be among the most important influences in their lives. When asked about the most salient feature of being Catholic, one of the younger leaders said: "It's my identity. It's who I am. It goes very deep. I have a love of Eucharist; I have an appreciation of the incarnation of God. I think in some ways that's why VOTF took off the way it did. It's like we already belonged to each other, even though we didn't know each other's names."

Another leader also pointed to the Eucharist as at the core of her being Catholic:

Why am I still here? Why is it that I can't feel that my spirituality would be fulfilled in another dimension? Two responses came to mind. I had been to a friend's church and to other denominational services. It was the Eucharist that was missing. And the other part of it was, "You know what, this is my church, and I will do my darndest to make it reflect the Jesus I know." It might take a little more time, but I am not going to be forced to leave because of the scandal.

One younger leader identified her family as Irish Catholic, "Pretty strong Irish Catholic." She admitted that she went through a period of discerning whether she wanted to remain with the Catholic Church; she continued: "Yet, I think I always identified myself as pretty strong Catholic. Somehow it fit. If you go to other services, they're fine, and if I had to I could get used to it, but at the end of the day, there's something that's not quite right, something that's missing."

For some, VOTF was a way to remain connected with the church through the disillusionment precipitated by the sex abuse scandal and cover-up. One of the women leaders explained:

The church meant everything to me. I was a lector and a church council member. I served funeral Masses. I sometimes was a eucharistic minister. After the scandal broke, I couldn't do any of it. I mean, gradually I pulled away from all those activities; being a lector was the last thing. It got ruined for me, and I don't know what's going to bring that back. I'm just hanging on, and Voice of the Faithful is the way I'm hanging on.

Despite the importance of the church in the lives of VOTF leaders, a significant minority of the men (43 percent) and a quarter of the women acknowledged that it was possible that they might leave the church. Personal interviews reveal the degree to which the scandal and its cover-up have affected the way they perceive the church and their future relationship to it. For some it has created a fissure between the practices of faith and the institutional church. One woman put it succinctly:

I feel my relationship now is more with the persons of the Trinity than with the institutional church. I have a cold spot in my heart right now toward the institutional church. I am suspicious of everything now. This is such a bad place to be; I'm sure I will get over it. It's different from my apathy from the past. You know, when I was a kid I was apathetic and would drift away from the church and then I'd come back. But this is different; I had made a huge commitment, heart and soul. I was ready to be a good Catholic for all my life — and now I question everything.

Another leader commented that for several months he found himself angry and unable to concentrate on the Mass. He then realized that his anger was aimed at Cardinal Law. "I finally said, 'This is wrong.' I just needed to separate my life from all this anger at the misbehavior of Cardinal Law, who was supposed to be our leader as a follower of Christ. So I find my life as a Catholic very confused. I think we are all struggling."

In spite of the shock and anger the scandal and its cover-up have precipitated, some leaders find that their long history of participation in the church gives them the strength to face the current turmoil. One leader commented:

I think back to the kind of mysteries that I encountered as an altar boy. My recollection of the church I grew up in was an old Romanesque church. It was a very dark church. Sort of dark and shadowy, and the candles cast shadows. Whenever I think back I actually think back to a funeral when I was an altar boy. And of course that was with the black vestments. The flashback in my adult life is of a church of life, with white vestments, and there's an openness and a spirit of enthusiasm that emphasizes the light, and I think it has been overwhelmingly a positive shift in terms of my sense of identity as a Catholic.

VOTF Leaders and Parish Life

With regard to parish life, all of the women and a majority of the men (64 percent) were registered members of a parish (Table 2.4). Large majorities of the men and women were members of at least one parish committee; 40 percent or more have served as lectors and eucharistic ministers, while smaller numbers were Mass servers or

Table 2.4: VOTF Leaders in Parish Life,
by Gender (in percentages)

	Total	Male	Female
Registered member of a parish	84%	64%	100%
Now or was:			
Member of a parish committee	76	57	90
Lector	36	36	37
Eucharistic minister	52	43	58
Mass server	22	31	16
In music ministry	28	23	32
CCD/RCIA teacher	56	40	67
Teacher in Catholic primary or high school	20	0	35

in the music ministry. Again, 40 percent or more taught catechism classes for youth (CCD) or adult converts (RCIA). Thirty-five percent of the women taught in Catholic elementary or secondary schools.

Participation in parish life has been an important dimension in the lives of many of the leaders and their families. A Vatican II generation VOTF leader reflects:

> We were teaching CCD and involved with our kids' social service work. We sang in the choir, were eucharistic ministers, and read at Mass occasionally. My husband was very involved with coaching CYO basketball.

The intimate relationship between parenting and parish participation is also reflected in the statement of another leader:

> I was a widow and he was a widower; then we merged two families. Together we have eight children, and they all went to Catholic high school. That was very important. I've been going to church all my life, once a week. In earlier stages I was very active in fund drives and a whole bunch of other things, but then we focused on the kids' activities.

Many VOTF leaders came from St. John the Evangelist in Wellesley, Massachusetts; they claim that the vibrancy of this parish played a crucial role in the establishment and development of VOTF. One leader reflected:

> Wellesley is a very affluent middle-class and upper-middle-class community. It is among the top three or four suburban communities in regard to per capita income. I think St. John the Evangelist is among the wealthiest parishes in the archdiocese. Demographically, it has the full range of people, not just gray hair people. There are the very young and the elderly. It has this wonderful mix of people, and this reminds you that the church is for people of all ages and ethnicities. St. John's School brings young families to the community. It is a very active parish with a lot of ministries and activities, including athletics. People are quite engaged in this parish. It is one of the most admired parishes in the archdiocese in terms of its range of activities. You have a lot of well-educated people in this community: lawyers and businesspeople, teachers and social workers. It is an unlikely place for a revolution to begin.

While a majority of VOTF leaders were active in one or more aspects of parish life, for some it was the emergence of VOTF itself that propelled them to action. One leader said: "I wasn't that active in my parish, but this issue turned me into an active Catholic, and my commitment to the church increased through VOTF."

Participation in Life beyond the Parish

More than 40 percent of the VOTF leaders, both men and women, have participated in a Catholic social movement such as Catholic Worker or Christian Family Movement, while a third (36 percent) of the men and almost half the women are or have been members of at least one organization promoting social justice, such as Pax Christi, Bread for the World, Habitat for Humanity, or the Society of St. Vincent de Paul (Table 2.5). And one in five of the leaders has been a member of a diocesan committee.

The literature read by VOTF leaders nourishes an ecclesiological orientation rooted in the spirit of Vatican II and encourages active

Table 2.5. VOTF Leaders beyond Parish Life, by Gender (in percentages)

	Total	Male	Female
Now or ever			
Member of a diocesan committee	21%	21%	21%
Participated in a Catholic social movement	46	46	45
Member of a social justice organization	40	36	42
Subscribed to*			
America	46	39	50
National Catholic Reporter	46	54	40
Local diocesan newspaper	28	33	25
Commonweal	24	23	25
Political self-identification			
Conservative	13	31	0
Moderate	56	54	58
Liberal	31	15	42
Political party affiliation			
Republican	14	25	6
Democratic	55	33	71
Independent	31	42	23

*The four publications listed are the only Catholic journals or newspapers to which 10 percent or more of the leaders reported subscriptions.

lay participation. About half of the men and women subscribed to the *National Catholic Reporter* and *America*. This was followed by the local diocesan newspaper and *Commonweal*. These were the only Catholic periodicals to which 10 percent or more of the leaders subscribed.

With regard to political self-identification, a third of the men but none of the women called themselves conservative; more than half the men and women said they were moderates, while a minority of the men (15 percent) and three times as many of the women (42 percent) called themselves liberals. When asked their political party preference, more than twice as many women (71 percent) as men (33 percent) called themselves Democrats; a quarter of the men but only 6 percent of the women identified themselves as Republican.

More of the men (42 percent) called themselves Independents; only one in four of the women declared themselves to be Independents.

We asked the leaders how features of American society such as pluralism and democracy might have influenced how they thought about themselves as Catholics, or about the Catholic Church. Their responses suggested that most of them had compartmentalized the way they thought and acted within the broader framework of American society. One leader expressed it this way:

It's not something I think I have ever significantly pondered until Voice of the Faithful. I don't ever think I looked at it as, "Gee, I'm from a democratic society, so how come the church is like this?" I'm a typical person on the go; we don't have a lot of time to think about these kinds of things. Perhaps because I am a product of Vatican II, I instinctively realized that the way the church was operating didn't seem like what the church was all about. The more I began to hear about the scandal, the more it seemed like we had just taken, as a church, a whole different path from the way the Church originally was.

A Vatican II–generation male leader reflected on the changes that had taken place in American society during his lifetime and concluded that the church had been at odds with scientific knowledge and the public sense of the appropriate positions on human sexuality:

It begins with birth control and it continues on with homosexuality, and with the big conflict we are having over gay marriage in Massachusetts. So that is one great fault line. The other great fault line that cuts right across the first is the role of women. In my lifetime we have seen the role of women go from being second-class citizens to becoming if not exactly equal then largely equal to men in every way you could measure. Back in the 1960s women made up only 12 percent of all medical students. I just saw in the paper the other day that women are now a majority of all medical students. They've gone from 12 percent to 52 percent in our lifetime. The existence of well-educated, professionally competent, highly able women is a tremendous

demographic shift, and it creates a tremendous thirst on the part
of women for full involvement in every part of life. It's equal opportunity in the workplace; it's also a call for equal opportunity
in the church, and those pressures are enormous, and I think the
church is caught amid these two fault lines.

Another Vatican II–generation leader expressed her concerns about
the future of the church and of American society in these words:

> I've done a lot of reading about ecclesiology and thinking about
> it and about how democracy has influenced the way I think
> about the church. I mean, the church didn't have to become a
> monarchy. Jesus didn't even found a church; Jesus founded a
> community. Over time it became a monarchy at the same time
> that the monarchies were developing. It mirrored those societies,
> but it didn't have to be that way. And it doesn't have to stay that
> way. It seems to me that would be more true to the community
> that Jesus drew together and that established itself in the early
> days of the church. You just have to believe that the Holy Spirit is
> with the community, that the Holy Spirit does not whisper in the
> ear of the bishops; that the Holy Spirit lives in the community.
> We as a church need to become a discerning community. As a
> discerning community, our task is not to discern and take a vote
> on whether God exists or not. But we need to be true to the
> tradition that comes to us from Jesus and the apostles. And I
> am influenced in my thinking by my being an American. We
> have created institutions that God knows are not perfect, but
> institutions where we have a constitution, where we affirm a set
> of core values and ways of making decisions. There are a lot
> of things from our democratic institutions that can work in the
> church. It's just I think that the notion that Jesus set up for all
> time our present hierarchy is just not historically correct.

Conclusion

The founders and leaders of VOTF during its first three years represented an elite group of men and women drawn primarily from the

Boston archdiocese and disproportionately from one parish, St. John the Evangelist in Wellesley. As a group, they were dominated by pre-Vatican II and Vatican II Catholics who pray daily, regularly participate in the Mass, see the church as one of the most important influences in their lives, and have been active in the multiplicity of activities that make Catholic parishes vital. St. John's of Wellesley embraces an extraordinary number of people with high levels of education and professional skills that, when brought together, made it possible for them to do something that surprised the local church — and even surprised them. Some indicated that even one day before the explosion of news about the scandal and cover-up they would never have imagined organizing and standing up for change in the church as they did. The clerical sexual abuse scandal was the catalyst that brought people together for a common purpose, uniting them in a commitment to bring about change in the church, to promote justice for the victims of clerical abuse, and to work for the protection of children in the future.

Chapter Three

VOTF Members

Who They Are and Why They Stay

"VOTF raised the most important and fundamental questions about the church's response to the abuse crisis. I will support it as long as it keeps up that good and necessary work."

"I want to be an active member of the church. I want my voice to be heard. I have the right to speak."

"To remain Catholic, I needed to see a forum within the church taking action to address the scandal of sexual abuse. Otherwise, the pain my family experienced would have caused me to leave for another faith tradition. VOTF gave me some hope."

Who are these Catholics who want to remain in the church, give voice to their concerns, and support an organization that challenges the structures that enabled the sexual abuse of minors by clergy and its systematic cover-up?

In this chapter we examine VOTF members, who they are and what they have in common. We begin by taking a general look at VOTF members, their family backgrounds and economic status. Next, we examine in detail their levels of education and whether there are differences between those who did and did not attend Catholic schools. We then look at their commitment to the Catholic Church, manifested by their attitudes, beliefs, and behaviors. Special attention is placed on Mass attendance and its possible effects. When comparable data are available, the characteristics of VOTF members are compared to those of the general Catholic population based on the 2005 survey conducted by D'Antonio et al. Finally, we address the question of why in the face of such great challenges brought about by the betrayal of church leaders VOTF members choose to remain as active Catholics.

The Demographic Overview

The split between women and men in VOTF is nearly 60 percent to 40 percent. We invited respondents to indicate their ethnic ancestry, including multiple roots; almost two-thirds claimed some Irish heritage. Latinos and African Americans made up only a small percentage of the membership.

An examination of family background affirms that VOTF members have strong roots in Catholicism. One member expressed this in the following way:

> Being Catholic is part of who I am, especially being Irish Catholic. I chose a profession of service — nursing — and my dedication to health care and my students is part of my own sense of vocation.

Another said:

> I feel like it's part and parcel of who I am, almost a part of my DNA. Try as I might, I can't dump it and I can't fully reconcile myself to it. And I'm lazy, don't want to go to church very much, and, of course, feel terribly guilty about it being Irish Catholic.

Not surprisingly, almost all were cradle Catholics, as were most of their parents. The great majority (85 percent) was also registered in a parish (true of 68 percent of the national population, based on the 2005 survey). Two out of three VOTF members were married, and of these the overwhelming majority indicated they were in sacramental marriages recognized by the Catholic Church. Most of those that were married have children, and about half of these children attended parochial schools. They estimated that one in three of their adult children attended Mass regularly. Eight percent of VOTF members were divorced. Fifteen percent were single; this may reflect the percentage of priests and professed religious among their members.

Almost half of the VOTF members were employed, while a third were retired. These figures reflect the imbalance of generations in VOTF, which leans heavily toward the pre-Vatican II and Vatican II– generations. About a third were in professional occupations, followed by business owners and managers, and academics. Less than one in ten identified themselves with clerical, service, or skilled trades oc- cupations. The high levels of academic, professional, and business achievements were reflected in their income levels, with 30 percent stating annual household incomes of $100,000 or more, and another 50 percent with incomes between $75,000 and $100,000.

Formal Catholic Education: A Key Feature of VOTF Membership

One of the most distinctive characteristics about VOTF members is their high level of education. Many came from highly educated par- ents; a third of their fathers and a quarter of their mothers were college graduates. The vast majority of VOTF members (nearly nine in ten) had at least a college degree; six out of ten had graduate or professional degrees (Table 3.1).

Furthermore, a majority was educated in Catholic schools, from a high of 70 percent at the elementary level and over 60 percent at the high school level to a majority at the college level. Almost a quarter of VOTF members had earned a degree in either theology, canon law, or scripture studies; half said they had taken an extensive

---

Table 3.1. VOTF Members and Catholics in General by Levels of Education (in percentages)

Educational Level	VOTF Members	2005 National Survey
High school or less	2%	32%
Some college	10	35
College graduate	27	19
Graduate degree	61	14

number of theology courses, and almost as many had taken diocesan or parish-sponsored theology courses, as one woman shared: "My husband and I attended a two-year pastoral formation institute in our diocese." It is not surprising that one in four VOTF members had some experience of formation for priesthood or religious life. One man reflected on his history: "I am a married priest, currently active in my local parish. I am on the pastoral council, am a catechist, and participate in activities with my children, who attend the parish school." Twenty-two percent of the men and women professed religious vows; 16 percent of the men had been ordained and some remain in active ministry. While these figures may be astonishing, they were consistent with the VOTF national office's profile of the membership. Thus, a small but important minority of VOTF members has very deep roots in the Roman Catholic Church, through ordination and religious profession.

These high levels of education, and Catholic education in particular, distinguish VOTF Catholics from the general Catholic population. Seventy percent of VOTF members had a Catholic elementary school education, 61 percent a Catholic high school education, and 58 percent attended a Catholic college or university. By contrast, about half of the general Catholic population attended Catholic elementary schools, less than a third Catholic high schools, and only about one in ten a Catholic college or university (2005 Survey). It may be suggested that VOTF Catholics represent the fulfillment of the U.S. bishops' vision of an educated, professional Catholic public when in 1884 they formally established the parochial school system in the United States (Table 3.2).

Table 3.2. VOTF Members and Catholics in General by Amount of Catholic Education (in percentages)

Catholic Education	VOTF Members	2005 National Survey
Elementary	70%	49%
High school	61	29
College	58	12

VOTF members who graduated from Catholic colleges display particularly high levels of commitment to the Catholic Church. Graduates were more likely:

+ to attend Mass somewhat more frequently;

+ to participate in programs or activities to help the needy on a weekly basis;

+ to say the church was the most or among the most important parts of their lives;

+ to say they would never leave the church.

The possible influence of Catholic education is more evident in their differential participation in church life. For example, the Catholic college graduates were significantly more likely to have been members of parish committees like the liturgy committee and the school board, and to be lectors and eucharistic ministers, CCD teachers, Catholic grade and high school teachers, or RCIA leaders. They were also more likely to be members of Small Christian Communities and movements like Call to Action,[1] a Catholic reform movement with its earliest roots in the Catholic Action movements of Chicago.

The Catholic college graduates were twice as likely to have read all the documents of Vatican II and less likely to report that they had not read any of them. During 2004 two important reports about the Protection of Children and Young People were produced, one by the National Review Board, and the other by the John Jay College of Law. The Catholic college graduates were also more likely to say that they had at least some knowledge of these studies. Religious reading habits also varied significantly by whether or not members went to a Catholic college; those who did were significantly more likely to subscribe to the National Catholic Reporter and America, and slightly more likely to get the diocesan newspaper and Commonweal.

Differences on the ideological items and party identification were very small. The Catholic college graduates were more liberal and moderate on political and social matters, and more moderate on economic matters, while a majority of both groups were Democrats.

Regarding attitudes toward church policy, there were no significant differences between those who went to Catholic colleges and those who did not. Nor did this distinction have an impact on participation in VOTF. However, Catholic college graduates were a bit more likely to have invited others to VOTF meetings and to be members of a VOTF affiliate. Overall, while there is evidence that formal Catholic school education makes a difference, even among VOTF members, the differences are not great. This may be because in general highly educated persons tend to want input into associations of which they are members, and in the face of an event like the scandal they are likely to want to take an active role in promoting reform.

Measures of Commitment

When asked how important the church is to them personally, 62 percent said it is the most or among the most important parts of their life. Only 44 percent of American Catholics in the general population said this (2005 Survey). At the other end, only 6 percent said it was not very important to them. One VOTF member added: "The Catholic Church is an important part of my life because I look to it for an example of how to live the gospel, to have the courage and conviction to see truth, to have the opportunity to share and express my faith with others."

Two additional questions examined VOTF members' degree of commitment to the church and its teachings. Since Vatican II, the church has stressed "a preferential option for the poor." We asked how often, if at all, they served the needy in programs such as soup kitchens or tutoring programs; a quarter said weekly, and another quarter said at least once a month. Only a fifth responded seldom or never. One person reflected: "I am disabled now, but when in good health I volunteered in a soup kitchen and served in an AIDS agency, running a support group and coordinating services for persons with AIDS."

A final question asked about knowledge of the Second Vatican Council. About one in five had read all of the documents. About half of them said they had participated in seminars on Vatican II and its documents. One man commented on how knowledge of Vatican II influenced him. "Education about the church and particularly about the call of Vatican II to 'full, conscious and active participation' in the life of the church and liturgy has transformed me from passive and submissive into an active, fully engaged Catholic."

VOTF Members in Parish Life

Nearly half were members of parish councils or on liturgy committees. One in four served on parish school boards or finance committees, while two-thirds reported serving on other parish committees. Nearly half served as lectors or eucharistic ministers while others were Mass servers, music ministers, greeters, or ushers. Over half reported teaching in religious education programs or on RCIA teams; and a quarter said they had taught in a Catholic grade school or high school. One woman commented: "The church has been very important to me throughout my life. When my children were young, I spent several years teaching in our parish religious education program, developing curriculum and teaching junior high and First Communion classes." Another reflected: "I taught CCD for my parish for eighteen years and continue to help with the Confirmation classes." Yet another said: "I participate in numerous service activities. I have taught CCD for six years, worked on the retreats for three, and I am on several other lay ministries."

Two out of three were members of small faith-sharing groups, including parish RENEW groups. One woman commented: "Since we made a Marriage Encounter, our faith and belonging to a faith community has been a vital part of our marriage and our life." A man added: "My wife and I have been co-coordinators of our parish Small Christian Community program for six groups for twelve years, and we have facilitated one of the groups for fourteen years."

In sum, VOTF members demonstrate extraordinary levels of participation in the intellectual and sacramental life of the Catholic Church, as well as in its mission and organizations.

VOTF beyond the Parish

VOTF members were active in a variety of groups beyond the parish level. Five percent were members of organizations under the U.S. bishops' sponsorship; one in four was a member of the diocesan pastoral council; a majority was in some other diocesan council or committee. One member indicated: "I am a Knight of Malta, and my wife and I are a Lady and Knight of the Equestrian Order of the Holy Sepulcher of Jerusalem. I also served six years on the state Catholic Conference." Another said: "I have met with the Pontifical Academy of Science and met Pope John Paul II on several occasions."

One in four participated in Marriage Encounter, Cursillo, or Call to Action (CTA). Smaller numbers were active in the charismatic movement, the Christian Family Movement (CFM), the Catholic Worker movement, the Right to Life movement, Young Christian Students, Dignity, or Catholics for a Free Choice.

VOTF members also belonged to traditional Catholic organizations: of the men, 33 percent and 16 percent respectively were members of the Knights of Columbus and the Holy Name Society. One member even indicated: "I was Grand Knight for three years." Women were less active in specifically women's groups: only 6 percent were members of the National Council of Catholic Women, and only 1 percent belonged to Catholic Mothers or Daughters of Isabella.

Thirty-one percent overall were in the St. Vincent de Paul Society. One member shared: "I volunteer weekly at a children's center that mostly has volunteers from St. Vincent de Paul. I also participate in other Faith-to-Justice programs at my church, and I'm currently training to be a liturgical minister." Eight percent of the members had served in the Jesuit volunteers, most probably in their immediate post-college years. One of them shared: "I spent two years as a full-time volunteer. One year was in the Jesuit Volunteer Corps, and the second year was at a young adult volunteer program in the archdiocese." Both programs included community living. Four in ten were affiliated with organizations such as Pax Christi and Habitat for Humanity.

VOTF Attitudes toward Participation
in Church Governance

Such broad and extensive participation in various aspects of church life have provided VOTF members the opportunity to develop strong views about the church. VOTF members are in almost unanimous agreement that decision making, not involving the creedal parts of the faith, should include wider participation by the laity. As one member stated: "The hierarchy must realize that we are educated, caring people who are invested in the realization of God's kingdom." For example, they all say the laity should have the right to participate in "Deciding how parish income is spent." This is not unlike the national survey, where 89 percent said the same (2005 Survey). As for the selection of priests for their parishes, 84 percent of VOTF Catholics and 71 percent of the national survey said that the laity has the right to participate in their selection. Eight out of ten VOTF Catholics also believe they should have a role in selecting bishops for their dioceses.

To get an indication of the salience of these beliefs, we asked VOTF members about the amount of time and resources they would be willing to invest to promote meaningful participation by the laity in church decision making. Almost half said they would devote two to five hours per week, of their time, while an additional 7 percent said they would devote six to ten hours per week and another 6 percent would devote more than ten hours per week. Only 12 percent were not willing to devote any time.

Regarding giving financial resources to VOTF, a small number (6 percent) were willing to give more than $500 a year, while one in five were willing to donate between $100 and $500 a year. Sixty-percent were willing to give up to $100, and only a minority of 14 percent said they were not willing to give any money to such a cause.

One in four members was not familiar with either the report of the National Review Board or that of the John Jay College of Law; 11 percent had a great deal of knowledge about them, and about four in ten said they had some knowledge of each group and of their respective study and report.

Members gave overwhelming support to the three goals of VOTF: to support victims of clerical sexual abuse (86 percent), to support priests of integrity (85 percent), and to shape structural change in the church (91 percent). Under half (44 percent) are in an affiliate group, almost a third attended an affiliate meeting during the past year, and a third donated money to a local affiliate, while 45 percent have donated money to the national office in the past twelve months. More than half the members signed the VOTF Petition for Reform, a petition addressed to the church hierarchy seeking accountability and reform of church structures (see *www.voiceofthefaithful.org*). The overwhelming majority (82 percent) saw the national office as providing effective day-to-day leadership, enabling VOTF to persist and fulfill its mission. The same percentage said the elective officers and the board of trustees were charting an effective direction for VOTF to persist and to fulfill its mission. Likewise about 80 percent saw the Representative Council doing an effective job. Overall, VOTF members were very satisfied with the leadership and the new structures.

In February 2002, Dr. Mary Jo Bane, a professor in the Kennedy School of Government at Harvard University, wrote an op-ed piece in the *Boston Globe*.[2] She began by saying: "The crisis in the Archdiocese of Boston tragically illustrates the consequences of a culture of secrecy and deference in the church. It is time for lay Catholics who love the church to challenge that culture. We can do so by withholding our contributions to the archdiocese until the church becomes more open and participatory."

To ascertain the level of support for this idea, we asked if the members agreed with this statement: "When the hierarchy is unresponsive to the views of the laity on matters which concern the good of the church, withholding financial contributions is an appropriate means for getting their attention." Sixty-six percent of VOTF Catholics strongly agreed with this statement. VOTF saw other deficiencies in the leadership of the hierarchy. More than eight of ten strongly agreed that the "hierarchy is out of touch with the laity."

VOTF members also did not believe that priests appreciated their leadership skills. Most of them strongly or somewhat agreed that "priests generally see laity as followers." As for the job performance of priests, three-quarters of VOTF members strongly or somewhat agreed: "priests generally do a good job." More than nine out of ten respondents to the national survey offered these same responses (2005 Survey). Nearly three-quarters of VOTF members strongly or somewhat agreed, "Parishes are too big and impersonal."

In response to a question about the Catholic periodicals they read, nearly four in ten said they subscribed to their local diocesan news-paper and a third subscribed to the *National Catholic Reporter;* a quarter received *America* and about one in ten read *Commonweal,* *St. Anthony Messenger, U.S. Catholic,* or VOTF's online newsletter, *In the Vineyard.* Smaller numbers subscribed to *Our Sunday Visitor, Crisis, First Things,* and the *Wanderer.*

Almost half described themselves as politically liberal, as economically moderate, and as social-cultural liberals. Just over one in ten described themselves as conservative on any of the three. Almost two out of three identified with the Democratic Party and almost a fifth with the Republican Party.

Mass Attendance as a Control Variable

Church attendance is an important variable in measuring the impact of religion on values, beliefs, and practices; this was especially stressed in analyses of the 2004 national election. In this section we examine the correlation between Mass attendance and differences in the values, beliefs, and practices of VOTF members. VOTF members claim high levels of Mass attendance, with two out of three attending Mass at least once a week. By comparison, the 2005 national survey reported that only a third of the general Catholic population attends Mass at least once a week. So high levels of Mass attendance is itself an important characteristic of VOTF Catholics (Table 3.3).

The overwhelming majority of VOTF Catholics who attend Mass daily or at least weekly are registered members of parishes, and their marriages are formally recognized by the church. The daily or weekly Mass attendance also correlates with levels of personal prayer and service to the needy. While eight out of ten VOTF members report

Table 3.3. VOTF Members and Catholics in General by Levels of Mass Attendance (in percentages)

Mass attendance	VOTF Members	2005 National Survey
At least weekly	66%	34%
At least monthly	23	30
Never/seldom	11	36

praying once a day or more, for those who attend Mass daily or weekly it increases to nine in ten. Half of those who attend Mass daily or weekly help the disadvantaged at least once a month.

There is a positive relationship between daily or weekly Mass attendance and the importance VOTF members place on the church. Three-fourths of VOTF members who go to Mass daily or weekly say the church is the "most" or "among the most" important parts of their lives. Again two in three daily or weekly Mass goers say they would "never leave the church," while only 14 percent say they might leave.

Higher levels of Mass attendance correlate with membership on the parish councils, liturgy committees, and other parish committees. Yet even some of those who now attend monthly or seldom also claimed that they had participated in the parish council (25 percent), finance council (10 percent), and liturgical ministries (40 percent). Daily or weekly Mass attendees were significantly more active in church ministries that seek to pass on the Catholic faith such as CCD and RCIA activities. They were also more likely to have participated in RENEW, Small Christian Communities, Marriage Encounter, Call to Action, and Cursillo.

Regarding VOTF members' attitudes and behavior toward church policy, Mass attendance rates had no effect on their insistence about more extensive participation in church decisions, nor did it affect perceptions of the hierarchy as out of touch with the laity. Those who seldom attended Mass were more likely to have more negative views of priests and to say the laity should withhold financial contributions to gain the attention of the hierarchy.

More than half of the "at least weekly" Mass attendees were willing to give at least two hours a week to promote church reform; those who attended less were less willing to give of their time. Mass attendance did not affect the willingness to give money to promote church reform.

Do Catholics with different patterns of Mass attendance differ in their knowledge of the events of Vatican II? We inquired about knowledge of Vatican II, and, as expected, daily or weekly Mass attendees were almost twice as likely as monthly attendees to have read all the documents. With regard to the National Review Board and its Bennett Report, higher percentages of "at least weekly" Mass attendees claimed at least some knowledge. This pattern held regarding the John Jay College Study. Daily or weekly attendees also were more likely to invite others to attend VOTF meetings.

One feature that emerges through this comparative reading of Mass attendance is that it is not a constant and may fluctuate over time. One VOTF member reflected: "The church was very important at one time, but that is no longer true. I have been in a state of flux since 2002; I took a break from being a catechist and don't attend Mass as often as I did." This suggests that for at least some the scandal had an impact on Mass attendance. Another VOTF member wrote: "I stopped attending Mass on a regular basis because the pastor who married us four years ago went to jail as part of the scandal, and the church basically swept it under the carpet after the initial outcry." Another wrote: "After a couple of years of regular church attendance, I have fallen away, very much discouraged by developments in the church. It doesn't help that we moved away from our old parish; we have been desultorily looking for a good new one." VOTF sustains for some of them at least a minimal level of interest in the church.

Participation in VOTF Activities

The next set of items attempts to help us understand how members became involved in VOTF and the degree of their participation. A majority went to their first VOTF meeting alone while some went at the invitation of another. More than half invited others in turn to attend VOTF meetings.

The manner in which the parish pastor dealt with the sexual abuse scandal seemed to have an influence on the decision to participate in VOTF. More than half said their pastors publicly responded to the scandal; of these pastors, more than a third were supportive of VOTF. One VOTF parishioner reflected: "With the cooperation of my pastor I organized an exploratory VOTF group, and after meeting weekly we ultimately voted to become a VOTF affiliate, which I chaired. It included a multiweek seminar discussion format for all parishioners." Another parishioner said: "My pastor encouraged the parishioners to meet, and the outcome was the founding of VOTF."

A little over a third of VOTF members declared their pastors neutral on VOTF, and a quarter said their pastors were unsupportive.[3] From these parishioners came such comments as the following: "He [the pastor] said 'pray for the church, pray for the priests.' He did not mention the victims." Another noted that at first "my pastor was supportive of VOTF," but then "he subsequently denounced VOTF and all its members as evil and divisive." Other pastors acknowledged the scandal and then tried to draw attention away from it. "Our pastor mentioned it in the beginning but has avoided any discussion and has not encouraged VOTF." Another parishioner reported, "My pastor's response to the scandal was to tell us it was unimportant. He promised never to mention it again from the altar. I thought that was terrible." And finally, this comment: "My pastor wrote to our local paper and cited Cardinal Law as a scapegoat who would never had [*sic*] done anything to harm children."

Over half of VOTF members are not members of an affiliate. These are some of the reasons given to explain this situation. "I joined VOTF from another city and do not know of any meetings here." For some the Internet is a medium of affiliation. "I am a Boston College graduate — a friend who still lives in Boston referred me to VOTF a couple years ago. I have forwarded email bulletins on to family members and friends."

Leaving and Staying in the Catholic Church

Respondents were asked to indicate where they stood on a seven-point scale ranging from 1 ("I would never leave the Catholic Church") to 7 ("I might leave"). Slightly less than half of VOTF members said they would "never leave" the Catholic Church. They slightly trail the general Catholic population in this response. In Table 3.4 we see that VOTF members were more likely to say they "might leave" (22 percent) than were the general Catholic populace (2005 Survey). How can this be explained?

We have seen that VOTF members display levels of commitment to the Catholic Church that are higher than those of the general Catholic population. This is shown by their frequency of Mass attendance, prayer, active participation in church life, and service to the needy. At the same time it is more likely for a member of the general Catholic population to say "I will never leave the church," and it is more likely for a VOTF member to say "I might leave." How do we understand this seeming contradiction between expressed intention and action?

Hirschman's classic work *Exit, Voice, and Loyalty* (1970) discusses the behaviors of consumers and members in firms and organizations, and he notes these come in two types. Some are inert or non-critical, and others are alert and critical. Non-critical consumers are likely to stay with a particular supplier as long as their basic needs are met.[4] There is little need to think about leaving. If a consumer becomes critical and there is a viable alternative, the consumer can leave one supplier and go to another; here exit becomes an option. Rodney Stark and other sociologists have characterized the American religious landscape as a vast market and explain religious switching in just this way. However, when one is a member rather than a consumer, the variable of loyalty enters the picture and the exit option becomes more costly. Our study indicates that VOTF Catholics tend to see themselves as members, and thus they are both active and critical.

The profile of VOTF members shows that they are highly educated, hold professional positions, have high incomes, and are active in their professions and communities. They are people with influence in the daily life of their community. This profile is consistent with previous

Table 3.4. VOTF Members and Catholics in General by Projections to Stay In or Leave the Catholic Church

	VOTF Members	2005 National Survey
Response 1–2 "Never Leave"	48%	56%
Response 6–7 "Might Leave"	22	14

research on loyal members, who remain with troubled organizations in order to reform them. The ability of VOTF members to influence outcomes in other forums has affected their understanding of how one can act as a member of the Catholic Church. Instead of giving up on the church they want to bring to bear their personal resources to reform the church.

Hirschman asserts that voice and exit can be complementary, and the former does not rule out the latter. Citing Banfield's 1961 study of political influence,[5] he proposes that interested parties will make efforts to engage an organizational decision maker in proportion to the advantage to be gained from a favorable outcome multiplied by the probability of influencing the decision. "If customers [members] are sufficiently convinced that voice will be effective, then they may well postpone exit."[6] This suggests why VOTF Catholics can on the one hand show a higher level of commitment to Catholicism and on the other express a higher likelihood that they "might leave" the church.

Theologian Paul Philibert predicts: "We can expect to see more examples like Voice of the Faithful and more exasperated defections from the Catholic Community until meaningful lay consultation and participation become a greater part of parish and diocesan life."[7] Further discussion of Hirschman's theory will be found in chapter 9, William Gamson's "The Virtues of Loyalty," and in the concluding chapter.

Conclusion

VOTF Catholics tend to come from families with deep Catholic roots; their high levels of Catholic education reflect this. Likewise, their high educational attainments place them in professional, academic, and executive occupations that are responsible for their generally high economic status. VOTF Catholics are active participants in the Catholic Church. They have high levels of Mass attendance, personal prayer, service to the poor, and participation in parish life. The scandal made visible their dissatisfaction with the hierarchy's management of the church and its capacity to understand the concerns of ordinary lay Catholics. Yet, at least at this point, they would rather raise their voices and devote their efforts to reform the church than cease being active members of the Catholic Church. It may be said that VOTF members possess a critical fidelity to their church.

Chapter Four

VOTF Members

Gender, Generation, and Region

In chapter 3 we found that Voice of the Faithful Catholics have deep roots in the Catholic Church anchored in family, enriched by Catholic school education, and shown in their Mass attendance, which is twice that of the overall American Catholic population. In this chapter we examine how gender, generation, and region of the country may be predictive of differences within VOTF membership, as well as with the general Catholic population.[1]

The Role of Gender

Gender and Changing Opportunity Structures

Like race and ethnicity, gender significantly shapes one's life chances. Catholic women and men of the pre-Vatican II era were expected to follow the prescribed roles assigned to each regarding sexuality, child rearing, and financially supporting a family. A woman's place was considered to be the home while men were designated to go out and work on behalf of the family.

The 1960s was a time of rapid social change. The feminist movement brought dramatic and continuing changes in the socialization of women and men. These changes had great impact on women's identity and roles. There was a rise in the numbers of women attending and graduating from college; this, in turn, increased their career opportunities. From 1950 to 1980, married women's share of the labor market rose from 24 percent to well over 50 percent. Many women postponed marriage to pursue careers. Gradually, child bearing and child rearing became only one part of their identities and roles. Both men and women went outside the home to work on behalf of the family, and increasingly to further their own careers.

The changing social conditions of Catholics contributed to what may be the most important change in the lives of many modern Catholic men and women: a shift in where the locus of moral authority is seen to reside. Before Vatican II, Catholics commonly perceived the proper locus of moral authority to reside in the bishops and ultimately in the pope. But events of the past half-century have changed that. A wide range of research shows that Catholics have changed from a predominant reliance on external authority to greater reliance on internal authority — their consciences. This shift is consistent with the strong tendencies toward individualism and personal autonomy that mark modern American society. Likewise it also reflects the new emphasis on freedom of conscience and personal responsibility found in the documents of Vatican II.

These changes of worldview, as well as the new opportunities that have developed for lay Catholics after Vatican II, have transformed the role of the laity in the church. Today one takes for granted the multiplicity of roles for laymen and laywomen in worship and parish life. Many of these roles — such as lector, eucharistic minister, and lay catechist — did not exist fifty years ago, or religious sisters or brothers performed such functions. Today they have engendered a growing sense of personal responsibility of the laity for the local parish community.

In addition, the growing shortage of priests and nuns has increased opportunities in the church for paid employment for men and especially women. Traditionally the Catholic school system was the major location of lay employment within the church; now there are over thirty thousand paid lay jobs in parish and diocesan offices.

Other research has found women and men being appointed by bishops to administer parishes without a resident pastor. In 1992, Ruth Wallace published *They Call Her Pastor,* a book about women taking on much of the administrative and symbolic role of coordinating a parish community.[2] Wallace stressed that the assignment of this position to women gave them a major responsibility for the life of the local church.

In 2003 she published *They Call Him Pastor,* the story of laymen administering these parishes.[3] In 1992 there were about three hundred such parishes in the United States, but by 2003 the number had grown to three thousand. Wallace's research suggests that a number of bishops look to local parish members to help them select the parish administrator. Given the growing number of these parishes, we may expect to find this an area of great opportunity for interaction and participation by both women and men in the governance of the church at the parish level.

The Demographics of Gender in VOTF

Our survey of VOTF Catholics found only small gender differences across generations; a higher proportion of men were found among pre-Vatican II Catholics while the reverse was true among Vatican II Catholics (Table 4.1). Men were more likely to have earned a graduate degree (68 to 55 percent), to be employed full time (50 to 40 percent), or retired (41 to 31 percent). They were also more than twice as likely (24 to 11 percent) to be in managerial and executive occupations.

Men and women were equally likely to be cradle Catholics, to be registered parish members, to have had similar Catholic school-college educational levels, and to have parents who were Catholic (Table 4.2, Appendix F, page 227). They were also similar in their religious beliefs and practices.

Participation in Church Life

Men and women were equally likely to serve as lectors and eucharistic ministers (Table 4.3, Appendix F, page 228). Still, there were remnants of the more traditional pre-Vatican II church in some of their activities. VOTF men were five times as likely to have been Mass servers. Men predominated on parish councils, on finance and school boards; women in liturgy committees and as CCD teachers. This couple is representative of a more traditional distribution of roles in church life: "For parish service, I am a member of Knights of

Table 4.1. Demographic Profile of VOTF Members,
by Gender (in percentages)

	Total (%)	Female (%)	Male (%)
Generation			
Pre-Vatican II	41	38	46
Vatican II	48	50	44
Post-Vatican II	11	12	10
Ethnicity (many respondents checked more than one ethnicity)			
Irish	63	67	58
English	22	22	21
Western European	24	24	22
Eastern European	9	9	10
Latino	2	1	1
All others (includes African Americans)	33	32	33
Education			
High school	2	3	1
Some college	10	13	5
College degree	27	28	25
Graduate degree	61	55	68
Married	75	71	80
Employment			
Full time	44	40	50
Part time	13	18	7
Retired	35	31	41
Nature of Employment			
Academic	21	21	20
Professional	30	30	30
Managerial/Executive	17	11	24
Business Owner	5	4	6
Other	27	33	19
Annual Household Income			
Under $49,999	25	27	21
$50,000–$74,999	18	19	18
$75,000–$99,999	15	14	18
$100,000 and more	29	26	33
No Answer	13	14	10

Columbus. My wife is the president of the parish Home and School and a volunteer in the school and for the annual parish carnival." VOTF men were more likely to participate in gendered organizations such as the Knights of Columbus than women were in comparable women's groups.

Behavior and Attitudes toward Church Policies

Large majorities of VOTF men and women agreed that the hierarchy is out of touch with the laity, that they have a right to participate in church governance at all levels, especially in deciding how parish funds are spent and how priests and bishops are selected (Table 4.4, Appendix F, page 229).

While economic, social, and political ideologies don't translate directly into church policies, they do suggest possible areas of support for or opposition to social legislation of interest to the bishops at the state and federal levels. Thus, it is important to note that in regard to ideological orientations toward politics and socio-cultural issues, women were more liberal than men. In economic matters, the moderate position dominated, with women significantly more moderate than the men. Less than a fifth claimed to be conservative in any area, but men were twice as likely to call themselves conservative. When asked about political party identification, nearly two-thirds said they were Democrats.

Participation in VOTF Activities

Differences appeared between the men's and women's participation in VOTF and their evaluation of the movement and its goals (Table 4.5). Women were significantly more likely (63 to 44 percent) to have invited others to meetings and to belong to a VOTF affiliate (49 to 36 percent). Only 44 percent of the total are members of affiliates. Women were more likely than the men to sign the Petition for Reform (55 to 45 percent). Women also had a more positive attitude about the effectiveness of the national office, the officers, and the National Council (by an average of 14 percentage points).

Table 4.5. Participation in VOTF Activities, by Gender (in percentages)

	Total (%)	Female (%)	Male (%)
First Attendance at a VOTF Meeting			
On my own	59	58	61
Invited by another person	16	15	17
Invited others to attend VOTF meetings	55	63	44
Member of VOTF affiliate – yes	44	49	36
In last twelve months, has			
Donated money to VOTF National	32	31	32
Donated money to local affiliate	24	25	23
Attended VOTF meetings	32	35	29
Attended regional conference	12	13	10
Signed Petition for Reform	51	55	45
National office provided leadership	82	87	75
Officers, trustees chart effective direction	81	88	73
Representative council providing			
effective guidance	78	85	70

The Significance of Generation

An aerial view of the first VOTF convocation in July 2002 would have shown a sea of silver, making apparent that the younger generation of Catholics was not well represented at the first gathering. VOTF leaders and members tend to be older Catholics. One member wrote: "At our regional and parish Voice meetings there are mostly 'gray tops'; the young people are absent from our group." Why is this the case? Is this an issue that is peculiar to VOTF? Is it important? To examine these questions we will begin with a consideration of generational change.

Sociologists use generation as a key variable to explain differences between groups. Researchers assert that the historical and cultural phenomena one experiences in adolescence and young adulthood affect one's worldview for life.[4] In studies of Catholics, the Second Vatican Council has been used as a reference point to distinguish generations of Catholics.[5] "Pre-Vatican II Catholics," born in 1940 or earlier, came of age before the council. "Vatican II Catholics," born between 1941 and 1960, experienced their formative years during the council. Those born from 1961 on are "Post-Vatican II Catholics." For them, Vatican Council II is a piece of history; they have no first-hand memory of the events that took place between October 1962 and December 1965. We find this tripartite differentiation useful in our examination of VOTF members.

The contexts in which these generations developed were different. The pre-Vatican II church conceived of itself as *a perfect society:* a self-sufficient organization without need for secular institutions. Catholics formed a parallel society removed from mainstream America.[6] The hierarchy strictly regulated the means to salvation, mediating salvation via the church's laws and sacraments.[7] Catholic parents supported this system by encouraging intellectual heteronomy (obedience to authority) over intellectual autonomy.[8]

Vatican II (1962–65) precipitated a big shift; tight boundaries were expanded. The church's perception of the world changed, as is made clear in Vatican II's Constitution on the Church in the Modern World. The modern world was no longer considered to be the enemy of eternal truths, and the church acknowledged modern progress as beneficial to humankind. The church sought to dialogue with the modern world.[9] From this time, Catholics' reliance on external authority decreased and reliance on internal authority, conscience, increased.[10] The comments of two VOTF members reflect this shift away from reliance on external authority to reliance on conscience: "My faith is the most important part of my life." "The Catholic Church does not define my faith completely. My Catholic faith is a very important part of my life and is my guide for many important decisions. However, the organizational Catholic Church is not very important to me."

Research shows that the pre-Vatican II generation is most loyal, church-going, and prayerful. They lived through the Great Depression and World War II, and many belonged to the "Greatest Generation," as Tom Brokaw called them in a book with that name. Many remember the prejudice and discrimination against Catholics that marked the first half of the twentieth century. This was the generation that finally convinced other Americans that it was possible to be a good Catholic and a good citizen, and it was the generation that gave us our first Catholic president when Senator John F. Kennedy of Massachusetts was elected to the highest office in the land. They were involved in building the Catholic infrastructure of parishes and schools. They have deep roots in the church, and they were most devastated by clerical malfeasance. As one member wrote: "The senior set has too many years and too much heart invested [in the Catholic Church] to take a hike." Today they are retired and have the time and resources to devote to reforming the church. Putnam's *Bowling Alone* suggests they were the last generation to display high levels of organizational engagement; it is not surprising that they are so well represented in VOTF.[11]

The Vatican II generation grew up during a period of transition from stability to change. Many remember the 1950s when a war hero, Dwight Eisenhower, sat in the White House and the nation experienced post–World War II tranquility as well as the tensions that mounted with the Cold War, a period when mutually assured destruction (MAD) made possible by nuclear weapons was our policy toward Communist regimes. They watched *Father Knows Best* and trusted strong and fatherly men to lead the nation and the church. The 1960s brought a change in national and church leadership. The Irish-Catholic John F. Kennedy, a World War II hero and U.S. senator, was elected president, as noted above. Pope John XXIII, an avuncular prelate who experienced the tragedy of World War II as a member of the Vatican diplomatic corps and knew the threats of annihilation by nuclear weapons, called an ecumenical council. The period that followed was one of radical changes. This generation is committed to the spirit of Vatican II and the importance of conscience and collaboration. Many are disappointed now by what they perceive as a deceleration of the reforms of the council. As one member said, "We are the 'over the hill gang' in love with the changes promised in the Vatican II documents only to find that our hierarchy 'deep-sixed' them and hoped we would forget." Such sentiments fuel their participation in VOTF.

The post-Vatican II generation raised in the 1970s and 1980s knew little, if anything, of previously accepted forms of discrimination.

Church officials accepted this trend in society, but balked when some suggested changes in the central institution of the priesthood. The Watergate break-in at the Democratic National Headquarters and cover-up of the break-in during the presidency of Richard Nixon exposed hypocrisy at the highest levels of government power; the average citizen became less trusting of institutions and even of others, and sought to become more self-sufficient. Church and community experienced the effects. This generation is most affected by the American ethos; they rely more on their own judgment and are less committed to institutions. A portion of this generation seeks comfort in trying to reproduce the security they imagined existed in a 1950s world. These factors do not encourage membership in VOTF.

One VOTF member commented: "All or nearly all are white senior citizens. The youngest person I saw at any of the six meetings I attended was my daughter, age thirty-five." Another expressed a desire to have younger members but concluded that most of them "are suspicious of institutions, and are also raising their kids at this time" and thus too busy to join VOTF. Another echoed this sentiment: "VOTF needs more 'boomers' and young people. It appeals to the upper class, not ethnics. The young are not into the reform of institutions — 'if it's broke throw it out,' they say."

Comparing the Demographics of the Generations

Table 4.6 shows the generational contrast between Catholics in the general population and VOTF members.

Table 4.6. Comparison of VOTF Members and U.S. Catholic Population, by Generations*

	Pre-Vatican II	Vatican II	Post-Vatican II
2005 National Survey of American Catholics	17%	34%	49%
Survey of VOTF Members	41%	48%	11%

*Data for U.S. Catholic population provided by 2005 national survey, D'Antonio et al.

VOTF members are older than Catholics at large. At least nine in ten VOTF members are over forty; almost half of American Catholics are under forty. With such a large number in the Vatican II generation, VOTF has a major proportion of members who have the resources and time to devote to the mission of the church (Table 4.7). They are rapidly moving into their peak earning years and are likely to be beyond the responsibilities of child rearing. They are also likely to be in good health and to live longer.

Irish ethnicity predominates in all three generations. There are few Latinos (2 percent) and most of them are in the post-Vatican II generation (5 percent). One member wrote: "I'm forty-four and clearly one of the youngest members in our group. We have no people of color and no young people." Another member said: "We need more Hispanics, African Americans, and younger members." But others recognize that wanting them will not produce them unless they see the relevance of the mission of VOTF to their participation in the church.

The vast majority of VOTF members across the generations are married; the largest proportion of single members is in the youngest generation, the post-Vatican II group. This may reflect modern marital trends in which the young — and especially Catholics — tend to marry later, in sharp contrast to their pre-Vatican II grandparents. Across the generations VOTF members are highly educated, and 60 percent have graduate degrees. As expected, the parents of the latest cohort, the post-Vatican II Catholics, are more highly educated than those of the earlier ones.

Beliefs and Practices across Generations

Across the generations, nine in ten VOTF members are cradle Catholics, coming from families where both parents are Catholic. Though they have been exposed to relatively high levels of Catholic education at every level, we see a decline in Catholic education between the older and younger generations (Table 4.8). The structural issue of the decreased availability of Catholic schools over time as well as significant increases in the cost of tuition may have had an effect on the latest generation's attendance.

Table 4.7. Demographic Profile of VOTF Members, by Generation (in percentages)

	Total	Pre-Vat II	Vat II	Post-Vat II
Education				
College degree	27	27	27	33
Graduate degree	61	60	60	59
Father – college graduate	34	27	35	60
Mother – college graduate	24	17	26	44
Married	75	80	74	67
Employed full time	45	16	65	67
Employed part time	13	12	15	12
Retired	35	70	12	0
Nature of Employment				
Academic	20	25	17	19
Professional	30	24	35	36
Managerial, executive	17	18	17	14
Annual household income				
Under $49,999	24	23	17	21
$50,000–99,999	35	29	36	34
$100,000 and more	29	15	39	36
Ideological orientations				
I am a political conservative		15	13	7
I am a political moderate		37	39	32
I am a political liberal		48	48	61
I am an economic conservative		21	19	14
I am an economic moderate		48	52	50
I am an economic liberal		31	29	36
I am a socio-cultural conservative		10	9	4
I am a socio-cultural moderate		36	38	33
I am a socio-cultural liberal		54	53	63

One-third across the generations have studied theology. In each of the earlier generations, a quarter of them were at one time enrolled in a seminary or religious formation program; this decreases to 14 percent in the youngest generation. This is still a relatively high number, since seminary enrollments and the number of religious sisters and brothers have declined by over half since Vatican II.[12]

Table 4.8. Religious Beliefs and Practices of VOTF Members, by Generation (in percentages)

	Total	Pre-Vat II	Vat II	Post-Vat II
Catholic education				
Grade school	70	72	72	56
High school	61	64	61	49
Catholic college	57	62	55	43
Marriage recognized by the church	91	94	89	94
Children attended Catholic schools	48	53	47	32
Attend Mass				
Daily/weekly	65	77	61	38
At least monthly	25	15	26	45
Seldom/never	10	8	12	17
Pray, apart from Mass				
Daily and more	79	83	78	69
Weekly/occasionally	19	15	20	29
Help the Needy				
Weekly	28	34	27	17
At least monthly	52	46	54	59
Church importance in my life				
Most/among most important	65	70	62	56
Quite important to me	29	25	32	36
Possibility of leaving the church				
1–2. Never leave	50	63	42	34
3–5.	27	22	29	38
6–7. Yes, might leave	23	15	29	28

Across the generations, nearly eight out of ten VOTF members pray at least once a day and help the needy at least once a month (Table 4.8). Seventy percent of pre-Vatican II Catholics in VOTF consider the Church "among the most important parts of my life." For the later two generations a little over half say this. Across the generations VOTF members give the church more importance than does the general Catholic population.

Table 4.9. Comparing VOTF and U.S. National Surveys,
At Least Weekly Mass Attendance by Generations

	Pre-Vatican II	Vatican II	Post-Vatican II
2005 National Survey of American Catholics	60%	41%	20%
Survey of VOTF Members	77%	61%	38%

When VOTF members are asked about the possibility of leaving the church, 63 percent of the pre-Vatican II Catholics said they would "never leave"; this drops by twenty and thirty percentage points respectively in the younger generations. VOTF members of the Vatican II generation are nearly twenty percentage points less likely than their counterparts in the general Catholic population to say they "would never leave." Post-Vatican II VOTF members were slightly less likely than their national counterparts to say they would never leave. When inquiring about who "might leave," the only significant difference was with the Vatican II and the post-Vatican II generations; four in ten VOTF Catholics said they might leave, in contrast to the general Catholic population's one in six.

Table 4.9 indicates the rates of Mass attendance for VOTF members and compares them with the rates for the general population of American Catholics (2005 Survey).

Mass attendance rates decline between earlier and later generations for both surveys. However, there is also a significant difference between the attendance rates of VOTF members and the general population of American Catholics; in each generation Mass attendance rates are about 20 percentage points higher for VOTF members.

Participation in VOTF Activities

Table 4.10 shows that VOTF members were most likely to attend their first VOTF meeting on their own. Pre-Vatican II members were more likely to invite others to attend meetings and to be members of a VOTF affiliate than were post-Vatican II Catholics. Pre-Vatican II members were more likely to donate money to the national office

Table 4.10. Participation in VOTF Activities, by Generation (in percentages)

	Total	Pre-Vat II	Vat II	Post-Vat II
Attended first VOTF meeting on my own	60	54	63	67
Was invited by another person	15	13	16	21
Invited others to attend VOTF meetings	55	61	53	38
Member of VOTF affiliate	44	51	42	26
Donated money to national office	32	40	27	20
Donated money to local affiliate	24	32	22	6
Attended VOTF meetings	33	40	30	17
Attended regional conference	12	16	10	6
Signed VOTF Petition for Reform	51	49	54	47

(40 percent) and to a local affiliate (32 percent), attend VOTF meetings (40 percent) and regional conferences (16 percent). The youngest generation was least likely to do any of these things while the Vatican II generation was in the middle on all forms of participation.

Participation in Church Life

Across the generations VOTF members show high levels of participation in liturgical ministries and religious education. They have a relatively high rate of participation in parish committee work, but, as expected, the older generations have been more active than the youngest (Table 4.11, Appendix F, page 230). A member of an earlier cohort reflects on her husband's participation: "My husband was president of the parish council, president of the diocesan pastoral council, a member of the diocesan financial committee, chairman of the Lay Advisory Council to the U.S. Catholic Bishops, and named a Knight of St. Gregory." A quarter of the older generations have participated in RENEW, a third in Small Christian Communities, a fifth in Marriage Encounter, Cursillo, or Call to Action, and one in ten in Right to Life or the charismatic movement. This consistent involvement is reflected in the following comments: "I made Cursillo in '79, and since then have been lector, regional rep, and team member." My husband and I have participated in Marriage Encounter, Engaged Encounter, and Cursillo and Life in the Spirit. The only movements

Table 4.12. VOTF Members' Knowledge of Vatican II and Other Documents, by Generation (in percentages)

	Total	Pre-Vat II	Vat II	Post-Vat II
Knowledge of documents of Vatican II				
Read all	31	33	33	16
Read none	36	30	37	48
Participated in seminars on Vat II	40	41	42	28
Knowledge of National Review Board on Protection of Children and Young People				
Not familiar with it	25	22	26	39
A great deal of knowledge	10	11	10	9
Familiarity with Report of National Review Board (Bennett Report)				
Not familiar with it	25	23	24	42
A great deal of knowledge	10	10	11	7
Familiarity with John Jay College Study				
Not familiar with it	25	22	26	37
A great deal of knowledge	9	9	11	7
Household subscribes to:*				
Local diocesan paper	40	46	37	27
National Catholic Reporter	32	39	30	13
America	22	26	21	12
Commonweal	13	17	12	8

*The four publications listed are the only papers or journals to which 10 percent or more of VOTF members subscribed. *St. Anthony Messenger* and *U.S. Catholic* were next with 9 percent and 8 percent respectively.

in which more than 10 percent of the post-Vatican II generation had participated were Right to Life and Marriage Encounter.

Knowledge of Vatican II and Other Documents

Knowledge of the documents of Vatican II and of current matters in the church varies across the generations (Table 4.12). One member of the pre-Vatican II generation indicated: "I was a *peritus* in the last session of Vatican II." More generally, one in three of the pre-Vatican II and Vatican II generations have read all of the Vatican II documents; only one in six of the post-Vatican II generation has. One in three of the older cohorts have read some of the documents, while two in five of the youngest cohort have.

At the June 2002 meeting of U.S. bishops in Dallas, measures were taken to respond to the abuse of children by priests. The National Review Board for the Protection of Children and Young People was established. A fifth of VOTF members across the generations had heard of the board; very few claimed a great deal of knowledge. A larger proportion claimed some knowledge, with a significant minority admitting they were not familiar with it.

In February 2004, the National Review Board published a report known as the Bennett Report. At the same time the John Jay School of Criminal Justice issued its report on the clerical sexual abuse scandal. Table 4.12 shows a significant number across the generations were not familiar with the documents, and only about 10 percent claimed a great deal of knowledge about the Bennett or the John Jay reports. We do not have data on the general Catholic population to compare it with VOTF members on this matter.

The last item in Table 4.12 examines subscriptions to Catholic newspapers and journals. About two-fifths of the older generations and over a quarter of the youngest generation read their diocesan papers. The *National Catholic Reporter* is the most read of the national periodicals listed in the survey. Controlling for generation, 39 percent of the pre-Vatican II and 30 percent of Vatican II generations subscribe to NCR; only 13 percent of the youngest generation does. Nearly a quarter of the older generation reads *America*, the second most read national periodical; about 12 percent of the youngest cohort subscribes.

Behavior and Attitudes toward Church Policies

Table 4.13 presents the responses of VOTF members by generation to a series of behavioral and attitudinal questions. Across the generations VOTF members agree that there should be more participation of the laity in church governance. Across the generations they favor wider participation by the laity in church decision making at the parish, diocesan, national, and world levels. The generations concur that laity should have input into decisions about the use of parish income

Table 4.13. VOTF Members: Behavior and Attitudes toward Church Policies, by Generation (in percentages)

	Total	Pre-Vat II	Vat II	Post-Vat II
Strongly agree that				
Hierarchy is out of touch with laity	84	82	86	83
Priests expect laity to be followers	44	47	43	38
Catholic parishes are too big	28	31	28	16
Amount of time willing to devote to church decision making				
1 hour per week or less	45	41	44	61
2–5 hours per week	48	50	50	34
6–10 hours or more per week	7	9	6	5
Money per year willing to give to VOTF for laity's role in church governance				
None	16	15	15	22
$50 or Less	36	38	34	41
$51–$100	30	26	33	27
More than $100	18	21	18	10

and the selection of priests and bishops. They are split on whether "Priests expect laity to be followers." To measure the salience of their views, we asked how much time VOTF members would be willing to give to church decision making. Half of the older cohorts said they would be willing to give two to five hours a week, while a third of the youngest generation would be willing to do so. We also asked how much money per year members would be willing to give to VOTF to promote the laity's role in the church. Half of the two older generations were willing to give $50 or more, with a fifth saying they would give more than $100 per year.

In sum, we found more differences based on generation than we did on gender. We conclude with a look at VOTF members who reside in different regions of the country.

The Role of Region

The church in the United States can be differentiated according to geographic regions, as a result of the history of settlement, the ethnicity of the settlers, and the geography and economy of the area. The cradle of Catholicism in the United States is the mid-Atlantic region, more specifically the city of Baltimore, the location of the first diocese in the United States. Its first bishop, John Carroll, was also the first Roman Catholic bishop in the United States. Initially he fostered a church with a clear American identity, but he never secured the collaboration of others in the church hierarchy needed to effectively extend his vision.

Charles Morris, in his book *American Catholic* (1997), has documented how Northeastern Catholicism became ghettoized and defensive; the Irish-led church lived in the shadow of unfriendly WASP elites and stood apart from society.[13] The largest dioceses, such as New York, Boston, and Philadelphia, were headed by cardinals and were the hubs of the feudal ecclesiastical empires that permeated the East. By the beginning of the twentieth century twice as many Catholics lived in the Northeast as in the Midwest, and the Northeast set the tone for Catholicism throughout the country.

Midwestern Catholicism enjoyed greater pluralism. Poles, Germans, and Irish sought to establish their own spheres of influence, as did other smaller ethnic groups, resulting in a greater toleration of diversity. The largest diocese in the Midwest was Chicago, but moderate-sized dioceses, such as Milwaukee, the headquarters of German Catholicism, and St. Paul, also exercised influence in the region. Archbishop John Ireland of St. Paul was the champion of a more American style of Catholicism, but the Vatican hindered his efforts.

The Catholic Church in Chicago was embedded in the social movement culture of the city. From the 1940s, Chicago Catholicism's pioneering role in social, liturgical, and ministerial reforms as well as lay activism was expressed in the Catholic Action movements that cultivated a spirit of participation and activism among the laity.

The seeds of California Catholicism are found in the Spanish missions tended by the Franciscan friars. Irish and Italian transplants formed the church in San Francisco. A wartime boom in the 1940s affected the development of the area and of the local church. After

World War II a typical Catholic family was headed by a professional, a veteran of the Second World War educated on the GI Bill and staunchly anti-communist; his wife tended the house and children. Such an upstanding citizen was not subjected to anti-Catholic prejudice, but was welcomed warmly by the Protestant business elite.[14]

In the Southwest, the metropolitan archbishop of Texas, Robert E. Lucey of San Antonio, advocated social justice by criticizing racism and segregation and supporting labor. He encouraged a progressive social agenda while he wielded his ecclesiastical authority without qualms.[15]

This sketch of Catholic regional diversity raises questions regarding how that variable may have influenced the way VOTF Catholics responded to our questionnaire. This section examines these differences.

The Demographics of Region

Similarities stand out when looking at VOTF members by region; the generations of pre-Vatican II, Vatican II, and post-Vatican II are evenly distributed (Table 4.14, Appendix F, page 231). In regard to ethnicity, the only notable variation is that there are fewer members of Irish and Italian descent in the Midwest, and more Latinos in the West.

VOTF members living in the West were more likely to identify as political and social liberals, while in the South they were more likely to identify as political conservatives. Across the regions they tended to identify themselves as economic moderates. The majority of VOTF members across the regions identify with the Democratic Party. Between a fifth and a quarter identify as Republicans. In Massachusetts one in four identified as an Independent or Green Party member.

Religious Practices and Attitudes

Similarity characterizes the religious practices of VOTF members across the geographic regions (Table 4.15, Appendix F, page 232). There were small regional differences in the percentages of VOTF members who went to Catholic schools, with the East and Midwest having the highest averages overall, and the South the lowest.

Mass attendance ranged from a high of 70 percent weekly or more in the East to a low of 60 percent in the West. These rates are significantly above the attendance rates of the general Catholic population in any region. Across the regions, with the exception of Massachusetts (22 percent), close to a third of VOTF members help the disadvantaged on a weekly basis. In all the regions about half or more are engaged in works of mercy and social justice at least monthly.

Participation in VOTF Activities

Although VOTF originated in Boston, it quickly spread to other parts of the Northeast, and then to other regions of the country. Boston and the Northeast acutely experienced the initial outrage that was the seed for VOTF. It soon became evident that sexual abuse and cover-up were national and not just local to New England; perhaps the spread of VOTF to all areas of the country reflects that growing awareness.

Table 4.16 shows that in all geographic regions nearly 60 percent of VOTF members went to their first VOTF meeting alone. Half of the members in Massachusetts and the East are members of VOTF affiliates; in the South and Midwest it is over a third, but only 27 percent in the West. It may be that the availability of more local affiliates in the East and Massachusetts encourages increased participation in local groups, while the lack of local affiliates in other regions discourages affiliate membership. One member from the West commented: "I attended VOTF in California, but when we moved to Utah in 2003 there is no chapter here." This lack of opportunity for local affiliate membership was corroborated by others. "Living in Texas, I am too far [away] to go to a VOTF meeting, but I have used VOTF tapes." Finally, "There are no VOTF chapters in Hawaii. This diocese is far behind in recognition of the role of the laity."

In Massachusetts and the East about a third have donated money to local affiliates, in the South and Midwest about 15 percent, and in the West one in ten have done so. Two out of five attend meetings in Massachusetts and the East; this drops to about one of five in the

Table 4.16. Participation in VOTF Activities by Region
(in percentages)

	Total	MA	East	South	Midwest	West
N=	1200	281	443	158	195	123
First attendance at VOTF meeting:						
On my own	59	61	56	65	58	61
With another person	25	28	30	16	18	13
Was invited by another person	16	11	14	19	24	26
Invited others to attend VOTF meetings	54	59	59	53	47	43
Strongly identify with VOTF stated goals						
Support victims	85	85	87	87	82	81
Support priests of integrity	85	84	85	91	83	83
Shape structural change	90	89	89	91	95	93
Member of VOTF affiliate – yes	44	54	49	36	38	27
In the last 12 months, have you: ("Yes" Percentages)						
Donated money to VOTF national office	31	25	37	32	33	29
Donated money to a local affiliate	24	34	30	16	15	10
Attended VOTF meetings	32	39	40	21	24	23
Attended regional conference	12	15	18	4	4	9
Signed VOTF Petition for Reform	50	52	52	48	55	48

South, Midwest, and West. These figures mirror the levels of affiliate membership across the regions and suggest that the existence of local affiliates may be helpful to spur involvement.

Participation in Church Life

VOTF members in the Midwest and West have been more active in parish council and other committee activities. Again, Midwest and West VOTF members were more likely to be serving the parish in the range of liturgical ministries. VOTF members in Massachusetts were least likely to have participated in church programs like RENEW and Small Christian Communities (Table 4.17, Appendix F, page 233). There are small differences across the regions in Catholic social movement activity, with members in the Midwest tending to be a bit more active.

Knowledge of Vatican II Documents and Other Documents

When asked about their knowledge of the Vatican II documents — the four constitutions, nine decrees, and three declarations — about one in ten VOTF members said they had read all the documents; in the West, one out of five said they read some of them; in the other regions it is again one out of ten. Across the geographic regions, close to half participated in seminars on Vatican II (Table 4.18, Appendix F, page 234). Regional differences regarding VOTF members and their knowledge of the National Review Board established by the U.S. Conference of Catholic Bishops in 2002 to help the bishops to develop a plan of action to deal with clerical sexual abuse, and subsequent reports providing analysis and recommendations (the Bennett Report and the John Jay College Study) were small.

VOTF members read a variety of Catholic newspapers and journals to keep informed regarding the church. In the South and Midwest they were the most likely to read the local diocesan newspaper. The *National Catholic Reporter* (NCR) is the most read national publication. Across the regions, around a third read NCR, and in the East it crests to 40 percent; only Massachusetts is low with a readership of 21 percent. Over a quarter read *America,* with the exception of the South and Massachusetts, where it is one in ten. Across the regions, one in ten read *Commonweal.* Less than one in ten read *In the Vineyard,* the newsletter for Voice of the Faithful.

Behavior and Attitudes toward Church Policies

The profile of VOTF members shows them to be people who are accustomed to actively participating in professional, community, and church life. It is expected that those more highly committed to the church will also be more concerned and critical about shortcomings in the institutions that claim their loyalty. Because they see themselves as part of the organization this can be a form of self-criticism focused on a sense of responsibility to reform an unsatisfactory status quo. This is displayed by the responses of VOTF members to questions about church policies (Table 4.19, Appendix F, page 235).

When asked if "priests expect the laity to be followers," nearly half the VOTF members in the East, South, and West responded, "Strongly agree"; in Massachusetts and the Midwest it was over a third. When asked about the size and atmosphere of Catholic parishes, over one in five in Massachusetts, the East, and Midwest strongly agreed: "Parishes are too big and impersonal." In the South and West about a third strongly agreed. Regarding the salience of their beliefs, between 41 percent (Eastern and Southern regions) and 50 percent (Massachusetts) said they would be willing to devote an hour a week to church decision making. Between 4 percent (Massachusetts) and 12 percent (West) said they would be willing to devote six to ten hours per week to such activity. The same figures apply to those who would devote two to five hours.

VOTF members seemed to be more willing to donate money than time. Half the members in Massachusetts, the East, and the South said they would be willing to donate $51 or more to promote the laity's role in church decision making. The figures were closer to four in ten for the Midwest and West.

Conclusion

In this chapter we compared VOTF members across three important variables: gender, generation, and region of the country. We found more similarities than differences in these comparisons. We noted that women predominate in VOTF membership and in membership in affiliates. There is significant agreement between the women and men on issues significant to VOTF, especially its three major goals.

In regard to generations VOTF leans heavily toward the pre-Vatican II and Vatican II generations. VOTF Catholics share similarities with other Catholics and their cohorts; however, even in the youngest cohort, the post-Vatican II group, the commitment to the church is higher than that in the general Catholic population. The two older generations have deeper roots in the church, have read more deeply and widely in theology, and are more familiar with the documents of Vatican II and the reports and studies that followed the sexual abuse scandal. The pre-Vatican II and Vatican II groups are also highly educated, have the most resources to bring to VOTF, especially time and money at this time in their lives. Perhaps most important, the two older generations are living longer and healthier lives than Catholics of a prior generation. They seem to have accepted the responsibility to lead in this struggle for reform of the church. Knowing that they will be around for more than a few years before having to hand over leadership to the next generation provides them a unique opportunity to frame a strategy for change and then to embark on it with the knowledge that both history and church doctrine support them in this cause.

Slight differences were noted among the regions. What remains clear is that VOTF members are among the most active and knowledgeable Catholics in the United States.

Chapter Five

The Social Sources of Dissent

Voice of the Faithful in a
Changing Catholic Church

Nancy T. Ammerman

In 1929, Protestant theologian H. Richard Niebuhr published a book called *The Social Sources of Denominationalism*.[1] In it, he traced out the divisions that have plagued American Protestant churches — race and region and ethnicity, but also social class. He pointed to Methodists north of the Mason-Dixon line and Methodists south of that line and asked what theological differences justified their division. He pointed to white Baptists and black Baptists and asked the same question, just as he pointed at his own German-language Lutherans and wondered why they couldn't share communion with Lutherans who speak Swedish. He also noted the disturbing regularity with which religious groups that start out as an expression of ordinary working people eventually become established and comfortable and disdainful of the very people whose discontents birthed them. Such, he said, were the social sources of denominationalism. People whose lives are shaped by different social realities often find it difficult to remain part of a single religious group.

Fifty years later, my own work on the Southern Baptist Convention revisited this question.[2] Here was a denomination that had originally been birthed by just the racial and regional forces of division that Niebuhr described. It had been held together for more than a century by a combination of regional solidarity and organizational

prowess; but by the late 1970s, it was undergoing tumultuous internal conflicts that would eventually lead to its transformation
into a conservative political powerhouse and to the departure of its
progressive wing. While the rhetoric of the battle was full of theology (and there *were* theological differences at stake), the words
reflected the very different social worlds of the "conservatives" and
"moderates" who were using them. One of the many things that
spelled the doom of the movement that tried to counter the fundamentalist takeover was that they did not live in the same social
world inhabited by the vast mainstream of that denomination. Even
where there was substantial theological agreement between progressives and the mainstream, movement leaders had forgotten how to
talk to the people who might have become their allies. And even
where there was substantial *disagreement* between the fundamentalists and that same mainstream, fundamentalists knew the social
terrain on which the battle was being fought. It is no surprise that
fundamentalist activists won the battles and got to keep the spoils,
while the more progressive wing has retreated into a variety of new
organizational homes.

Denominations, of course, are a Protestant phenomenon, and one
of the remarkable things about the Roman Catholic Church has been
its ability to hold together immensely varied social worlds. So what
can Catholics really learn from what happened to a Protestant denomination? As we will see in the conclusion, there are indeed limits
to this analogy; but the lessons to be learned lie in the way social
worlds shape people's relationship to their church, as well as how
they hear messages about the need for reform. So it is worth asking,
How is the world of Voice of the Faithful different from the world of
others in the church who are not part of that movement? In any religious group, it is worth paying attention to the ever-present mix of
religious and social factors — some holding people together in spite
of themselves and some creating new lines of division. So, what social changes have made it possible for Voice of the Faithful to emerge,
and what does that tell us about the shifting terrain on which these
battles are being fought?

The Origins of Dissent

The first thing to be said about members of Voice of the Faithful is that they are, by many measures, very good Catholics. The vast majority (93 percent) were born into the church. Both parents were baptized Catholics, and these, their children, began life as baptized infants. Indeed they have been thoroughly immersed in the church's culture and institutions for their whole lives. While only 15 percent of American adults went to any sort of religious school, an astonishing 70 percent of VOTF members and leaders went to Catholic grade schools, and 61 percent continued into Catholic high schools. Even the rest of the lay Catholic population is considerably less likely to have been to Catholic schools (Table 5.1).[3] Nor did they leave their good Catholic habits behind as adults. Today they are more likely than the general Catholic population to be registered at their parish and to be regular weekly attenders.[4] In all sorts of ways VOTF members and leaders are as Catholic as they come. They have been formed by Catholic families and schools and parishes for their whole lives.

Table 5.1. Catholic Upbringing

	VOTF members	American Catholic laity
Cradle Catholic	93%	?
Attended Catholic grade school	70%	49%
Attended Catholic high school	62%	29%
Attended Catholic college	57%	12%

Nor is this a pattern of surface commitment. VOTF members are also very likely to say that their faith is among the most important things in their lives — again more likely to say so than the average American Catholic (Table 5.2). They pray even when they aren't at church — 79 percent of them daily or more — and their prayers have hands and feet. Nearly half (43 percent) participate in service ministries more than once a month. If high-commitment Catholicism includes both Mass attendance and personal faith, spiritual piety and good works in the world, then meetings of VOTF must surely be one of the best places to find a collection of high-commitment Catholics.

Table 5.2. Current Catholic Commitment

	VOTF members	American Catholic laity
Registered in parish	85%	67%
Attend Mass weekly or more	65%	34%
Pray daily or more (outside church)	79%	62%
Faith is among the most important things in life	62%	44%
Help needy more than once a month	43%	?

Among the most important social sources of this movement, then, is the church itself. VOTF members differ from other Catholics in their high degree of devotion to the church.

While that is a necessary starting place, deep formation in the church is not a sufficient explanation for this movement. There are more mundane social sources at work as well. The descriptive tables from the survey stop short of allowing an assessment of which factors are most important, but we can nevertheless begin to see in them some of the "social sources" of VOTF. There is a good deal of similarity across the generations of VOTF members, but it is useful to think about each of them in turn.

Dissent among the Elders

The oldest generation of VOTF members, born before 1941 and shaped in the pre-Vatican II church, is remarkable in a number of ways. Partly they are remarkable because there are so many of them. Forty-one percent of VOTF's members are over sixty-five, compared to just 17 percent of the overall Catholic population. Sometimes called the "Greatest Generation," this cohort has consistently invested in lifelong organizational membership and leadership. Their habits were to join young and work their way up.[5] Their commitment to building institutions has been critical in sustaining churches and volunteer organizations of all sorts. Not only is this generation continuing their organization-building habits, but today many are retired and have available time (and reasonable resources of health and money) for doing the work. We should not be surprised, then, to find a disproportionate number of older members lending their energies to this new organizational effort.

But these are not simply typical retired Catholics with the time and inclination to volunteer. They are the best educated and most experienced leaders of that generation. While only about 12 percent of Catholics in this generation graduated from college,[6] 87 percent of older VOTF members have a college degree or more. Indeed, nearly half of this older generation of VOTF members has a *Catholic* college degree. In the years surrounding World War II, they were surely in the vanguard of Catholics moving into the American middle class. In all the ways that higher education shapes a life, they have experienced broader horizons and opportunities, more diverse neighbors and friends, and a greater willingness to question authority.[7] For several decades, this select group of American Catholics, now the church's senior citizens, have lived in a very different social world from the one inhabited by others in their generation. The typical Catholic of the pre-Vatican II generation was shaped in a world where neighborhood and ethnicity, family and parish often formed a more narrow social horizon.[8]

This highly Catholic-educated older cohort has also occupied key positions within the church. They were the natural leaders who sat on school boards (24 percent) and finance committees (21 percent), parish councils (41 percent) and other committees (60 percent). Over half (54 percent) have taught the next generation of their parish's children in CCD or PSR (Parish School of Religion), and nearly that many have served as lectors (47 percent) or eucharistic ministers (44 percent). They have been willing to serve, but they have also had the skills to do so. These are people who have been respected Catholic leaders all of their adult lives.

Dissent among the Boomers

Following behind them is the Vatican II generation. Roughly coextensive with the boomer generation, it is defined in this study as those who came of age in the midst of the changes brought by the Vatican Council. Almost half the members of VOTF and 60 percent of the founders fall in this generation, compared to only 41 percent of the overall Catholic population. This is the generational center of gravity in the movement. Boomer Catholics are very similar to the older members in their trajectory through Catholic homes, Catholic schools, and on to Catholic colleges (and Catholic marriages). When they were growing up, weekly Mass attendance was still normative, and parish schools were still plentiful. Even if they were living in the suburbs, the church was an important part of their growing-up years.

Then they went off to college. Like their older VOTF colleagues, boomer VOTF members are also considerably more likely to be college graduates than the average lay Catholic of that generation (88 percent vs. 23 percent). Across all the generations, VOTF members are disproportionately likely to have been to college and for that college to have been a Catholic one. For older VOTF members, a Catholic college education provided knowledge and skills for being leaders in their parishes (and for successful careers). For boomer VOTF members it may also have been a profoundly transformative experience.

Combining what this survey tells us about college attendance with what it tells us about the age of VOTF members, we find that fully 27 percent of the VOTF members who responded to this survey were in Catholic colleges during the formative years surrounding the Second Vatican Council. They are no more likely to have received a Catholic education than was the older generation, but the education they received came in the midst of cultural and religious revolutions that are likely to have had long-term impacts. Being at Boston College in the 1940s or early 1950s, for instance, was considerably different from being there in the 1960s and 1970s. In both cases, the result is Catholic college graduates who are more knowledgeable and more active than those who didn't go to Catholic colleges. But my hunch is that the ideas and activities experienced on Catholic campuses in the 1960s and 1970s played a particularly formative role in the lives of those who have been drawn to VOTF. In the thick of movements for change, everything seemed possible.

D'Antonio and Pogorelc quote one member saying, "We are the 'over the hill gang' in love with the changes promised in the Vatican II documents only to find that our hierarchy 'deep-sixed' them and hoped we would forget." I heard a similar sentiment from a sixty-ish woman recently. She proudly reported the astonishment of a young reporter who visited their VOTF group and was surprised to find so many old people there. This woman said, "We're old people who are still revolutionaries!" They have been formed by the revolutions they have been a part of, but distinctively formed by experiencing those revolutions in a deeply Catholic environment.

In these experiences, boomer Catholic progressives parallel their Southern Baptist counterparts. The leaders of the SBC progressive wing were also more likely to have attended a Baptist college than were the conservatives. Likewise, many of them cut their revolutionary eye teeth in the civil rights movement. They had learned to work for and expect change, and they had learned those lessons from within a deeply Baptist environment. In the 1960s and 1970s, at least some of the revolutionary fervor of the culture was fueled by commitments nourished on the campuses of religious colleges, campuses that combined deep religious roots with active social engagement.[9]

Both the pre-boomer and the boomer VOTF cohorts left those college campuses to become exceptionally knowledgeable, active, and loyal Catholics. Not only were these Catholic college grads especially likely to be in leadership roles in their parishes, but they were also likely to have read at least some of the council documents (63 percent) and to have taken theology classes (36 percent). To this day, they stay informed both through their active participation in the church and through reading Catholic periodicals.

What they didn't do in any great numbers is join the traditional Catholic men's and women's societies. Except for the 33 percent of VOTF members who are in the Knights of Columbus and the 10 percent in the St. Vincent de Paul Society, the Catholics who would eventually end up in VOTF were unlikely to be found in the ethnic and social groups that marked the Catholic experience of earlier generations. They were as likely to participate in the Catholic Worker movement as in the Holy Name Society and far more likely to have participated in Cursillo, a Marriage Encounter, RENEW, or a small Christian community. The new forms of gathering that cropped up in the years since the council provided arenas in which lay participation was linked with faith. These were faithful people who had been exercising their voices for some time already.

The absence of ties to those gender-based Catholic organizations is a hint that gender practices are one of several ways in which the social world of VOTF members is distinctive. Given that nearly half of the leaders of the movement are Vatican II–generation *women* should tell us something. Highly educated, boomer-generation women were the pioneers in second-wave feminism — more interested in *women's* groups than in *ladies'* societies, more committed to using their own unique leadership skills than to doing whatever the priest asked them to do.[10] Over the last forty years, many Catholic women and men have come to understand that "feminist Catholic" is not an oxymoron.[11]

That gender is a defining issue in the formation of VOTF members can be seen, ironically, in the absence of gender differences among the VOTF members. Men and women across the generations are equally Catholic, equally knowledgeable and active, and equally well-educated. In a church that has historically been experienced by men and women in very different ways, this gender-uniformity is striking. There are small lingering differences within the oldest generation in education, work experience, and which roles they've had in their local parishes, but otherwise there are remarkably few differences between the men and the women in the movement. The one exception to this pattern is that VOTF women are more politically and economically liberal (42 percent politically liberal) than VOTF men (15 percent). Apparently one can be a politically conservative man in VOTF (31 percent of male members say they are), but it's highly unlikely that a politically conservative woman will find a home here (no female members say they are). Otherwise, VOTF men and women seem to share very similar backgrounds and similar levels of engagement — and to be equally unhappy with the way the church is being run.

Dissent among the Younger Generation

The most recent generation of Catholics, growing up since the council, is considerably underrepresented in the ranks of VOTF. Still, those who are there have a story that has varied only slightly from that of their older compatriots. They are just as likely to be cradle Catholics, but less likely to have gone to Catholic schools (56 percent for grade school vs. 72 percent of the older two cohorts) and still less likely to be sending their own children to Catholic schools (32 percent vs. 50 percent of the older two cohorts). Compared to the older members, they are considerably less active participants in the Mass (38 percent vs. 68 percent attend weekly or more), but that is still ahead of the average post-Vatican II lay Catholic (26 percent). The strong Catholic culture of the earlier generations has not been as present for this younger cohort. Younger VOTF members, like older ones, are the more active Catholics of their generation.

Given their stage in life, it is probably not surprising that younger VOTF members are less active in some forms of parish leadership and in VOTF itself. Preoccupied with family formation and establishing a career, volunteer commitments of all kinds often take a back seat. They have also not been especially active in RENEW, Call to Action, Cursillo, and the like. Perhaps as a result of all these things taken together, they are somewhat less informed than older VOTF members. In the midst of raising kids and establishing themselves, they are simply not as organizationally invested as the older generations.

Looked at from another angle, this younger generation is not one of the prime "social sources" from which VOTF gains its strength. Only to the degree that members of this generation have been shaped by an especially deep Catholic upbringing and especially high current commitment do we find post-Vatican II Catholics making their way into the ranks of this movement.

The Defining Issues

Like their older colleagues, post-Vatican II VOTF members are there in large measure because they are unhappy with priests and bishops who abused their trust and failed to protect their children from the sexual misconduct of priests. One of the interviewees recalled:

> What got me the most was Father Geoghan was one parish away, in Weston, . . . and Father Shanley was one parish away in Newton, okay, and my little boy . . . in their heyday, when they were working their mischief in these two parishes, my boy was a ten-year-old altar boy. He was a cherubic, beautiful little kid just ripe for the picking. And I thought, "Oh my God, one parish away."

Not only was the reality of the abuse overwhelming, but the negligence of the hierarchy was infuriating. Another interviewee linked the decision to participate in VOTF to "my outrage at the bishops' behavior; they failed the laity." Another said, "I've had enough of people who are out of touch making decisions that impact me without so much as lending an ear to hear if I had anything to say about it." If they had not been convinced already, the entire sex abuse episode demonstrated to potential VOTF members that the hierarchy is out of touch and that priests aren't doing an especially good job (Table 5.3). VOTF members are now far more likely than the average parishioner to be unhappy with the way they are treated by priests. Given the birth of VOTF in the cauldron of the clergy sex abuse scandals, it is hardly surprising that priests and the Catholic hierarchy are held in less than high regard.

Table 5.3. The Issues

	VOTF members	American Catholic laity
Hierarchy is out of touch	85% strongly agree	19% strongly agree
Priests see laity as followers	44% strongly agree	17% strongly agree
Priests do a good job	76% somewhat or strongly agree	92% somewhat or strongly agree
Laity should have a say in parish financial decisions	99% agree	89% agree
Laity should have a say in selecting priests	84% agree	71% agree

The solutions called for by VOTF largely revolve around greater lay involvement in decision making at every level of the church. Said one interviewee, "The faith experience of all the People of God should be equally valued in decision making in the church. The elevated clerical power must go." Here, however, VOTF members are not especially distinctive. Ninety-seven percent of American Catholics think that laity ought to have at least some role in making decisions about parish finances, and 14 percent think laity should have the final say. There is broad national support for lay participation at the diocesan level, as well. While the average lay Catholic may not be as disillusioned with official church leadership, VOTF is not out of the mainstream in its call for laypeople to take more decision-making responsibility in church life. Nor is there any significant difference within VOTF on these issues. In fact, there is remarkable uniformity among members and leaders on what's wrong and what ought to be done about it. To the extent that this is a movement about lay participation, the movement's own message is unanimously supported by its members, and the ranks of possible recruits are legion.

Social Sources Revisited

So why aren't more lay Catholics joining VOTF? My hunch is that the problem is not the message, but the social world of the messengers. VOTF is simply a different world from the mainstream of the American Catholic Church. The differences we see in this survey are rarely differences *within* VOTF. There is little variation across gender or generation or region. Generation matters, for instance, but not because younger VOTF members are especially different from older ones. Generation matters because so few of the younger generation of Catholics are VOTF members. Gender matters because most of the church would find the world of well-educated feminist Catholics rather alien, even if feminism wasn't overtly on the agenda. Education matters, not because one group within VOTF is more educated than others, but because the rarified world of high-powered professionals and people with graduate degrees is not the world of most American Catholics (Table 5.4). And ethnicity matters, not because

Table 5.4. Demographics

	VOTF members	American Catholic Laity
Age: under 35	11%	49%
Age: 65 or over	41%	17%
Have college degree or more	87%	32%
Latino	2%	25–29%
Household Income > $75,000	42%	40%

there are divisions within the ranks of VOTF, but because there aren't. VOTF has formed a strong and cohesive social movement out of the social world its members share. They have had very similar upbringings, share very similar educational experiences, and are very similar in their comfortable place in American culture. And they are overwhelmingly white. The rest of the church isn't joining because when they walk into a meeting, they don't see anyone who looks like them.

Here perhaps a brief cautionary tale from the Baptist Battles may be in order. As I watched progressive Baptist leaders attempt to mobilize a movement to oppose the conservative takeover, my research assistants and I were struck by how different the two sides *looked*. The progressives (in the 1980s) were likely to be in tweeds and button-down collars, and they were more likely to carry a briefcase than a Bible (although there very well might be a Bible inside the briefcase). The people who ended up following the conservatives, on the other hand, often carried very big and very visible Bibles, and the women sometimes carried theirs in what a friend of mine calls a "Bible cozy." Conservatives loved it when the music leaned in the direction of country styles, and the cut of their clothes was likely to be less "classy." Now there is nothing theological about any of those differences, but somewhere along the way, progressives had learned to think of Bible cozies as tacky and country music as lowbrow.[12] It's little wonder that they had a hard time convincing those folks that they, the progressives, were real Baptists, even if they did have sterling Baptist credentials.

Like those progressive Baptist leaders, these very differences give VOTF members and leaders formidable religious and cultural capital to expend in the movement. They can draw on their income, education, and status in American society to make a case to which the larger culture may be sympathetic. They can also draw on their deep Catholic upbringing and education to give them rhetorical advantage and legitimacy within the church. Given the enormous investment VOTF members have in their church and the impressive Catholic credentials they bring to the table, they can even make a plausible claim that they are the "real Catholics."

The only problem with that claim is that it will inevitably get all mixed up with the other ways in which the world of VOTF is not the world of the rest of the church. How is the world of VOTF different from the world of the rest of American (not to mention global) Catholicism? What is glaringly obvious is that this is not a voice that speaks for the growing immigrant population in the church. Nor is it a voice that speaks for Catholics who are less educated. Nor, at least yet, is it a voice for the younger generation. And, ironically, it is probably not a voice for the less-faithful Catholic who has much less invested in the future of the church. Right now Voice of the Faithful speaks from and to people of sterling Catholic credentials, but finding a broader base for the movement will require some intentional recognition of the social sources that shape the immensely diverse worlds in which Catholics live their lives.

Concluding Questions

The diversity within the church is, of course, not new. Even the existence of a dissenting movement within the church is not new. This is where the "social sources" argument reaches its limit. While those social sources help us to understand where this movement has come from and who is likely to join, they do not tell us *how* the movement is likely to progress. Unlike Baptists, even the most disgruntled Catholics can't vote out their leaders. Indeed, the most crucial faithful voice is not a lay voice at all. The irony of this movement is that it is dependent on the very authority it opposes to grant it what it desires.

So some intriguing questions remain: What if Voice of the Faithful really did become the voice of all the laity, but the official hierarchy refused to change? What then? Or, more likely, what if Voice of the Faithful continued to grow, kept its deep Catholic sensibilities, but continued to be rejected by the church's official leaders? What if it attained significant organizational strength and an increasingly distinct identity, even if the majority of Catholics did not join? When progressive Baptists were finally forced out of the SBC, they grieved, but they fairly easily moved toward starting new Baptist groups. They simply assumed that they had the option to move out on their own. That is not the Catholic pattern. So no matter how thoroughly VOTF may transcend the social barriers to create a massive, unified Catholic social movement, polity still counts. While more VOTF members are willing to consider leaving the church than are ordinary Catholics (23 percent vs. 14 percent), it's still not very many. The years ahead will bring new challenges as this organization continues to explore both what it means to have a voice and what it means to be faithful.

Chapter Six

Bringing Doctrine Back into Action
The Catholicity of VOTF Catholics
and Its Imperative

Michele Dillon

The Historical and Institutional Context
of Lay Catholic Activism

Voice of the Faithful (VOTF) sprung into action from the deliberations of a small number of upper-class professionals living in an upscale Catholic parish in one of the most affluent Boston suburbs in response to the very specific circumstances of the priest sex abuse crisis and its institutional cover-up whose epicenter was the Boston archdiocese. Like many Catholics, VOTF's founding members were by-and-large churchgoing individuals appalled at what the abuse scandal unveiled about the church's clerical culture and corporate practices and concerned about the short- and long-term impact of the crisis on the church. Critically, however, some of VOTF's leadership corps also had a history of social activism on economic and geopolitical issues far removed from Catholicism and religion in general. Pooling their founders' shared activist background provided VOTF with a stock of experiences and resources that are much needed in any social movement, not least one that embarks on confronting the Catholic Church, a global transnational organization with a rich, two-thousand-year-old, multifaceted institutional and doctrinal tradition.

Notwithstanding the specific site and circumstances of VOTF's origins, the emergence of Voice of the Faithful as a social movement in the Catholic Church extends a long history of lay activism among American Catholics. Although the activism of VOTF was spurred by the particular context of the sex abuse scandal, the concern among lay Catholics for greater accountability and transparency in the institutional structure and practices of the church is not a new development. As far back as the late eighteenth and early nineteenth centuries, the issue of lay trusteeism, the assertion of the rights of the laity to control parish property and decision making, presented such a critical challenge to the authority of the fledgling American Catholic Church that it constituted a crisis for the First Provincial Council meeting in Baltimore in 1829.[1] The American Republican political emphasis on democracy and individual freedom coupled with the anti-elitist and populist emphasis on the rights and competence of ordinary Americans to move toward religious and political self-determination[2] coalesced to undermine the smoothness with which the European, Roman model of the church as a tightly controlled hierarchical structure was imported into American Catholicism.[3]

The democratic lay impetus was squelched by the bishops (though there was support for it among some individual bishops) in favor of episcopal and hierarchical authority. The Baltimore Council legislated against the laity holding church property titles, reaffirmed the rights of the bishops to hire and fire pastors, and generally put an end to lay patronage of Catholic parish congregations.[4] As is well documented, this resolution allowed the bishops to become the key definers of American Catholic identity and the sole legal owners of diocesan church property.[5] By the end of the nineteenth century there was little doubt about the primacy of hierarchical authority in the church. Most notably, the First Vatican Council (1869–70) formally institutionalized the principle of papal infallibility, and soon thereafter the papal decrees against Americanism (Leo XIII, 1899) and Modernism (Pius X, 1907) sent the unambiguous message that from Rome's perspective the rights of the laity and any cultural ideas that might affirm such rights had little relevance to the institutional identity of Catholicism.[6]

History didn't end with Vatican I, however. Close to one hundred years later, the Second Vatican Council (1962–65), celebrated a different kind of church. In church history, Vatican II is widely considered a revolutionary event, as especially evidenced by the wide-ranging scope of the issues it discussed and the transparent, dialogical manner in which it conducted its deliberations.[7] The strong consensus among sociologists, historians, and theologians is that Vatican II redefined the church from a rigidly hierarchical, authoritarian, imperialist, anti-modern institution to one that became more engaged in and relevant to the modern world. In particular, Vatican II represented a shift toward a participatory church that recognized lay interests, competencies, and experiences.[8]

From the perspective of lay activism, it is highly significant that Vatican II affirmed the equality of membership in the church of the laity and the ordained as the one "People of God" and provided Catholics with a rationale for lay emancipatory activism.[9] Using the liberal democratic language associated with political change, the council proclaimed the "rights of man," and while cautioning that emancipatory movements should be "penetrated by the spirit of the gospel," it praised the "dynamic movements of today by which these rights are fostered" (*Gaudium et Spes,* no. 41). Articulating a coherent, integrated view of religious and social identity, the council observed, moreover, that there cannot be a "false opposition between professional and social activities on the one part, and religious life on the other" (*Gaudium et Spes,* no. 43). The scope of the emancipatory agenda envisioned by the council was further expressed in its insistence that the laity be given "every opportunity [to] participate in the saving work of the Church" and that laypeople were not only permitted but were indeed obliged to express informed opinions on issues pertaining to the "good of the Church" (*Lumen Gentium,* nos. 33, 37).

One interpretation of this statement is that lay participation extends to saving the church from practices that contravene its own ideals of human dignity and equality, a stance further supported by the council's recognition of the importance of human agency and collective action in remedying the many contradictions in social and institutional practices. Specifically, the council stated that "by their combined efforts" laypeople should "remedy any institutions and conditions of the world which are customarily an inducement to sin, so that all such things may be conformed to the norms of justice" (*Lumen Gentium,* no. 36). Presciently, the council acknowledged that gap between theory and practice in the church's own institutional life and declared that it too should be redeemed: " . . . it does not escape the Church how great a distance lies between the message she offers and the human failings of those to whom the gospel is entrusted" (*Gaudium et Spes,* no. 43).

Following Vatican II's affirmation of collective action and paralleling the emergence of a broad array of social movements in the American political sphere in the late 1960s and 1970s, several Catholic activist organizations were also founded during the early 1970s. Catholic mobilization was largely driven by groups committed to progressive institutional changes in the church that were in keeping with the lay emphasis articulated at Vatican II, but conservative groups opposed to doctrinal and institutional change also emerged. Progressive activist groups included the Women's Ordination Conference (established in 1975), Dignity, an association of gay and lesbian Catholics (1969), the Association for the Rights of Catholics in the Church (1980), and Catholics Speak Out (1981). Although separate groups, these and other pro-change Catholic activist organizations eventually came under the umbrella of Call to Action (CTA), a broad-based lay movement for transformative change in the church that originated in the late 1970s and that today, or at least until the founding of VOTF, was the primary force advocating institutional changes in Catholicism.[10]

In sum it is important to recognize that the activism of VOTF fits with a long tradition of American lay Catholic activism dating at least to the late eighteenth century and in more recent times as part of the broader post-1960s cultural advocacy of progressive social and institutional changes in favor of equality. The legitimacy of VOTF's collective focus on changing the church is further bolstered from within the church's own institutional and doctrinal tradition. Most notably, the affirmation by the church hierarchy itself during

Vatican II that Catholics are obliged to take a responsible role in remedying the gaps between Catholic ideals and values and the institutional practices of the church can be seen as lending additional validation to VOTF's project. Clearly, although some bishops, priests, and lay Catholics may well argue that VOTF is not a legitimate Catholic organization in the sense that it does not have a mandate or an imprimatur from the collective body of American Catholic bishops, from a sociological perspective, VOTF's activism can be seen as being well grounded both in American secular culture as well as within the Catholic tradition.

Are VOTF Catholics Good Catholics?

While VOTF presents as a legitimate religious-based social movement working for change in the church, a more pressing question is whether its leaders and members are good Catholics. In other words, are they errant Catholics simply looking for a cause around which to rally and get energized, or do they have a deeper immersion in the Catholic tradition? And how do the attitudes and habits of VOTF members compare with American Catholics as a whole? These are important questions that the extensive data gathered by William D'Antonio and Anthony Pogorelc in their representative survey of VOTF founders (N=35) and members (N=1273), and in combination with D'Antonio et al.'s 2005 survey of Catholics nationwide (N=875) allow us to answer.[11]

The short answer to the question of whether VOTF Catholics are good Catholics is "Yes, they are!" Almost all of the VOTF members attend Mass on a weekly or almost weekly basis (84 percent) and pray daily (80 percent).[12] Close to half teach or have taught in CCD, the children's religious education program (53 percent), and are eucharistic ministers (45 percent) or lectors (43 percent). Similarly, many report helping the needy more than once a month (44 percent). Clearly, in light of the doctrinal significance of the Mass in the Catholic tradition and the teaching of the *Catechism of the Catholic Church* (no. 1341) affirming the Eucharist as the "center of the church's life," VOTF Catholics are squarely at the core of the church. And, in fact,

VOTF Catholics (66 percent) are twice as likely as American Catholics in general (34 percent) to attend weekly Mass. They are also more likely to be registered parish members (85 percent of VOTF members and founders compared to 68 percent of American Catholics).

Some of the difference in weekly Mass and parish commitment between VOTF and other Catholics has a generational explanation. VOTF members are older than Catholics nationwide; 41 percent of VOTF members are part of the pre-Vatican II generation and another 48 percent are in the Vatican II generation, leaving only 11 percent of members born after Vatican II. By contrast, 49 percent of American Catholics were born after Vatican II. This younger generation has a lower rate of church attendance than is true of older cohorts, thus depressing the rate of weekly attendance for American Catholics as a whole. Nonetheless, despite this generational caveat, the greater involvement of VOTF in the life of the church stands out.

VOTF Catholics are also distinguished by their deeply Catholic backgrounds. Almost all are "cradle" Catholics (93 percent). Between two-thirds and three-quarters of VOTF members went to Catholic elementary (70 percent) or high schools (62 percent), and over half (57 percent) graduated from Catholic colleges or universities. These figures are substantial. American Catholics in general attend Catholic schools and colleges at a much lower rate. For example, only 12 percent of Catholics in the national survey are graduates of Catholic colleges (though again this too has a generational component, with post-Vatican II Catholics less likely than others to have attended Catholic colleges).

Irrespective of whether or not VOTF members went to a Catholic college, these rates also point to the remarkably high level of educational attainment in VOTF. Eighty-seven percent of VOTF members are college graduates, and a staggering 60 percent of these have a graduate or professional degree (compared to 33 percent and 14 percent respectively for American Catholics). As we would expect, VOTF members' educational advantage translates into socio-economic success. They populate the high-status professional (30 percent), academic (21 percent), and managerial (17 percent) occupations; their modal annual household income is $100,000 or more, while at the low end of the spectrum only 25 percent have a household income under $50,000.

In line with their thoroughly Catholic background and their high level of education and social status, VOTF members also show a high degree of doctrinal competence. Close to half (46 percent) have participated in seminars on Vatican II, a third (32 percent) report having knowledge of some or all of the documents of Vatican II, and over a third (37 percent) have taken theology courses. Similarly, many VOTF households subscribe to the lay weekly newspaper, the *National Catholic Reporter* (32 percent), or to the Jesuit weekly magazine, *America* (22 percent). Not surprisingly, VOTF members' deep immersion in the Catholic doctrinal and institutional tradition penetrates how they think of their self-identity. Close to two-thirds (62 percent) say that the Catholic Church is among the "most important" aspects of their life, and once again, this figure is substantially higher than that reported by American Catholics as a whole, 44 percent of whom say that the church is among the most important aspects of their life. It is somewhat surprising that a relatively similar proportion of VOTF leaders (60 percent) and members (62 percent) said that the church is among the most important things in their life. Given their commitment to VOTF and by extension to the church, one might have expected more leaders to endorse this higher importance response and fewer to endorse the less salient "quite important" option (31 percent). Nine percent of leaders and 11 percent of members said that the church was not very important in their lives or were unsure about its importance.

D'Antonio and Pogorelc analyze their VOTF survey data across five major social variables that frequently emerge as significant sources of differentiation in people's attitudes and habits across diverse samples and topics. These variables are gender, birth cohort or generation, region of the country, Catholic college education, and frequency of Mass or church attendance. The resulting analyses indicate remarkably few differences among VOTF members as a group and instead largely highlight the overall homogeneity of their backgrounds, interests, and habits. There are nonetheless some differences, and the most striking are based on gender. Most notably, more women (59 percent) than men (41 percent) are members of VOTF, and this is also true of the founders/leadership group, 60 percent of whom are women and 40 percent men.

There is also evidence that women members are slightly more committed than men to the VOTF organization. For example, they are more likely to attend meetings (35 percent vs. 29 percent) and to have signed the VOTF Petition for Reform (55 percent vs. 45 percent), and, indicative perhaps of women's more collaborative or relational style, they are also more likely to have invited others to attend VOTF meetings (63 percent vs. 44 percent). Women (58 percent) are also more likely than men (45 percent) to have taught CCD, though the reverse is true of service on the parish school board: 28 percent of men have served compared to 19 percent of women. Similarly, VOTF men have a greater rate of participation in Catholic organizations largely because these have tended to be exclusively male. It is nonetheless noteworthy that a rather substantial one-third of VOTF men (33 percent) are or have been members of the Knights of Columbus, an organization generally seen as representing a more traditional Catholic base, and 16 percent are members of the Holy Name Society. Women (50 percent), on the other hand, are more likely than men (42 percent) to have participated in a social justice organization such as Pax Christi, Habitat for Humanity, or Bread for the World, though some women, too, about half as many as men, have participated in the St. Vincent de Paul Society.

Another interesting gender difference is VOTF women's greater tendency than men to think about the possibility of leaving the church. Whereas 55 percent of men say they would never leave, the comparable figure for women is 47 percent. This difference is reflective perhaps of the tension for women between, on the one hand, their greater commitment to the church and to change in the church (as indicated, for example, by the greater presence of women in VOTF), and, on the other, their simultaneous awareness that the church offers women a limited opportunity structure, crystallized by the church's opposition to women's ordination. This is a de facto reality that is orthogonal to VOTF's organizational agenda, and yet it is understandable that many VOTF women (as suggested by some of the responses in the open-ended survey questions) see change on this issue as part and parcel of any meaningful structural change in the church. They are perhaps, then, more likely than men to get frustrated with the church and its pace of change and to voice this impatience with the threat of exit, while nonetheless working with much doctrinal agency within the church to effect change.[13]

In addition to gender, there are a couple of other noteworthy sources of variation. American Catholicism has a regional subnarrative, and we see some evidence of this in VOTF. Catholics in the Midwest (33 percent) are more likely than those from other regions (approximately 23 percent) to have participated in the Chicago-based Call to Action, the Catholic organization that VOTF members as a whole are most likely to have participated in, though many too have participated in Marriage Encounter (19 percent), and Cursillo (17 percent) — in addition to men's participation in the Knights of Columbus (33 percent), for example. Catholics from the West (47 percent) and the Midwest (44 percent) are more likely than those from the East (37 percent) and South (36 percent) to have participated in a parish Small Christian Community. And, pointing to the largely regional accent of the sex abuse scandal, VOTF members living in the South are the least familiar with the Bennett Report and the John Jay College Report issued in the aftermath of the scandal than Catholics elsewhere.

Not surprisingly, perhaps, VOTF members who are Catholic college graduates (60 percent) are more likely than others (43 percent) to have taught CCD. But it may be a surprise to some that Catholic college graduates are also more likely to be members of Call to Action (28 percent vs. 15 percent). This finding could be interpreted as suggesting that the more Catholics know about the Catholic tradition, the more likely they are to push for change in current church doctrines and practices.

What Do VOTF Members Think of the Hierarchy and of Priests?

VOTF members' deep immersion in the Catholic tradition and their commitment to the Eucharist as the core of Catholic identity and practice stand in stark contrast to their attitudes toward the church hierarchy and toward priests. A startlingly high proportion of VOTF members, 85 percent, think that the "hierarchy is out of touch." We know from earlier surveys of American Catholics that a majority are critical of the hierarchy and disagree with official church teaching on several issues (including birth control, divorce, celibacy, women's ordination, homosexuality, and the legalization of abortion). Nevertheless, the substantial number of VOTF members who regard the hierarchy as out of touch still seems unexpectedly high. Moreover it is remarkable that this negative view is expressed almost as evenly by the VOTF members who are at Mass every Sunday (80 percent) as by those who are less frequent or lapsed in their church attendance (85 percent who attend church monthly and 92 percent of non-attenders).

VOTF attitudes toward the hierarchy are at odds with the current views of American Catholics in general, only 19 percent of whom, even in the wake of the sex abuse scandal and dismay over parish closings, endorse the view that the hierarchy is out of touch. In short, VOTF members' responses indicate a wedge between them and non-VOTF Catholics and unveil an intense anger and impatience with the hierarchy. These negative sentiments were fully expressed by VOTF members whose written comments on the survey are well captured by the following selection of quotes used in regard to the hierarchy:

+ "Too powerful"
+ "Not accountable"
+ "Steeped in hypocrisy"
+ "No relevance"
+ "Imperious"
+ "No imagination"
+ "I simply ignore the hierarchy...."

Of course, just because VOTF members are highly critical of the hierarchy, this does not necessarily mean that they would also be critical of priests, those who play such a central role in the pastoral life of Catholics. VOTF members' views of priests, however, offer a very bleak assessment. Only 18 percent strongly agree that priests "do a good job." This figure increases to 76 percent if we include those in the much weaker response category "somewhat agree." This still puts VOTF members' assessment of priests lower than that of American Catholics in general, 92 percent of whom agree (either strongly or somewhat) that priests do a good job. In any event, the fact that fewer than one-fifth of VOTF Catholics have an unreservedly positive view of priests is quite striking. And it does not seem to be driven by VOTF members' negative experiences in dealing with priests' attitudes toward VOTF: only 26 percent said that their parish priests were unsupportive of VOTF.

VOTF attitudes toward priests raises an interesting tension for their activism. One of VOTF's explicitly stated goals is to "support priests of integrity," an objective that finds extensive support in the VOTF survey: 86 percent of members strongly identify with this goal. The tension I see here is how can VOTF both as an organizational strategy and as a practical matter support priests of integrity when so many of its members think that priests (most of whom presumably have integrity) do not do a good job. It is not apparent from the survey what exactly VOTF members regard priests as not doing well, though 44 percent say that "priests expect the laity to be followers," and this may certainly undermine VOTF members' appreciation for how well priests do their job. We know from other research, however, that the laity may perceive deficiencies in the priest's sermons, in the quality of the liturgy, in his pastoral outreach abilities, in his personal style, and in his parish management skills.[14]

Studies conducted in 2000, before the public visibility of the sex abuse scandal, indicated that Catholic laity gave their priests a much lower rating than Protestants gave their clergy on specific dimensions of the pastoral role.[15] Among the job performance dimensions assessed were preaching, sympathetic counseling, working with young people, and worship services. Based on these survey results, Greeley concluded that "a quarter of the Catholic people think that their priests do a miserable job on almost all of their pastoral activities, and a sixth say that their priests are doing a fine job."[16] These data on attitudes toward specific dimensions of priests' jobs show that VOTF members are more closely aligned with American Catholics than the D'Antonio and Pogorelc survey data on the more general question assessing whether priests do a good job. Nonetheless, as I see it, one challenge for VOTF is to address what specific initiatives it can take to improve the quality of the job done by priests in view of VOTF's goal of supporting priests of integrity. If VOTF seriously embarks on this challenge, the organization clearly will do a great favor for the church as a whole. As we know, if Catholics don't like their priests or think they are doing a poor job, they are less likely to attend Mass,[17] even though in the case of VOTF (as discussed earlier), we see very high church attendance rates notwithstanding their negative assessments of priests.

What Solutions Does VOTF Offer?

A second challenge facing VOTF derives from the negative views that they have, as we saw, of the hierarchy. The survey results do not offer many clues as to how VOTF proposes to make the hierarchy more in touch with or relevant to the laity. One set of responses affirms VOTF's commitment to ensuring wider lay participation at all levels of the church — local (98 percent), diocesan (96 percent), national (94 percent), and international (90 percent), aims that are supported by virtually all of the members. More specifically, VOTF members favor lay participation in decisions about parish spending (98 percent), the selection of priests (84 percent), and the selection of bishops (85 percent). An interesting anomaly here is that although VOTF members want greater lay participation in the church, many of them have not availed themselves of the opportunities that already exist for lay decision making at the parish level. For example, just over a third have served on the parish council (37 percent), and a fifth have served on the finance council (21 percent). Another interesting gender difference is apparent here. Paralleling the male structure of the church, men are more likely than women to have assumed these executive-type roles.[18]

In any case, VOTF members' overwhelming support for its organization's focus on ensuring lay participation in decisions about parish finances deserves further comment. Where does this preoccupation with parish finances come from? And how does it fit with the long-embedded strand in Catholic activism toward integrating American cultural values with the Catholic hierarchical structure? Since its inception VOTF has unequivocally defined one of its three goals as shaping structural change in the church (in addition to supporting victims of sex abuse and priests of integrity), an objective with which 90 percent of VOTF members strongly identify. For VOTF, structural change has come to pivot around access to participation in parish financial decisions. Much of VOTF's activism can be summarized with the commanding call of "Show me the money!" — a slogan that fits well with the American capitalist tradition.

Lay access to church finances can certainly ensure some transparency in church management practices and encourage the accountability of priests to their parishioners and by extension the accountability of bishops in accounting for diocesan finances. However, it does not necessarily do anything to change the structure of the church, and equally important, will do little to change the clerical culture on which so much blame for the sex abuse cover-up is laid. VOTF's focus on money stems largely, I believe, from VOTF's insistence that it wants to change church structures but not church doctrine. Trying to keep its eyes on structure alone, VOTF settles for what it knows best. As well-heeled professionals in the secular world, VOTF founders and members know well the language of finance. It's a language and competency with which they are comfortable. Thus, by focusing on parish finances, they are taking on the church on terms they know and understand best. But in doing so, they are also affirming their own structural disempowerment in the church — the fact that they are the dispossessed laity trying to repossess the church. VOTF apparently assumes that it can accomplish structural change in the church by accessing its money. But this objective certainly cannot be attained as long as VOTF avoids talking about doctrine and recognizes that it cannot maintain a split between doctrine and structure.

It is sociologically and theologically naïve to assume that doctrine and structure, or culture and structure, are separate domains. In the secular world the doctrine of democracy gets translated into specific structural processes and procedures that reflect and enhance democratic ideals. In the Catholic Church, the doctrine of apostolic succession, and the belief that the pope and the bishops are in a continuous line back to Peter and to Jesus, means that the church's hierarchical structure is something that Catholics cannot ignore. For their part, Catholics can certainly disagree with the hierarchy (Catholicism prides faith and reason), but they cannot consider the bishops irrelevant to the church's and their Catholic identity. By the same token, the hierarchy cannot ignore the laity. The hierarchy's relations with the laity do not have to follow the authoritarian model that has so often dominated the hierarchy-laity relationship; rather, there is much doctrinal validity to the possibility that it can be collegial, communal, and dialogical as so elaborated by Vatican II.

In sum, whereas VOTF Catholics show themselves to be "good Catholics" by their Mass attendance, their general church participation, and their background in and knowledge of Catholicism, their Catholicism appears less attuned to the larger Catholic tradition when we take account of their attitudes toward the hierarchy and their compartmentalization of structural change from its doctrinal context.

The imperative for VOTF then is to desist splitting the goal of structural change from talk of doctrine. Instead, the inherently Catholic question that VOTF needs to ask is: "What in the doctrine can be used to empower structural change?" There is nothing unusual or contradictory in lay Catholics articulating a doctrinally grounded case for structural change in the church. Rather, using doctrine to change doctrine and the church's structural practices is compatible with the Catholic tradition's conjoint emphasis on faith and reason. Doctrinal reflexivity is the modus operandi of the church itself (during Vatican II, for example)[19] and of much of the discourse of professional theologians. And it is characteristic of how pro-change Catholic activists prior to VOTF have articulated arguments for changes in Catholicism.

VOTF leaders and members, as we saw from the survey results, are well grounded in Catholicism and specifically in the teachings of

Vatican II. It is puzzling why they don't use this immersion to speak with a more confident doctrinal voice. Perhaps they are constrained by their own founding slogan and by a political context in which they do not want to be seen as doctrinal upstarts. But if VOTF really wants to accomplish structural change in the church, it needs to specify what those changes are, and couch those changes in doctrine. In this new scenario, VOTF, clearly, can continue to advocate participation in parish financial decision making if it continues to judge this goal as being at the heart of its mission. But in doing so it would be well advised to ground its claims in doctrinal understandings of lay obligation and stewardship rather than simply in terms of the corporate language of financial control and accountability.

There is probably no better place in which to begin to find the doctrinal context and justification in which to couch VOTF goals than in the decrees of Vatican II. Among other affirmations, they acknowledge the complexity of today's challenges, the special expertise a competent and informed laity can offer to the whole church, and the critical importance of a communicative church in which the laity and the hierarchy alike engage in mutual and reasoned dialogue. Such reasoned dialogue, not church exit or silent protest, offers a way out of the polarization crystallized by VOTF members' attitudes toward the hierarchy and the negative appraisals made by some bishops in their a priori judgments of VOTF. As VOTF and the church as a whole move forward, it is fitting to close with a reminder that the hierarchy and the laity are collaborators in building the church and maintaining the vibrancy of Catholicism, as so declared in the emancipatory words of Vatican II's Pastoral Constitution on the Church in the Modern World:

- Let the layman not imagine that his pastors are always such experts, that to every problem which arises, however complicated, they can readily give him a concrete solution, or even that such is their mission. Rather, enlightened by Christian wisdom and giving close attention to the teaching authority of the church, let the layman take on his own distinctive role (no. 43).

- ... the church requires special help, particularly in our day, when things are changing very rapidly and the ways of thinking are exceedingly various. She must rely on those who live in the world, are versed in different institutions and specialties. ... It is the task of the entire People of God ... to hear, distinguish, and interpret the many voices of our age and to judge them in the light of the divine Word. In this way, revealed truth can always be more deeply penetrated, better understood, and set forth to greater advantage (no. 44).

- It is necessary for people to remember that no one is allowed ... to appropriate the church's authority for his opinion. They should always try to enlighten one another through honest discussion. ... All the faithful, clerical and lay, possess a lawful freedom of inquiry and of thought ... and the freedom to express their minds ... about those matters in which they enjoy competence (nos. 43, 62).

Chapter Seven

Voice of the Faithful Survey

An Ecclesiological Reflection

Mary E. Hines

William D'Antonio and Anthony Pogorelc have done a great service with their sociological study of the Voice of the Faithful as a social movement within the Roman Catholic Church. As a Bostonian as well as a theologian, I have followed the foundation of VOTF and its rapid spread beyond the Boston area. It has obviously responded to concerns deeply felt within much of the Catholic population, and particularly among laypersons. VOTF is at an important moment in its brief history as it assesses its past and looks to its future. This survey should be an excellent impetus to look back at past contributions and strengths and to assess limitations that may need to be addressed in order to continue to make the positive impact on the church that is VOTF's goal. The results of the survey are provocative and challenging. I hear in the comments of both leaders and members that there is some falling off in interest and commitment as we get away from the original critical moments of the sex abuse revelations. I also hear some concern about membership and a beginning recognition that while VOTF is surely *a* voice of the faithful and has made a great contribution to calling attention to problematic church issues, it is not the only voice of the faithful. The demographics of the study are very interesting in this respect. There needs to be further analysis of why the central issues that engage VOTF have not captured the attention of younger people, African American Catholics, or Hispanic Catholics in large numbers.

I hope that my reflections on the survey data can assist in this process of moving to the next phase of VOTF's life. My task, as I understand it, is to offer some ecclesiological context and assessment of the emergence and growth of this predominantly lay group and its call for structural reform of the church in response to the sexual abuse crisis. I have drawn data not only from the survey itself, but also from other material that articulates VOTF's self-understanding.

A Canonical Response

One way to approach evaluating VOTF's emergence is through canon law. After all, the first ecclesiologists were canonists, or at least the first specifically ecclesiological tracts were produced by canonists. Are such groups as VOTF canonically legitimate? Do the laity have the right to form such associations? Some of the episcopal responses to VOTF, such as the refusal to allow meetings on church properties, might indicate that they are not allowed by church law. However, the canonical answer to the question of the legitimate emergence of this group, as VOTF very well knows, is that the faithful have the right to form private associations as long as they do not purport to teach Catholic doctrine in the name of the church or include the word "Catholic" in their title (canons 215, 216, 298, 299, 300, 301). The literature of VOTF frequently assures us that it is not questioning or raising questions of doctrine. Even so, canon law is not enthusiastic about such associations, and canon 298.2 recommends associations that are "erected or praised or recommended by competent ecclesiastical authority." VOTF has done its homework here, consulted canon lawyers, Ladislas Orsy, for example, and is aware of the canonical legitimacy of its emergence as a social movement within the church. It has, however, already experienced the possibilities for conflict arising out of canon 298:2.[1] Similar guidelines for the formation of associations within the church are found in the Vatican II document on the laity, *Apostolicam Actuositatem,* no. 4. I am not going to go any further down the canonical path that seems pretty clear. My reflections will rather focus on the theological/ecclesiological self-understanding that reveals itself in the survey material.

The very rich and extensive material provided us by the survey suggests many avenues of exploration. I have chosen to focus on three particular, interrelated, and fairly obvious areas and to offer some conclusions that may suggest avenues for further thought.

1. What ecclesiology or ecclesiologies animate this group? What images of the church are central? What vision of the church do they hope for the future?

2. How do VOTF's leaders and members see the relationship of their call for the reform of the church's institutional structures to other dimensions of the church's reality, particularly its mission?

3. What is VOTF's vision of lay leadership in a post-Vatican II church? Can leadership in administrative areas be divorced from issues of doctrine? How much of this vision comes from an internalization of Vatican II and how much from American culture, particularly the call for more democracy?

4. Conclusions: Some questions and concerns as VOTF enters its next phase — or continues its own institutionalization process.

One of the points made frequently in the literature that has followed the sex abuse scandal suggests that the sex abuse crisis exposed serious problems with the church's institutional structures that long preexisted the present situation. I suggest that it also concretely reveals the conflict of interpretations of Vatican Council II that has been increasingly evident since the 1985 synod held to celebrate the twentieth anniversary of the conclusion of the council.[2] The synod exposed a divergence of views regarding the purpose and goals of the council that continues today. Many saw, and see, in the council an as yet unrealized call to the very reforms that VOTF finds essential, e.g., more collegiality among bishops, more attention to the historical and cultural realities of the many local churches that make up the church universal, less secrecy, more lay involvement in church decision making. Others interpret the council as intending little significant change from the very centralized institutional model in place on the eve of the council and feel that efforts made toward bringing about some of these reforms in fact represent a deviation from the mind of the council fathers. Because of this debate the foundation of VOTF and the issues it raises have considerable significance for the church as a whole, even beyond the very tragic circumstances that called it forth. Reading the survey material provides a concrete window into the struggle over the reception of the Vatican Council, still in its relatively early stages forty years after its last session.

My first point attempts to identify the operative ecclesiology of the group.

> What ecclesiology or ecclesiologies animate this group? What images of the church are central? What vision of the church do they hope for the future?

Ecclesiology is reflection on the mission, nature, and structures of the church. A great deal depends on where one starts this reflection. This clearly plays out in VOTF and its relationship with church authority. Let me describe in brief and necessarily overly simplistic terms two basic approaches to understanding the nature of the church. The first, often called "ecclesiology from above," starts with the Christological origin of the church and assumes that all authority and leadership in the church are delegated by Christ to the hierarchy of the church. It is they who have the sole responsibility of teaching and leading the faithful. An "ecclesiology from below," on the other hand, begins with the origins of the church in history and assumes that structures of authority and leadership evolved in the church under the guidance of the Holy Spirit, who is given to all the faith-filled people. This second approach is sometimes described as emphasizing the pneumatological dimension of the church. As in so many of the ecclesiological positions at issue today, both approaches can be found in the council documents. *Lumen Gentium*, chapter 1, "The Mystery of the Church," represents primarily an ecclesiology from above, while chapter 2, "The People of God," focuses on the church from below in its more historical dimensions. Responding to this discussion, the Dutch theologian Edward Schillebeeckx famously said there should really be no dichotomy between above, the Christological dimension of the church, and below, the church in history, focused more on its pneumatological dimensions, because in a spirit-filled community in fact what comes from below does come from above. Christ acts in his church in and through the whole spirit-filled community.[3] Properly understood neither of these two positions excludes the other, though this point is often ignored — and starting points, or emphases, remain important. This distinction in starting points, or emphases, is clearly illustrated in an incident recounted in *Keep the Faith, Change the Church*:

> At one point, Father Oliver said that revelation is given to the hierarchy. Mary Scanlon objected. "I believe God reveals himself to all of us in different ways. God reveals himself in family experiences and work experiences and as laity we have a special wisdom that comes from being a layperson."
>
> Father Oliver said that wasn't the main source of revelation. He said that God was revealed primarily through the hierarchy and the hierarchy was in a position to translate revelation to lay people.[4]

The survey and written material from VOTF implies an understanding of the church as originating in history where the Spirit is given to the whole church, including, but not exclusively, to the hierarchy. It implies a church where many structures are contingent and able to be changed in response to changing social and cultural realities. It describes a church where all have something to contribute — echoing the description of the many gifts needed to make up the whole church in 1 Corinthians 12. There is a clear, if implicit, critique of an *exclusively* Christomonistic descending model that emphasizes the hierarchy as the source of all authority in the church. There is also a clear assumption in the VOTF literature that the Vatican Council intended a new way of doing things within the church where laypersons would have more voice, even if that has not been actualized in the period following the council. Vatican documents on the church and on the laity are appealed to frequently for support. It is several times noted that there are structures of consultation provided for at Vatican II, but that they have often been co-opted by an authoritarian way of exercising them on the part of the hierarchy.

VOTF then seems to have primarily an ecclesiology from below for which it draws inspiration from the documents of Vatican II. Its primary images of the church are "People of God" and institution, which may at first seem contradictory.[5] "People of God" reflects the ecclesiology from below that emphasizes the gifts of the spirit given to the whole community that develops through history. Use of this image also points to the impact of Vatican II on most of the survey respondents who were energized by the power of this image in the immediate wake of the council. The survey reveals that the membership of VOTF is drawn most heavily from those in age groups likely to have been influenced by the council and disproportionably from those educated in Catholic schools, also likely to have knowledge of the council and its teachings. "People of God" was the image that captured the minds and hearts of involved Catholic laity in the first exciting years after the council. This again, however, points to the complexity of interpreting conciliar documents that include diverse and sometimes apparently contradictory images of the church. *Lumen Gentium* in its use of many biblical and patristic images for the church implies that none of these images is adequate in itself to capture the complex reality of the church and that a diversity of images is needed. There is a danger in thinking that any one of these images completely defines the reality of the church. Exclusive focus on any one image can ultimately become ideology. VOTF literature recognizes the need for a deeper study of the council documents and their meaning for the church today. This in itself is a major contribution to the ongoing process of receiving and interpreting the council.

My second point raises a concern about the other major image of the church operative in VOTF literature, the church as institution.

How do VOTF's leaders and members see the relationship of their call for the reform of the church's institutional structures to other dimensions of the church's reality, particularly its mission?

A danger in this central focus on institutional structures is that while critiquing the exercise of church authority and structure, VOTF itself sometimes seems to divorce institutional dimensions of the church from its wider reality. The discussion about reforming structures sometimes seems to take place in a vacuum without a clear articulation of the overall mission of the church to which they are in service.

VOTF leaders understandably focused on structural reform as an immediate response to the American hierarchy's handling of sexual abuse. They pointed out that the abuse by individual priests was exacerbated and enabled by bishops who relied on the secrecy endemic to a hierarchical system and seemed to place preserving the institution above protecting its most vulnerable members. An institutional crisis provoked an institutional response. It is instructive to compare the emergence of VOTF in this context to the emergence of other reform groups in the church. Obviously this is not intended to be exhaustive but merely evocative.

Reform movements often arise out of the charismatic or prophetic dimension of the church and often arise in response to an overly institutional understanding of the church. In earlier church times when there was no obvious active role for the laity, these reform groups usually became religious orders, some not without a struggle. Johannes Metz notes that they often originated "as movements that started on the fringe or margin of society as it had been... [and often functioned as]... a kind of shock therapy instituted by the Holy Spirit for the Church as a whole."[6] The Franciscan movement comes immediately to mind. Apostolic orders, founded to carry out the church's social mission in the world, had their own struggles with the institutional church as they developed structures to carry out their founding charisms. A distinctive note of these earlier movements is that their first concern is the church's ability to carry out its mission in the world. Any concern for internal structural issues arises out of this primary commitment. In a post-Vatican II church that recognizes the baptismal call of the laity to mission and ministry it is not surprising that VOTF understands its ethos to be consciously lay, though it has clerical and religious members. In the light of the history of the emergence of such groups, it is also not surprising that VOTF is experiencing some conflict with ecclesiastical authority.

The relatively recent emergence of another consciously lay group in the United States, Call to Action (CTA), provides a particularly interesting basis for comparison. I noted in comments from both members and leaders of VOTF an attempt to distance themselves from this group, among others, not always named but recognizable.[7] An incident recounted in *Keep the Faith* illustrates this point. "Mike was careful to differentiate our group from other Catholic lay organizations. He explained that we were focused on gaining greater lay involvement in the church and that we deliberately did not take positions on controversial issues such as women's ordination, divorce, birth control, and celibacy.... We are committed to working within the system.... This is what makes us different from many of the other organizations."[8] It is implied that CTA is more dissident, more to the left, more interested in meddling in doctrinal matters, etc. The question needs to be asked, if CTA is any of these things, how did it get that way? And what can VOTF learn from CTA's experience?

The origin of these two groups is instructive to compare. CTA was in fact brought together at the behest of the American bishops (as canon law would approve — within the system) as part of the bicentennial celebrations in 1976. Its original purpose was to make a contribution to the common good in the United States by bringing Gospel values and the church's tradition of social teaching to societal issues such as racism, militarism, and poverty. It accepted the Vatican II typology that the primary mission of the layperson in the church was to bring these values to the world. Laity were indeed called to mission and ministry through baptism, and their ministry was to be carried out primarily in the secular world. In the process of the conference, however, laypersons present recognized that issues could not be so neatly divided. The critical social issues under discussion had reverberations within the church. Their discussions of the mission of the church in the world led them to confront the structures of their own church and to recognize that a church calling for justice and human rights in the world needed first, or at least simultaneously, to address those issues within itself. In addition then to recommendations for justice in society, delegates developed recommendations regarding the internal life of the church. They began to see mission and structure as inextricably related. They raised issues such as the selection of bishops and pastors, annulment processes, roles for women in the church, church teaching on homosexuality, to name but a few.[9] Their discussion of mission led them to structure and to doctrinal issues — and ultimately to conflict with church authorities, who found laypersons raising such questions threatening. The lack of willingness to dialogue with CTA about these issues on the part of church authority has resulted in the adversarial situation alluded to in the anecdote from *Keep the Faith,* a situation surely not intended by the early participants in Call to Action — lay leaders not unlike VOTF members, educated, highly participant Catholics, very involved in their parishes, committed to the good of the church, very much within the system.

VOTF came from the other direction. Rather than beginning with a broad understanding of the church's mission in the world, its initial concerns focused appropriately around structural reform to address the particular critical issue of sex abuse and its cover-up. Going forward, however, this narrow focus on structure is in danger of becoming problematic and limiting. I suggest that the attempt to divorce structure from wider questions of mission and doctrine is artificial and ecclesiologically deficient. And as an attempt to avoid the conflict with church authority that other groups have experienced, this attempt to "work within the system" doesn't seem to have worked all that well.[10] As VOTF moves to its next phase I suggest that it will have to move to articulating a coherent vision of the church and its mission that will contextualize its call for reform of structures. It otherwise risks falling into the same problem as the very situation it critiques, isolating and absolutizing the institutional dimensions of the church, and perhaps further alienating those Catholics for whom institutional dimensions of the church's reality are not the most engaging, and I think of young people here.

Religious orders (at least historically), Call to Action, and other contemporary lay movements such as the Community of St. Egidio,[11] different as they are, suggest that movements for which a vision of the church's mission in the world and commitment to its actualization are central are more likely to last beyond the original founding impetus and to attract a wider diversity of members. At this moment in its brief history this is clearly a concern for VOTF. I do not mean to imply that a concern for the church's mission, particularly its social justice mission, is absent in VOTF — its individual members report involvement in social justice groups in the survey — but in a reading of the survey it does not come to the fore as a central preoccupation of the group as a whole.[12]

Point three also comes from my concern about the focus on institutional dimensions of the church, but this time in relation to VOTF's avoidance of doctrinal issues.

> What is VOTF's vision of lay leadership in a post-Vatican II church? Can leadership in administrative areas be divorced from issues of doctrine? How much of this vision comes from an internalization of Vatican II and how much from American culture, particularly the call for more democracy?

Is VOTF's vision of lay leadership in the church too restrictive? VOTF suggests that more involvement of the laity would have been a check on the secrecy and authoritarianism that allowed the sex abuse scandal to reach the level that it did. VOTF members see this situation as exposing the lack of implementation of a Vatican II theology of the laity. There is no question that an immediate result of the council was a sense of empowerment for the laity. This was already mentioned in the previous discussion of the image of the "People of God" as the symbol that most captured the new sense of empowerment of the laity that characterized the early years following the council.[13] The move from the pre-Vatican II Catholic Action model, which saw the laity as helping the hierarchy in their mission, to an understanding of the laity as called to mission and ministry in their own right at baptism (*Lumen Gentium*, no. 31; *Apostolicam Actuositatem*, no. 3) was a rallying cry in the early years following the council. The particular mission of the laity was primarily identified at Vatican II with the secular. The laity were to be a sort of a bridge from the church to the world (*Lumen Gentium*, no. 31). At this early stage it was thought important to identify a special mission for laity in their own right, distinguished from that of the clergy. Post-Vatican II experience soon exposed this typology as inadequate. The church is a complex reality, and it is not so easy to compartmentalize ministries and tasks on the basis of one's status in the church. The Call to Action experience is also illustrative here. Involvement in the church's mission to transform the world led to the recognition that these same issues existed within the church. As we saw, laypeople came to recognize that their gifts were also needed to transform the inner life of the church. VOTF starts there and focuses its energies on implementing structures at every level within the church that encourage active participation of the laity in decision making and provide for accountability of church officials. Involvement in finance and review boards and other administrative roles is promoted.[14] Election of bishops and the participation of the congregation in the call of pastors are also suggested as avenues into fuller participation of the laity.

There are a number of survey questions about the effect of the American democratic experience on these suggestions for lay involvement. While survey answers to these questions differ, most respondents seem to derive their inspiration from Vatican II. Undoubtedly also, however, VOTF members are influenced by their democratic experience as Americans, especially in their concern for participation and structure. In assessing this influence, however, it is important to remember that there are roots for these so-called democratic practices in the earliest history of the church[15] and in the theology of the church as spirit-filled community, as well as in the early experience of the church in the United States. Democratic practices are not necessarily as foreign to church governance as some suggest.

VOTF members, then, promote active and more democratic involvement of the laity in the administrative structure of the church, but I would raise the question here too, as I did with mission, whether this vision of lay involvement and leadership is too narrow. VOTF literature frequently asserts that its members do not intend to meddle in church doctrine. This seems to imply that while administration and governance may be the province of the laity, understandings of the church's mission and matters of faith belong exclusively to the hierarchy. This is not rooted in the early history of the church where, as Francine Cardman points out, the process of handing on the faith included both clergy and lay.[16] At Vatican II, the laity are clearly given a role not only in structural issues but in matters of discerning faith and morals. *Lumen Gentium* 12 says, "The body of the faithful as a whole, anointed as they are by the Holy One,...cannot err in matters of belief. Thanks to a supernatural sense of the faith which characterizes the People as a whole, it manifests this unerring quality when, 'from the bishops down to the last member of the laity,' it shows universal agreement in matters of faith and morals." This surely suggests that decisions on faith and morals arrived at without participation of the faithful are significantly deficient.

I would urge VOTF going forward not to excuse themselves from making their minds known on matters of faith as well as structure.[17] In that same section of *Lumen Gentium* church authorities are exhorted not "to extinguish the spirit, but to test all things." The Decree on the Apostolate of the Laity (*Apostolicam Actuositatem*) says, "The Holy Spirit who sanctifies the People of God through the ministry and sacraments gives to the faithful special gifts as well....From the reception of these charisms or gifts...there arise for each believer the right *and duty* [my emphasis] to use them in the church and in the world for the good of mankind and for the upbuilding of the church. In doing so believers need to enjoy the freedom of the Holy Spirit who breathes where he wills." Again there is a call not to extinguish the spirit (*Apostolicam Actuositatem*, no. 3). Pope Benedict, writing as a theologian during the council, reinforced this call: "The Church needs the spirit of freedom and of sincere forthrightness because she is bound by the command, 'Do not stifle the Spirit' (1 Thess. 5:19), which is valid for all time."[18] It is not clear whether Pope Benedict would write these words today, but the biblical and conciliar principles that he was invoking remain constant. VOTF's calls for structural reform are truly important and need to be continued, but laypersons are also responsible to make their minds known on matters of faith. Structure cannot be divorced from mission and doctrine without falling into the same overemphasis on institution that has led to the problems VOTF is addressing and ultimately to an impoverishment of our understanding of church.

As for the official church's reaction, the response of church authority to new and emerging groups, especially as they move beyond their foundational phase, has often been the impulse to control and institutionalize. New movements always have their birth pains. It will be a challenge for a lay group without the structures of traditional religious orders to keep focused and survive especially in a situation of conflict, but I suggest that if VOTF can keep its momentum, broaden its vision, and rethink what it means to operate "within the system" it can continue to be an important force in actualizing Vatican II's vision of a fully participant church.

Conclusions

Voice of the Faithful has played an important role in the response to the sex abuse crisis. It has galvanized the energy of already committed laity, involved the formerly less committed, and renewed the Vatican II call for active participation of the laity. Its predominant ecclesiology from below and its focus on the image of the whole church as the people of God provide theological underpinnings for the call for structural reform. A clearer articulation of the relationship of ecclesiology from below and from above might serve to allay the fears of some that the structural reforms called for are primarily inspired by American democracy, or that such an approach ignores the Christological dimensions of the church. I believe also that VOTF's calls for reform would be even more compelling and appear less narrowly institutionally focused if situated within a more wholistic understanding of church that articulates an understanding of mission and recognizes that laypersons' gifts are not confined to the administrative or structural dimensions of the church. According to Vatican II laypersons have not only the right but the duty to contribute to the faith of the church, and this means being willing to express views on some of the more controversial issues that VOTF has tried to avoid.

There is also a need to recognize explicitly that VOTF is one voice of a particular demographic and to reflect on how to call forth other voices that have not been energized by this narrow focus on structure and to find out why they have not been engaged. The survey points to the need for greater diversity of age, ethnicity, race, and economic levels.

Perhaps more attention to the wider mission of the church will serve as an invitation for more and diverse voices of the faithful to be heard who may not be so engaged by issues of structural reform. I appreciated throughout the survey material the commitment to ongoing theological education that many members mentioned in their survey responses and the sacrifices that entails in the midst of extraordinarily busy lives. I hope this can be sustained. Boston College deserves much appreciation for making so many opportunities available through its Church of the 21st Century Initiative.

Finally, having read the survey material and the other materials Bill D'Antonio and Tony Pogorelc have supplied to the members of this panel, I want to thank Voice of the Faithful — founders, leaders, and members — for their work in providing a beacon of hope in a period of great discouragement and disillusionment for many Catholics. I hope this reawakening of the laity to rights and responsibilities can be sustained and grow in the midst of busy lives. This is an important moment in the reception of Vatican II, which in its inception came from above. Movements like VOTF represent the grassroots reception and ownership of the council that has been lacking.

Chapter Eight

"The Faith We Are Called to Keep... and to Spread"

Robert P. Imbelli

I am thankful for the invitation to offer these reflections, drawing from the survey findings and interviews, as well as from other observations of Voice of the Faithful members and critics.

I am neither a sociologist nor a canon lawyer but have been asked to reflect from the perspective of a "systematic theologian." Where the sociologist may legitimately focus on organizational structures and dynamics, the theologian seeks to discern the content and comprehensiveness of the animating theological vision of a movement.

Moreover, though Voice of the Faithful understandably springs from a determinate history (to which I will refer), my own contribution hopes to address the future rather than merely to rehearse the past. I begin, then, with a general impression that others may confirm or correct. The inimitable Tip O'Neill once opined that "all politics is local." I strongly suspect that all Voice of the Faithful is local as well: strongly influenced by local situations and local leadership (both that of the local bishop and the local participants). Thus it strikes the observer that Voice of the Faithful is, in fact, a rather large tent under which many people and multiple agendas dwell.

If this is a fair observation, then ongoing conversation, discernment, and even mutual correction among the membership seem necessary for the movement's continued well-being and efficacy. In this discernment constructively critical voices should be welcomed and given a place and an attentive hearing. Though I have under-lined the local character of Voice of the Faithful, surely a significant national voice in the movement is that of James Post, the movement's president. Let me, then, refer to a recent event at which the respon-dent was James Post. The occasion was the seventh annual lecture of the Catholic Common Ground Initiative delivered this past June in Washington by Archbishop James Weisgerber of Winnipeg, Canada. The archbishop's lecture was entitled "Building a Church of Commu-nion." I would like briefly to touch on three points that Post made in his response to the archbishop's talk.

1. Speaking of his [our] generation he said: "We are the sons and daughters of [the World War II generation — Tom Brokaw's "greatest generation."] . . . we mirror the unique intersection of religious values, education, and worldly accomplishments that occurred in the late 20th century."[1]

I don't know whether Jim Post had seen the charts, graphs, and stats that we now have before us at the time he prepared his response. But I think his two sentences constitute an admirable summary of the findings. The members of Voice of the Faithful are, to a large part, the successful products of the impressive Catholic educational and social subculture that prevailed in the United States through the 1950s, up until the very dawn of Vatican II.

2. A second point was the following: "The clergy sexual abuse disclosures seared the conscience of baby boomer Catholics. The rev-elations of cover-up, deception, and concealment of predator priests infuriated us. This was the 'Catholic Watergate experience,' the betrayal of something fundamental that we deeply treasured."[2]

Once again, in only three sentences, Jim Post sums up volumes. One is moved time and again by the sense of outrage over innocence abused and trust betrayed felt by so many Catholics. Moreover, what-ever the good intentions of Voice of the Faithful in supporting "priests of integrity," many priests themselves feel tarnished by the misdeeds of their confreres and often abandoned by their bishops as well.

3. Post goes on to address the issues we face in terms of "leader-ship," "governance," and "accountability." He quotes approvingly Robert Bennett: "In order for the Church to achieve the goal set

out by the bishops of 'restoring the bonds of trust that unite us,' more must be done, through a process that involves transparency and substantial participation by the laity."[3]

I am in full agreement with each of the points Jim Post has made. Indeed, if I may interject a personal experience: I am a member of the board of trustees of the Blessed John XXIII Seminary in Weston, Massachusetts. I return from each meeting of the board newly thankful for the competence and commitment of the board's lay members. Transparency and participation are not only secular values; they are gospel values.

You might be interested in discovering that, in these matters, you may have a potential ally. A well-known writer recently had this to say: "Many bishops and pastors...expend their energies on micro-management, doing many things that laypeople could do as well or better, and only grudgingly entertaining the counsel of the non-ordained. This compulsive need for control is an aspect of the deadening disease of clericalism, which is widespread in the Church in America." The author then rises to a rhetorical climax: "Consultation, collaboration, participation, Yes." However, before you rush to the Voice of the Faithful website to discover the identity of this potential supporter, he then adds: "Democracy, No."[4]

Clearly, in this as in so much else, "The devil dwells in the details!"

Toward a New Narrative

Voice of the Faithful admits, somewhat ruefully, that some/many "misunderstand us, including members of our Church's hierarchy and lay Catholics who misinterpret our mission and goals."[5] This recognition leads to a commendable concern to explain the movement's mission and goals. But, as any organization knows, such clarification is not a once for all matter, but entails a continuing reflection and an ongoing discernment. How much more is this the case with a movement that situates itself "in communion with the universal Catholic Church," one that accepts "the teaching authority of our Church, including the traditional role of the bishops and the Pope."[6]

What service can a systematic theologian render, in particular one who is persuaded of the inseparable link between theology and spirituality, orthodoxy and orthopraxis, if you will? In pondering this question I was reminded of an intriguing statement in Peter Steinfel's important book *A People Adrift*. The book opens starkly: "Today the Roman Catholic Church in the United States is on the verge of either an irreversible decline or a thoroughgoing transformation."[7] You can hardly be more apocalyptic than that!

But anyone who knows or reads Peter Steinfels knows that he is not a "quick fix" man; he doesn't believe in unnuanced analyses or simple solutions. And so he goes on to write regarding the ecclesial situation in the United States: "All the parties ['Conservatives and Liberals'] that emerged from the Council have their mixed records of successes and failures, their vested interests, and their turfs to defend." Then he adds, in words that deserve to be engraved on our doorposts: "Perhaps no single point in this book is more important than this: the narratives that have framed the contending diagnoses of Catholicism's health are outdated and inadequate. It is time to cease forcing the data into simplified, partisan accounts, time to...expand the framing narratives to accommodate almost four decades of further experience."[8]

I asked Steinfels, when he came to Boston College, whether his own book provided this new narrative. He admitted it did not. Nor do I pretend to offer one. It is, I believe, one of the crucial challenges before us, toward which we must all collaborate. I hope that Voice of the Faithful can be a contributor to the urgent task.

Catholicism's Depth Grammar

But if I do not propose a "new narrative," may I at least suggest some elements of the comprehensive *Catholic grammar* that such a narrative must honor, if it is, indeed, to "keep the faith" in the full Catholic sense.

Just as the expert in linguistics Noam Chomsky suggests that a depth grammar underlies different spoken languages, so I want to recommend that we must pay heed to the distinctive Catholic depth grammar in the stories we tell, the articles we write, even the interviews we give, if our words are to build up in an authentic way the Catholic community. This imperative is especially challenging, since we are all tempted by sectarian, reductionist, and adversarial pressures. Nor is the situation rendered any easier by the media's incessant appetite for controversy reduced to sound-bite proportions. Fragmentation, not Catholic fullness, seems the order of the day.

Given the limits of a short article, I will briefly highlight four elements of such a Catholic grammar that may serve to guide and challenge our dialogue, our discernment, and our living of committed discipleship.

The Catholic "Both/And"

It has become a commonplace to say that the language of Catholicism tends to embrace *"both/and,"* rather than "either/or." Affirming this, however, requires of its proponents the spiritual maturity capable of supporting a tension that is both creative and soul-stretching.

In speaking of the church, then, we need to insist, with Vatican II, "that the society structured with hierarchical organs and the Mystical Body of Christ are not to be considered as two realities, nor are the visible assembly and the spiritual community.... Rather they form one complex reality which coalesces from a divine and a human element."[9]

Hence it would be a reductionist use of Catholic language to speak dismissively of "the institutional church" (as some do), as though there were some other church. The reform of institutions is a perennial task, but their abolishment is an impossibility. Indeed, there are structural realities, like episcopacy, that for the Catholic Tradition are of divine ordinance (*de jure divino*).

A similar, not uncommon, reductionist linguistic usage is to speak of "the hierarchy" in implied or explicit contrast to "the people of God." The great chapter 2 of *Lumen Gentium* focuses upon the "people of God." But this crucial ecclesiological term refers to the *entire* people of God: bishops, priests, lay faithful, and religious. Vatican II's epochal ecclesiological accomplishment is to consider all the baptized in their common dignity and responsibility, before going on, in subsequent chapters, to treat of the hierarchy (chapter 3), the laity (chapter 4), and religious (chapter 6) in their distinctive missions and ministries.

Catholicism's Christocentric Narrative

But with this insistence on the inseparability of the institutional and the spiritual (or "mystical") element of church, there is no doubt that the whole purpose of the institutional is to serve, to foster and promote, the spiritual and mystical. Indeed, the great Catholic theologian Karl Rahner predicted: "the devout Christian of the future will either be a 'mystic,' one who has experienced something, or will cease to be anything at all."[10] And this deeper spiritual dimension, which will last forever, is the living *Jesus Christ* himself, who through his resurrection has become "life-giving Spirit" (1 Cor. 15:45).[11] It would be congruent with Rahner's intention, then, to amend his statement: not so much experience "something," but experience "Someone."

One frequently hears today that Christianity, like Judaism and Islam, is a "religion of the Book." Though this is commendable as an effort to foster understanding and dialogue among the religions, it is most inadequate as a depiction of the distinct identity of Christianity. Far more than a religion of the Book, Christianity is a religion of the Person. As John Paul II affirms in his splendid Apostolic Letter *Novo Millennio Ineunte:* "We shall not be saved by a formula but by a Person, and the assurance which he gives us: *I am with you!*"[12]

The distinguishing identity of the people of God, then, is that it is the body of *Christ.* Vatican II's Constitution on the Church is entitled *Lumen Gentium,* the Light of the Nations. But the title is not self-referential: the church is not the light of the nations. The light of the nations is Christ himself. Hence Catholicism's depth grammar is always "Christic": centered on Jesus Christ. He must be the heart of the narrative we live and tell.

In a presentation given at Boston College Dr. Francis Butler outlined a "Professional Code of Ethics" for church leaders. The very first norm for ecclesial leadership that he articulates sounds precisely the right note: "I promise to do all in my power to deepen my understanding of the Church...as the body of Christ, and I will evaluate my service in the Church daily in the light of my relationship to the person of Jesus Christ and his command to love one another as he has loved us (John 15:12)."[13]

In a similar vein, Ronald Rolheiser in his fine book *The Holy Longing: The Search for a Christian Spirituality* makes this passionate plea: "Within Christian spirituality, long before we speak of anything else (Church, dogmas, commandments, even admonitions to love and justice), we must speak of Jesus, the person and the energy that undergirds everything else. After all everything else is merely a branch. Jesus is the vine, the blood, the pulse, and the heart."[14] I would only add to this splendid affirmation: even before we speak of participation and accountability. For, in the church, we are participants in the body whose head is Jesus Christ; and we are ultimately accountable to him who will come again to judge the living and the dead.

Realizing this Christic depth grammar of Catholic language leads to three further corollaries by which to test the adequacy of our own reflection and discourse:

1. Jesus Christ is much more than teacher, offering moral example and instruction. He is the living Lord of the church who continues to nourish us with his own body and blood. It is not the pope's church or the bishop's church or my church; it is Christ's church. The noontime prayer recommended on the Voice of the Faithful website serves as an important daily reminder: "Jesus, Lord and brother, help us with our faithfulness. Please hear our voice...."

2. Any reference to the church as "sacrament" (whether "sacrament of the unity of all humankind," or universal sacrament of salvation), if it is to be complete and faithful to the vision of Vatican II, must always stipulate: *"in Christ."*[15] Too often "sacramentality" is invoked in a rather free-floating manner, detached from its moorings and meaning in the reality of the risen Christ.

3. No appeal to the Spirit should be made in a way that might suggest the Spirit's independence from Jesus Christ. The Spirit is the Spirit of Christ. The Spirit will indeed "lead into all truth (John 16:13)"; but the Truth into which the Spirit leads is the Truth who is Christ. We do not run beyond Christ to some third age, a vacuous new age of the Spirit. We are called in the Spirit to follow Christ, to "catch up" to Christ in his fullness (see Eph. 4:11–16). Jesus Christ is ever the Lord and we the disciples.

The Pattern of Transformation

The third element of the grammar of Catholicism I would underscore is that it delineates a pattern of *transformation*. Here chapter 5 of *Lumen Gentium*, "The Universal Call to Holiness in the Church" is both radical and all-demanding. The council, recovering the New Testament and patristic tradition, teaches: "all the faithful of Christ, of whatever rank or status, are called to the fullness of Christian life and to the perfection of charity."[16]

It is crucial for us to recall that the proclamation of the Good News of what God has done in Jesus Christ is always accompanied by a call to conversion (*metanoia*) and transformation. From Jesus' own summons, "The time is fulfilled and the kingdom of God is at hand: convert, believe the Good News" (Mark 1:15), to Peter's proclamation on the first Pentecost, "Convert and be baptized every one of you in the name of Jesus Christ" (Acts 2:38), God's grace calls for human response and responsibility. If one has truly seen, one cannot remain unchanged.

Moreover, baptismal conversion is not a once and for all achievement. It must be daily renewed and must engender an ongoing transformation, whereby the entire self is given over to Christ and his gospel. The Letter to the Colossians expresses this imperative in particularly striking fashion. "Stop lying to one another, since you have put off the old self with its practices and have put on the new self which is being renewed in wisdom according to the image of its Creator. Here there is not Greek and Jew, circumcision and un-circumcision, barbarian, Scythian, slave, free: but Christ is all in all"

(Col. 3:8–11). How these words take on new resonance in light of the abuse scandal we have experienced! They summon each of us to a new realization of the many guises the "lie" can assume, and to an honest recognition of our own (not just others') propensity to self-deception.

In the implementation of Vatican's II's directives concerning the *aggiornamento* (updating) of the church's self-understanding and practices, appeal is frequently made to the Constitution on the Liturgy, *Sacrosanctum Concilium,* and its call for *participatio actuosa,* active participation by all in the liturgy of the church. But too often we have settled for a merely managerial distribution of external roles and functions. Perhaps that is why the "reform" frequently appears lifeless.

The true purpose of active participation (which can take place by profound silence or truly attentive listening, as much as by robust reading or singing) is the growth in holiness of the whole people of God. There are certainly diverse modes and styles of holiness. Perhaps a particular form that resonates with the needs and aspirations of our time is what John Paul II, in *Novo Millennio Ineunte,* identifies as "a spirituality of communion."[17]

In the Catholic Common Ground Lecture I referred to above, Archbishop Weisgerber drew heavily upon *Novo Millennio Ineunte* and concluded: "There will be no communion without holiness.... A communion based on holiness is a demanding vision and we need to recognize that the cross always stands at the center of such a vision."[18]

Allow me to suggest one salient way the cross enters into our conversations and writings. We all need to practice a stricter "asceticism of language." May I invoke here that secular saint George Orwell and his classic essay "Politics and the English Language."[19] Taking our lead from Orwell, we must learn to purify our speech: to avoid rhetorical inflation, to shun facile generalizations and the destructive polarization into "us and them" that does not promote, but rather undermines a spirituality of communion.

To be frank we need to prune language like that of a recent posting found on the Voice of the Faithful website under the title "The Synod and the Signs of the Times." The unnamed author speaks of "bishops in Rome trying to write rules on paper for millions of Catholics who are struggling to practice their faith in moral communion with Christ in a world made immoral by those who are supposed to lead the flock." Orwell, I think, would strike red lines through a few of the feverish generalizations.

Catholicism's Evangelical Dynamic

Fourth, and finally, a Catholic depth grammar structures an evangelical commitment and dynamic. The Catholic Common Ground Initiative is often (and rightly) associated with Cardinal Bernardin's concern to foster dialogue in the face of increasing polarization in the church. But dialogue, however important, is not an end in itself. If one reads the "Founding Documents" of the Initiative, it quickly becomes clear that dialogue is for the sake of discernment, and discernment is for the sake of discipleship and mission.[20]

Though "evangelization" may ring a Protestant note in some Catholic ears, it is an intrinsic dimension of the Gospel. Who can joyfully behold beauty without desiring to share it with all? Who can experience a life-transforming encounter with Jesus Christ without the urgency to share his friendship with others? Vatican II's ecumenical vision does not countenance a bland tolerance, but advances the respectful imperative to proclaim that Jesus Christ is indeed the light of the nations. The love of Christ requires no less of us. In sponsoring a "new evangelization," Pope John Paul II was the faithful interpreter of Vatican II.

An essential evangelical task of the church in every age and culture is to discern the signs of the times, both positive and negative. It is a task incumbent upon all of us whose defining identity is to be members of Christ's body, living in the most powerful nation of the early twenty-first century. For all the merits of late-capitalist American democracy (of which we are privileged beneficiaries), this society and culture also pose serious challenges to a Catholic faith vision.

For we live in a culture that many discerning observers characterize as marked and marred by a therapeutic and consumerist individualism. In such a culture religion often becomes but another commodity, tailored to one's personal preferences. None of us stands outside this culture. All of us are, in some measure, branded by it.[21]

In this culture we are called by Jesus Christ to be "salt of the earth, light for the world" (Matt. 5:13–16). We cannot dwell apart from this world; but we dare not collude with its less than gospel values. As Paul exhorts the Romans, he admonishes us: "I appeal to you, brothers and sisters, by the mercies of God, to present your bodies as a living sacrifice, holy and acceptable to God, which is your worship in the Spirit. Do not be conformed to this world, but be transformed by the renewal of your mind, that you may discern what is the will of God, what is good, and acceptable, and perfect" (Rom. 12:1–2).

However urgent the task of church renewal, a renewal that Voice of the Faithful aspires to further, we must never lose sight of the ultimate goal, the goal of Vatican II: the salvation and true life of the world in Christ. However righteous our cause, however legitimate our demand for transparency and accountability, it would be an unmitigated tragedy if, in its pursuit, we "consume and devour one another" (Gal. 5:15). For then we would be salt that has lost its savor, light that has been extinguished. Then Vatican II's vision of the church as "sacrament of unity in Christ" would be mocked by our divided and embittered state.

Conclusion

Many factors will affect the future of the Voice of the Faithful movement: wise and discerning leaders, loyal and committed members paramount among them. But, as I have suggested, the vitality of its Catholic future will also depend upon the fluency and competence with which both leaders and members articulate and enact a comprehensive and integral Catholic vision. I have attempted to offer some criteria in aid of discernment, a grammar in service of a new narrative. However, no one speaks "grammar." We use the grammar to tell stories, to preach sermons, to write articles, to give interviews, even to chant slogans.

Slogans and logos indeed have their place and purpose — and their limits. May I be bold to conclude, then, with a proposed revision of the VOTF slogan, in keeping with the "grammatical analysis" set forth.

> *"Keep the Faith/Change the Church//*
> *Spread the Faith/Change the World!"*

Chapter Nine

The Virtues of Loyalty

William A. Gamson

About thirty-five years ago, an economist named Albert Hirschman published a provocative book titled *Exit, Voice, and Loyalty* (1970).[1] It had a major impact on social movement scholars, and its arguments have become part of the shared knowledge of the field. As I reflected on the voluminous data that Bill D'Antonio and Tony Pogorelc have collected about the Voice of the Faithful leaders and members, I had a recurrent reaction: *Hirschman would use this case to illustrate his arguments if he were writing his book today.*

So I revisited his book to refresh my memory. First of all, the book has an important subtitle, which I had forgotten since it is rarely included in citations: "Responses to Decline in Firms, Organizations, and States." The term "organization" is a broad one, but it includes the Catholic Church. The church is, in sociological jargon, a transnational voluntary association to which members can make varying degrees of commitment and can leave if they so choose. Hirschman makes a few passing references to this type of organization but doesn't really attempt any serious analysis. Nevertheless, his analysis is extremely relevant for understanding the response to the current crisis in the church.

Hirschman is looking at the interplay between two options that members have when an organization to which they belong is experiencing difficulty. They can leave and put their energy into some other organization or into other pursuits, or they can try to change the organization. That is what Hirschman means by exercising voice. Which option they choose is a complicated matter.

First, there is a question of how easy or difficult it is to exit, including the availability of alternatives. If it is easy to leave and there is an alternative of equal or better quality, why hang around and invest effort in fixing the organization? But sometimes exit is not so easy. Hirschman uses the nation state as an example. One can leave one's country if one doesn't like the way it is governed and go to live in another country — that is, if one lives in the United States and not in a country that doesn't allow this option. But even in the United States, this is a complicated decision, precisely because it is not merely an economic matter — as Hirschman emphasizes — but involves a complicated mix of emotions, social networks, and other social and political issues.

In analyzing why and how people respond as they do to an organization in crisis or decline, Hirschman focuses on the concept of loyalty. His reasoning leads him to a fascinating paradox: "Loyalty is at its most functional when it looks most irrational, when loyalty means strong attachment to an organization that does not seem to warrant such attachment."[2]

Hirschman's central argument is that "loyalty holds exit at bay and activates voice."[3] The most quality-conscious and committed members are likely to be the first to recognize the problems, and hence, if they have no loyalty, they will be the first to exit.

> This tendency deprives the faltering firm or organization of those who could best help to fight its shortcomings and its difficulties. As a result of loyalty, these potentially most influential customers and members will stay on longer than they would ordinarily, in the hope or, rather, reasoned expectation that improvement or reform can be achieved "from within." Thus, loyalty, far from being irrational, can serve the socially useful purpose of preventing deterioration from becoming cumulative, as it so often does when there is no barrier to exit.[4]

The alternative of exercising voice is, as Hirschman recognizes, often problematic. Even nominally democratic organizations have tendencies to develop oligarchies and become staff-driven rather than member-driven. And in hierarchical organizations such as the Catholic Church, the problems of exercising voice are compounded. To those who would consider this option, the task is likely to seem daunting.

Here, Hirschman argues, "Loyalty . . . helps to redress the balance by raising the cost of exit. It thereby pushes [people] into the alternative, creativity-requiring course of action from which they would normally recoil."[5] Members who are locked in to their organizations a little longer because of loyalty, will "use the voice option with greater determination and resourcefulness than would otherwise be the case."

Nevertheless, "while loyalty postpones exit, its very existence is predicated on the very possibility of exit. . . . The chances for voice to function effectively as a recuperation mechanism are appreciably strengthened if voice is backed up by the *threat of exit,* whether it is made openly or whether the possibility of exit is merely well understood to be an element in the situation by all concerned." In other words, the effectiveness of voice is strengthened by the possibility of exit. Voice is most likely to be resorted to and to be effective when exit is always possible but is not too easy because of loyalty.

Voice of the Faithful

What a totally apt name. The "voice" part echoes the chosen option. The data set documents again and again the ways in which the leaders and members are the most committed and loyal of Catholics. These are not "recovering Catholics" (a term I learned from some of my Boston College colleagues' self-characterizations) or "cafeteria Catholics," but those who make their religious affiliation a central part of their identity and practice in everyday life. Eight out of ten members report that they pray once a day or more. These are the stalwarts who provide an active core of participants on parish committees and pass on the church culture to children.

On virtually every measure of what it means to be an observant Catholic, they are higher than those who self-identify as Catholics in national surveys. They are also highly educated and well-off, upper-middle-class or wealthy professionals. They are exactly the group whom Hirschman is thinking of as the "most quality-conscious" members who can best help the organization change. The slogan "Keep the Faith, Change the Church" is just a catchier way of saying what in Hirschmanese would be: "Stay loyal; exercise voice, not exit."

For very good reasons, D'Antonio and Pogorelc distinguish three generations: pre-Vatican II, Vatican II, and post-Vatican II. I find Hirschman's analysis helpful in understanding the different mix of exit, voice, and loyalty in these three generations.

For the pre-Vatican II group — those over sixty-five — exit is extremely difficult. These are people for whom being Catholic is central to their personal identity and their lives. Leaving the church would be like leaving their personal identity behind with it. As a VOTF member put it: "The senior set has too many years and too much heart invested to take a hike."

For the Vatican II generation it is more complicated. Their choice of the voice option seems more contingent, a combination of loyalty plus a belief in the potential effectiveness of voice. Here, the exit option appears to be more real and dependent on whether or not the church is capable of responding to their voice. The VOTF quote that says it best for me is: "We are the 'over the hill gang' in love with the changes promised in the Vatican II documents, only to find that our hierarchy 'deep-sixed' them, hoping we would forget."

This self-deprecating description is a little misleading since they are far from "over the hill." Because exit remains an option, they are the group most likely to be effective in exercising voice. They are held in by the vision of change in the church promised by Vatican II. They haven't forgotten this vision, and if the hierarchy continues to "deep-six" their efforts at change, they will eventually reach a point where their loyalty has its limits.

And then there is the missing generation — post-Vatican II, the under forty-fives. "At our regional and parish voice meetings, there are mostly gray tops." Not having a lifetime of commitment or the vision of Vatican II to inspire hope of change, exit is too easy an option. "The young are not into the reform of institutions — if it's broke, throw it out," to quote a VOTF member, or as one of my colleagues put it, "I don't have centuries to bring about change."

One VOTF leader observed that "many young adults are watching to see whether their middle-aged parents and grandparents are really going to make a difference. So I think they are watching even if they haven't committed to getting involved in a hands-on way. Many of them are pretty much at odds with the church, and they are not sure that it should be repaired. So they are watching and waiting." Voice is too hard, exit too easy, and there isn't enough loyalty to defer the exit option.

Passionate Politics: The Role of Emotions

For complicated reasons, the field of social movements went through a period of great distrust of accounts that emphasized emotions. The field had been dominated by explanations that had at their core the view that movements were a case of "people going crazy together." In reaction, many social movement scholars — including John McCarthy and myself — emphasized the rational side of participation in collective action. Issues of organization and the mobilization of resources were the focus, and emotions were given short shrift.

For the last twenty years or so, emotions have come back in — not to emphasize irrationality but to emphasize that both strategic thinking about opportunities and efficacy as well as emotions operate. Rather than thinking of movements as expressive or instrumental, we have come to see all movements as having both instrumental and expressive aspects. They are often blended so that certain emotions are necessary and desirable if a strategy of change is to succeed. And the most central emotion, in this analysis, centers on the concept of moral outrage and righteous indignation about injustice.

A few years ago, a trio of young social movement scholars — Jeff Goodwin, Jim Jasper, and Francesca Polletta — published a set of essays that brought together work on emotions and social movements. They called their edited volume *Passionate Politics*.[6] It would be hard to understand the reactions of the Voice of the Faithful without analyzing the emotional content of their voice and loyalty.

Goodwin et al. introduce the concept of "moral shocks" — often the first step toward recruitment into social movements. To quote the authors, they occur "when an unexpected event or piece of information raises such a sense of outrage in a person that she becomes inclined toward political action. . . . It implies a visceral, bodily feeling, on a par with vertigo or nausea." To quote a VOTF member, it felt "like being punched in the stomach."

In this case, the moral shock is in the betrayal of the faithful by the hierarchy, not in the misbehavior of priests, reprehensible as this may be. "They *knew* and they reassigned him to another parish!" The hierarchy was more concerned about protecting the reputation and institutional interests of the church than in protecting the vulnerable children of its faithful followers. Not being a Catholic, I don't personally experience that sense of betrayal, but I can fully understand and empathize with it.

From the standpoint of the social movement theory reviewed here, VOTF has the ideal combination of conditions for producing effective voice. One has the impetus to action and the energizing jolt provided by a moral shock plus the ideal blend of exit, voice, and loyalty. The most committed church members are those who are too loyal to exit easily but for whom exit remains an ultimate option. They choose voice for now but might eventually leave if the church is unable or unwilling to address the problems they see.

Problems and Obstacles to the Success of VOTF

Will the church be able or willing to respond to the challenge presented by the Voice of the Faithful? The first thing to emphasize here is that this is not merely about what is in the hearts and minds of individual members of the church hierarchy. There are social and cultural issues that shape the decisions in powerful ways — and this is what I will attempt to address here.

Cultural Contradictions. The Catholic Church is a hierarchical, transnational, voluntary association with its own organizational culture. Everywhere that it has a presence, there is a complex history of how this culture interacts with national political culture. The interaction in Italy, for example, is a fascinating story in its own right.

In the United States, the culture of the church exists in an American political culture for which notions of grassroots democracy have a deep cultural resonance. When Catholic women who are responsible professionals in their work lives say they feel like they are being treated as children in their church lives, they are reflecting this contradiction. American values create certain expectations about accountability and participation that become norms against which the church is inevitably judged.

"It is difficult to support a dictatorship after having been raised with democratic ideals," says one VOTF member. As one of the leaders puts it, "I guess maybe the American part of me is the very self-confident part of me, because I trust my conscience. So that fawning over priests really insulted the American part of me. I just thought that was anti-democratic."

From the standpoint of U.S. political culture, some of the reforms suggested by VOTF seem extremely modest and unradical. For a non-Catholic, the reaction is likely to be, "You mean you don't have that already?"

- The laity should have some voice in how the money they contribute to the parish is spent.

- The laity should have some voice in who serves as their parish priest.

But from the standpoint of the hierarchical culture of the church, these are not simple changes to make. They introduce a culture of democratic participation into what is essentially an incompatible, paternalistic culture. A lay opponent, David Zizik, addresses the cultural tension as a supporter of the organizational culture. He challenges the VOTF claim that they do not seek to change church doctrine.

In fact, the group's existence is predicated upon a view of ecclesial authority and lay-episcopal relations that rubs against the grain of Catholic doctrine and tradition. . . . The group's re-fusal to respect the bishops' governing authority compromises any hope that the group can contribute to church "reform" in a manner that is authentically Catholic.[7]

This is not to say that some creative accommodation cannot be found to blend the two cultures if there is a good faith effort to find one. But it suggests that this culture clash will be a recurrent tension and difficulty at each step along the path to change.

Camel Noses and Slippery Slopes. There is a long theme in the social movement literature about the reluctance of authorities to respond to challengers by changing their policies if they can, in-stead, exercise social control. Corporations challenged by unions, for example, hired their own mercenaries to break strikes and used a va-riety of repressive tactics before they came to terms with collective bargaining agreements.

You have your choice of metaphors here to express the fears of authorities. The first of these is the camel metaphor: "Once the nose of the camel is in the tent, pretty soon the whole animal will fol-low." The second is the slippery slope metaphor: "Once we make this concession, we will find ourselves on a slippery slope, having set in motion forces that we can't control that will force other, more radical changes."

In the case of the VOTF challenge, there are plenty of examples of members of the church hierarchy who express these fears. Arch-bishop John Myers of Newark, New Jersey, called the Voice of the Faithful "anti-church and, ultimately, anti-Catholic. . . . Through its words and deeds, we believe that this organization has as its pur-poses: to act as a cover for dissent with the faith; to cause division within the church; and to openly attack church hierarchy."

Myers goes on to voice the fears described above: "Married clergy, ordination of women, abolition of the tradition of celibacy, altering Church teaching on sexual morality, and defiance of the apostolic authority that has guided the Church since its founding two thousand years ago by Our Lord Jesus Christ, have all found a place in the ranks of Voice of the Faithful." A letter writer to *Crisis* magazine describes how "some of the people in attendance [at a VOTF meeting] were hushed or told to leave when they started asking questions about that slippery goal of VOTF to 'shape structural change in the Church.' "

One must also concede that these fears are not without some basis in reality. While the VOTF has quite deliberately not raised the "hot button" issues of reform such as ordination of women, allowing priests to marry, reproductive rights, and same-sex marriage, the data show that many and sometimes a majority of VOTF members would support significant changes in church policies on these issues. And even if VOTF leaders have no hidden agenda of this sort, increasing the influence of those who privately harbor such a vision of the church will still seem like a slippery slope.

Conclusion

From the standpoint of social movement theory, the Catholic Church is very lucky at this point in its history. Faced with a major crisis, it has produced from among its most committed members, a challenge by a group whose loyalty pushes them to exercise a voice for changing the church instead of deserting it. Cultural tensions and fears of camels and slippery slopes are difficult obstacles to overcome. But ultimately, the church hierarchy makes choices and sets policies. They can choose whether to be governed by fears and resistance or by a good faith effort to address the issues raised by Voice of the Faithful. The church can change. On whether it will, I hesitate to venture a prediction.

Chapter Ten

Fundamental Strategic Tasks for Leaders Organizing Grassroots Insurgencies, with Particular Reference to VOTF

John D. McCarthy

> If not now, When? If not us, Who?
>> VOTF Leader

In this brief essay I sketch a series of theoretical guidelines for think-ing about the fundamental tasks that confront leaders who organize insurgencies like the one VOTF has mobilized, and then go on to illustrate how the recent experience of VOTF raises crucial strategic issues for VOTF leaders as they contemplate their next steps.

My discussion draws upon a rich and extensive body of scholarship on social movements in the United States and Western Europe that has developed during the last three decades. I will very lightly sketch the outlines of four fundamental strategic tasks confronting leaders, and use each sketch to put into the context specific findings of the survey responses to the VOTF survey that was carried out by William D'Antonio and Anthony Pogorelc (as reported in chapters 2 and 3) as well as with additional information about the history and current operations of VOTF. These four strategic tasks relate to:

- defining and acting upon state political and organizational (eccle-siastical) opportunity structures;

- strategic framing of insurgent goals, means, and motives;

* creating and adapting organizational and tactical repertoires;
* mobilizing and sustaining supporters and resources.

State and Organizational (Ecclesiastical) Opportunity Structures

Insurgents face political and organizational structures that can sometimes constrain, through repression. These structures can also provide opportunities because of incompetence among elites, and some of the leaders of the organization may even facilitate the mobilization of a movement that aims to bring pressures for change.[1] A synthesis of the several elements of political opportunity structures[2] highlighted:

* the relative openness or closure of the institutionalized political system;
* the stability or instability of the broad set of elite alignments that typically undergird a polity;
* the presence or absence of elite allies;
* the state's [organization's] capacity and propensity for repression.

Most of the work I draw upon here pertains to collective insurgencies in states rather than those within organizations. And while insurgent processes in organizations, like churches, armies, and political parties, may not always parallel those in states, the strategic dilemmas that confront insurgent leaders are, for the most part, similar.[3] Nevertheless, insurgencies within organizations also occur within states so that insurgents may respond to political opportunities both within organizations and the states within which they are embedded, substantially complicating the impact of political opportunities on insurgencies. One of the most important factors in such situations is the possibility of "boomerang" effects whereby organizations may enlist the states within which they are embedded to pressure the organization within which they are acting to enact changes to which they are resistant.[4]

One of the central aims included in VOTF's mission statement is to bring about greater openness in the structure of governance of the Catholic Church out of widespread frustration due to the relative inability of faithful Catholics to have serious influence upon recent important issues that have affected the church.

In general, the hierarchy has not been very supportive of VOTF, and in many cases it has used direct repression by denying local groups access to church facilities, although several bishops have been supportive. On the other hand, the survey results suggest that an enormous reservoir of support exists among parish pastors. Thirty-six percent of the VOTF members reported their pastors to be supportive of VOTF, and 38 percent reported them to be neutral. Of course, these figures probably overestimate the extent of pastor support across local communities, since VOTF members are probably more likely to be concentrated in parishes with supportive pastors. Nevertheless, supportive and even neutral pastors represent opportunities for VOTF activists.

The VOTF membership is deeply embedded in parish life and as a result already has extensive access to existing decision-making channels at the parish and diocesan levels, even if such access is severely restricted. The membership in parish committees on the part of VOTF members is truly incredible — 37 percent report membership in parish councils, 21 percent in finance councils, 45 percent on liturgy committees, and 61 percent in other parish committees.

These are not isolated insurgents, but fully integrated members of existing parish (and sometimes diocesan) decision-making structures, being quite well situated to take advantage of present access to decision making at the parish level and to press for wider access in the future.

Strategic Framing Tasks

Insurgent leaders must effectively frame the problems they believe need to be resolved: What needs to be changed? Why and how? And they need to accomplish this in ways that, at minimum, appeal to their existing potential supporters and hopefully facilitate turning neutral observers into supporters with the ultimate goal of turning as many supporters as possible into members.[5] There is strong evidence that the content of some collective action frames facilitate the mobilization of supporters. For instance, nineteenth-century suffragettes were more successful in creating state-level organizations in those states where they framed gaining the vote for women around women's distinctive contribution to political debates than where they framed it as purely an issue of women's rights.[6]

Framing is strategic, accomplished by insurgent groups and organizations. These frames are embodied in media reports, organizational materials such as reports and press releases, and, in recent times, in the text included on organizational websites. Analysts distinguish among framing tasks, including diagnostic framing (what is wrong), prognostic framing (what needs to be done), and motivational framing (why supporters need to get involved to bring about needed changes).

One indication of the effectiveness of the strategic framing that has already been accomplished by VOTF leaders is the almost universal agreement by members with the stated goals of VOTF. Eighty-five percent of the members identify "strongly" with the goals of "supporting victims" and "supporting priests of integrity," and 90 percent "strongly" support the goal of bringing about structural change to the church (see chapters 2 and 3 for more detail). Although it may seem obvious that organizational members agree with the stated goals of an insurgent group, for a variety of reasons, levels of agreement as high as those seen for VOTF are quite unusual.[7]

VOTF leaders have done an especially effective job of framing its diagnosis of the problems to be solved, a set of proposed solutions, and a defense of its goals and chosen tactics in pursuing these changes as seen in materials available on its website, especially in its Frequently Asked Questions (FAQs) section. A few observations about the content of the group's presentation of self illustrate VOTF's adept efforts to locate itself in both the meaning structures of the church and the wider American society in light of the principles enunciated by framing analysts:

- VOTF has framed its message and actions as reflecting great loyalty to the church and as committed to working within the church for its improvement (William Gamson's chapter in this volume brilliantly assesses the great strengths of this message as a frame of interpretation).[8]

- VOTF has developed sophisticated justifications for its goals and methods of proceeding by drawing upon important church documents (especially those of Vatican II) and theological arguments.

- VOTF has framed its messages so that they resonate with deeply held values of the broader American culture concerning representation of citizens in collective decision making and institutional transparency. VOTF itself has maintained a stance of transparency in its own operations as it has asked for greater transparency in the operations of the Catholic Church. (D'Antonio and Pogorelc discuss these themes in chapter 3 in this volume.)

- Finally, VOTF has begun to elaborate a more sophisticated motivational frame, focusing especially on how members can become more active, through its Parish Voice initiatives.

Insurgent Organizational and Tactical Repertoires

Analysts of insurgent movements have shown that a wide ranging organizational and tactical repertoire is typically available to insurgent groups in any particular political and cultural context. Insurgents choose among the available alternatives, sometimes without much consideration of the full range of alternatives, and, for the most part, their choices are shaped by political, institutional, and status processes.[9]

Organizational Repertoires

Many observers have noted the recent trend in the United States for social movement groups to employ very weak forms of membership, sometimes termed checkbook membership or mailing list membership,[10] although not all analysts have decried the trend.[11]

VOTF has chosen a common and very widespread organizational form that is one of federated local groups.[12] Although VOTF aims to establish chapters in every parish in the United States, at present a significant proportion of members, based on the survey results, are not linked to a local group, and/or have not been active in any other way. Many such members are supporters only, illustrating the phenomenon of mailing list membership. The following results drawn from the VOTF membership survey demonstrate that a minority of VOTF members are linked to a local group through participation or financial support. Only a bare majority report even having signed a VOTF petition.

Percentage of Respondents Who Reported:

Member of VOTF affiliate	44%
Donated money to local affiliate	25%
Attended a VOTF meeting	34%
Donated money to VOTF National	32%
Attended a regional conference	12%
Signed a VOTF petition	53%

Members like many of VOTF's are sometimes also characterized as isolated members, describing the nature of their weak ties to the organization and the fact that they may have no interaction with other members. Research on similar insurgent groups shows that isolated members are very hard to retain, and groups that depend upon such members remain in a constant search for new ones.[13] The consequence of this state of affairs is that an organization must devote extensive scarce resources just to keeping the size of its membership stable while in constant search of new members. On the other hand, members who are linked to local groups through face-to-face contact are far more likely to remain involved with the group from year to year.

So at present VOTF exhibits a mixed structure of membership with a majority of members being isolated and the rest of the members networked into local VOTF groups (although it is not clear how tightly because the survey respondents were not given the opportunity to indicate the extent of their involvement). This is a common structure chosen by many insurgent groups in recent years in the United States.[14] VOTF is publicly committed to developing a local chapter in every U.S. parish, which, if largely successful, would enable linking previously isolated members to local groups.

Adopting a federated organizational repertoire obligates leaders to consider two important and interrelated questions: How will the far-flung local groups be connected to one another and what role will local groups play in the governance of the organization? The question of how to cluster local groups into intermediate structures appears to be in process for VOTF — there is evidence of regional clustering as well as state-level structuring. This remains an ongoing problem for groups that are federations of local groups: how to most effectively cluster local groups into intermediate structures is shaped by political opportunities (such as the structure of the target institutions and governments), economies of scale, and very importantly considerations of organizational governance.

At present VOTF reports the existence of about 150 local groups, but assuming that VOTF continues to grow at a rapid pace, by 2010 as many as 2,000 local groups might exist in parishes across the country. Such growth would not only put great financial strains on the organization, it would also create continuing issues concerning organizational governance which are chronic in large federated organizations like VOTF. At present there appears to be rather wide endorsement of the leadership of VOTF. Eighty-two percent of the survey respondents said that the VOTF executive office provided effective day-to-day leadership, 81 percent that the officers and board had been charting effective directions, and 78 percent that the VOTF representative council is providing effective guidance. But groups that are federated locals almost always experience ongoing conflict over goals, means, and, especially, organizational decision making, as local groups begin to assert their independence. So while continuing vigorous growth in membership and the formation of many more local VOTF groups may be a signal of a successful movement, such growth, if it occurs, will certainly bring with it serious growth pains, illustrating the well-known principle, "Be careful what you wish for."

Tactical Repertoires

Insurgent groups strategically develop sets of tactics designed to achieve the changes they seek. In recent years insurgent movements in the United States have typically employed tactical sets that include both inside and outside tactics. Inside tactics are those that work within the existing channels of decision making in the organization or state. Outside tactics are those that work outside of those channels, for example, as protest and boycotts.

I have already noted that VOTF members and local groups, based upon their survey responses, are well situated to pursue a wide variety of insider tactics such as petitions, meetings with bishops and pastors, resolutions in existing decision-making forums, and the like.

But in addition to the widespread use of insider tactics, VOTF has also employed several outside tactics, including protest demonstrations, employed effectively in the Boston area early in the development of VOTF and more sparingly elsewhere since. As well, VOTF has used a tactic that might be best termed a "donation strike," which a significant majority (66 percent) strongly support. The Boston "Voice of Compassion Fund" is the prototype. It asks parishioners who decide they must withhold their donations to parish collections and/or the bishop's special collections for reasons of conscience to instead donate funds to the National Catholic Community Foundation. That Foundation is managed by the laity and accountable to the laity. The Boston Voice of Compassion Fund represents a creative outside tactic, with strong support from the members.

The use of certain outside tactics such as protests has become more acceptable in recent years, leading analysts to characterize them as routine and now a "normal" part of the political process.[15] However, adopting certain outsider tactics, such as sit-ins, always runs the risk of alienating supporters and members.

Mobilizing Supporters and Resources

Even if the majority of Catholics in the United States do not support the goals of VOTF — although a recent national survey of Catholic attitudes showed that a majority (63 percent) said the church hierarchy was "out of touch"), there still remains an enormous pool of supporters who are potential members. VOTF presently reports having approximately 30,000 members. If VOTF achieved its goal of establishing a chapter in every parish in the United States and each chapter enrolled an average of twenty members, that would amount to a membership of more than 350,000 for VOTF.[16] Given the demographic composition of present VOTF members, the potential level of financial support for the group is huge.

Turning Supporters into Members

An extensive research literature exists that clearly specifies the important factors that are involved in the process of turning supporters of a social change into members of organizations that seek associated changes.[17] Key to this process is the *availability* of supporters who agree with the goals of the insurgent group and have time and money to contribute. We know from the many studies of movement organizations that recruiting members is most effectively accomplished through the social networks of current members. New members are most easily recruited through social networks (friends, families, co-workers, co-worshipers) that *connect them to current members.* Finally, mundane as it may seem, the best predictor of whether a connected and available person becomes a group member is *whether that person is asked to join.*

VOTF is blessed with members a large proportion of whom are engaged in the activities of their church, and consequently they are very well situated to effectively recruit new members who support VOTF's goals and are available. VOTF membership is deeply embedded in parish life. The extent of membership in parish committees is truly incredible: 37 percent report participation in parish councils, 21 percent in finance councils, 45 percent in liturgy committees, and 61 percent in other parish committees.

And they are widely engaged in other activities within the church, as can be seen in the following figures from the VOTF membership survey:

Percentage who report:

Member of any parish committee	> 61%
Participated in liturgical ministry	> 43%
Ever a teacher of Religious Education	> 53%
Participated in Catholic social movement	> 22%
Ever a member of a social justice organization	47%

The level of engagement of current VOTF members, then, represents a key resource for expanding the size of the membership. As noted above, potential members, however, must be solicited. Current VOTF members are already active in doing this, according to their responses to the membership survey. Seventy-five percent of the respondents reported attending a VOTF meeting, and of those 55 percent invited others to attend a VOTF meeting

When we look at the current membership, however, we see that the majority of the current members attended their first VOTF meeting on their own volition rather than being asked to attend. Concerning their first VOTF meeting:

Attended on their own	60%
With another person	25%
Invited by another	15%

This would appear to contradict the principle that most members need to be asked to join an organization like VOTF. This pattern is likely to be partially the result of the virtual nature of early involvement for many of them, and also because they represent the first cohort of members. Membership has to start somewhere. They are the early risers.

Turning Members into Activists

Beyond joining an organization like VOTF, members can provide their time and their material resources in an effort to help the group bring about desired changes. The members of VOTF possess manifold social capital (education and worldly experience, especially experience in a variety of other Catholic social movement groups), extensive financial capital (29 percent of them report earning over $100,000 a year, and another 34 percent earning between $50,000 a year and $99,999 a year), and a generous stated willingness to provide time to VOTF.

Assuming thirty thousand present members, and quickly calculating the available money and time that those members are willing to provide based upon a very conservative reading of the survey responses, the present membership appears willing to provide approximately 1 million dollars a year and more than 50,000 hours a month to VOTF.

If VOTF were to form a chapter in every U.S. parish with an average of twenty members, the available resources, assuming no change in the commitment of new members to support VOTF with their time and money, would translate into more than 15 million dollars a year and more than 800,000 hours a week in membership labor.

The present availability and the potential future availability of enormous amounts of members' time appear to be a blessing, but its availability requires serious attention. Committed members need to be integrated into the work of the group. Creating tasks for these activists will take great creativity. One explanation of diminished civic engagement in the United States in recent years is that associations and social movements have wanted the money of members, but not so much their time, since pursuing social change had become a more professionalized project. If VOTF is to engage its many members it must ask: *What will VOTF activists do?* Turning members into activists requires providing them meaningful tasks to accomplish, or it risks the stability of their long-term involvement.

One common strategy that federated movement organizations like VOTF have employed that both integrates large number of local members into social change activities and harnesses their diverse skills and enthusiasms is the use of a task committee structure. Allowing motivated members to spin off committees aimed at accomplishing specific tasks allows each local group to develop a distinctive portfolio of task committees adapted to the interests of its membership, while at the same time allowing members to be involved in creating their own social change tasks.[18]

The Future of VOTF

I offer some observations about VOTF's past and its prospects here and then summarize what I believe are some important lessons.

First is the issue of group assessment and reflection. It is now a common practice for a group like VOTF to regularly assess its strategies and tactics, and, consistent with its highly professionalized and Americanized leadership and membership, VOTF looks to be on solid ground on the reflection and assessment front. Rather than settle early on a rigid set of practices, modern organizations instead are more likely to constantly assess their present practices and look to improve them. Typically this process entails scanning the environment to see how similar organizations are attempting to solve similar organizational difficulties.

Second is the question of group momentum. VOTF has grown rapidly, but it has only, as I have suggested, barely tapped its potential among American Catholics who share a commitment to its three central goals of supporting victims of abuse, supporting priests of integrity, and shaping structural change within the church. VOTF was born in reaction to the egregious dereliction by elements of the church hierarchy in response to the abuse scandal. VOTF continues to be offered additional opportunities by elements of the hierarchy to dramatize the need for structural reform in the church. VOTF can take advantage of these opportunities to build the movement for structural reform, but, in my judgment, it needs to consider a longer-term strategy for continuing its momentum, one that builds on both its newfound knowledge of its present membership and some of the principles derived from past studies of movements like VOTF.

VOTF's *framing* of the broad problems it seeks to address needs over time to become less tightly coupled to the details and associated outrage of the abuse scandal, in my judgment. That scandal revealed the great need for transparency in church decision making and for broader structural change, but I strongly suspect that most leaders and much of the membership of VOTF will continue to believe in the necessity of such change as the abuse scandal fades into the historical past. In order to remain a vital presence in the affairs of the church, VOTF will be obligated to continually expand its focus to incorporate new substantive issues germane to the core question of structural reform of the church. The initial framing of the problem and its potential solution was accomplished without input from most of the current membership since they joined VOTF subsequently. The ongoing reassessment of VOTF's goals and tactics will, of necessity, include much wider membership involvement.

VOTF has been and will have to continue to be attentive to questions of what it means to be a VOTF member and what kind of relationship members have to one another and to VOTF. Such attention comprises, on the one hand, a concern with what type of *organizational repertoire* is most effective for VOTF, and, on the other hand, a concern with issues of organizational governance that I alluded to earlier. To the extent that VOTF continues to expand, it must attend to each of these concerns. Success in responding to these concerns almost guarantees that VOTF will experience *conflict over governance* in the not too distant future. Federated organizations such as VOTF that aspire to national scope are chronically vulnerable to conflict over governance for a variety of reasons, especially because its far-flung local groups tend to develop very different priorities. Since issues of governance of the church are central to VOTF's mission, the organization will be quite vulnerable when this conflict begins to occur. It is very important that VOTF remain committed to transparency in its own governance when this does happen. As a result, VOTF would be well advised to begin anticipating such problems before they actually occur.

I have painted a rosy picture of the potential for VOTF growth as an organized force for change in the church. Organizational growth, however, will not occur without great effort and resources being devoted to bringing it about. The present membership represents an extraordinary resource for helping to accomplish future growth because of their enormous social and financial resources, as I have argued. To become truly national in scope and to ensure its long-term future, however, VOTF needs to consider targeting growth outside of its original Northeastern base and among younger Catholics.

Currently, 60 percent of VOTF's membership is concentrated in the Northeast, Moreover, VOTF's membership highly over-represents older Catholics, and greatly under-represents young Catholics. Without success in recruiting younger members, VOTF will have difficulty establishing any long-term presence in parishes across the United States. Expanding VOTF local groups in under-represented regions (e.g., the Southwest) and among the young seem appropriate organizational priorities.

One possible strategic direction, based upon the success of the Church in the 21st Century program at Boston College, would be to target campus ministries for the development of local VOTF groups and to recruit younger members. And while campus ministries at Catholic colleges seem an appropriate starting place, the sheer size of Catholic student populations on large university campuses suggests that secular campuses with enrollments over 10,000 (there are approximately 250 of them in the United States) are also potentially fruitful targets. At Pennsylvania State University, for instance, approximately 25 percent of the over 40,000 students enrolled are Catholic, a sizeable target population. Many of the student movements of the 1960s built campus locals with the mechanism of circuit riders who went from campus to campus establishing campus chapters with volunteers assembled from open meetings aimed at interested students.

I offer these several suggestions in hopes that they may be useful to VOTF leaders and concerned members. Many of the monographs and research articles I have cited may also be of additional use to those who are struggling with how to carry on the important work begun with such vitality by VOTF.

Chapter Eleven

Conclusion

We conclude our study of Voice of the Faithful by reviewing our findings in the context of our goals. Simply put, our goals were to interview as many founders and current (2003–4) leaders as we could find in the Boston area, first to construct a narrative description of their responses to the scandal provoked by revelations of the clergy's sexual abuse of minors and its cover-up that erupted in Boston in January 2002 (chapter 1). Second, we wanted to explain how VOTF as a social movement came into being. To advance this understanding we studied the demographic characteristics of the movement's founders and leaders, as well as indicators of their religious beliefs, practices, and attitudes (chapter 2). Third, we conducted a survey of VOTF members to compare their demographic characteristics, and their religious beliefs, practices, and attitudes with those of the founders and leaders (chapters 3 and 4). To the extent possible, we have also provided comparisons between VOTF Catholics and the general population of American Catholics available through the 2005 national survey.[1]

Our goal was to present our findings to a public audience in Boston before the end of 2005. We accomplished this in collaboration with the Church in the 21st Century Project of Boston College by holding a symposium on this study on October 23, 2005, at Boston College. We invited six scholars noted for their expertise in the sociology of religion, social movements, and theology to critique our findings (chapters 5–10).

This review includes a summary of our study and of the major points made by the six scholars at the symposium.

VOTF in Context

Some would say that January 2002 was to the Catholic Church in the United States what the Enron collapse and financial scandal would be to the whole nation, a scandal that prompted the Sarbannes-Oxley legislation to protect shareholders and the general public from fraudulent practices. Revelations of clerical sex abuse and its cover-up by some members of the hierarchy shook the church's moorings and called forth a major response from the laity. The social movement Voice of the Faithful was in the forefront of this effort.

In early 2002, Catholics felt pummeled by the news, yet they also realized that without the modern media, this scandal might have remained hidden for a longer time. It was clear that the members of the hierarchy that orchestrated a cover-up were unlikely to come clean on their own and unable to police themselves. An underside of the church, known to only a few, had now been exposed to the American public. In early 2002, the *New York Times* alone carried news of the sexual abuse scandal on its front page for more than forty days.

What was frightening for many ordinary Boston Catholics was that the crisis was so local, and they were close to it without knowing it. Priests like John Geoghan of Boston, accused of sexual abuse by more than 130 people, might be in their parishes hearing confessions and giving them communion; they could be sitting beside him at parish events. And the same was true for their children. An event that began in one local church, Boston, quickly became a national event. And the pattern that was revealed there was soon to be observed in many other dioceses: criminal acts and cover-up, then discovery and outcry all over the land. The motives behind these cover-ups, whether well intended or not, made little difference.

This deeply hidden and ongoing secret was made public by the media: newspapers, television, radio, and the Internet took the secret and placed it at the front and center of the nation's consciousness. The events of January 2002 made prophetic the words of Esther Dyson — once dubbed by the *New York Times Magazine* as "the most powerful woman in the Net-erati" — to bishops from the Americas gathered at the Vatican in March 1998. She suggested that the effects of the information revolution might position bishops on the receiving end of a broad cultural shift.

> It's going to shake up every established authority in the world, including the Catholic Church.... Where the church is established, the Internet lets dissidents communicate. It erodes authority. It will challenge you to be more open, more human, more accountable.... Almost everything will be public, and that forces people to behave better. It will be more and more difficult to discuss things in corridors and behind closed doors.[2]

In January 2002 that day seemed to have arrived. However, only the future will reveal how the scandal of 2002 will affect the church over the long run. The cover-up of malfeasance by the corporate leaders of Enron brought forth the wrath of employees, the general public, and even political leaders. The Enron leaders were forced to resign and face trial and conviction for crimes. Only one church leader, Cardinal Law, was allowed by the Vatican to resign as a direct result of his handling of the scandal, and he was eventually given another assignment, to save face, in a prestigious Roman basilica. One bishop, Thomas Dupre of Springfield, Massachusetts, resigned and later received two indictments for abusive behavior when he was a priest. Other bishops have resigned their posts for similar past actions. To date three dioceses have filed for bankruptcy protection.[3]

VOTF began as a Boston organization, but with the help of modern media it quickly became national and international. Its first major event, the convention in Boston in July 2002, was a national event and even international. Neil Postman, author of numerous books of media criticism, noted that modern communications media, especially the Internet, takes issues beyond their own ground zero and makes them international. He asserts that this will eventually dilute the strength of certain power centers. "If indeed it takes power away from the center and gives it to the margins ... we can anticipate not tomorrow but in a hundred years the Vatican will be far less important in determining proper Catholic liturgy, theology and so on."[4]

Leaders and Members

Even though VOTF quickly moved beyond its local confines, there is homogeneity in the characteristics of its leaders and members. Women are in the majority. A large number claim some Irish heritage. They possess high levels of education, income, and occupational status, and have a strong sense of Catholic identity. Imbelli characterized them as "the successful products of the Catholic culture and education system."

Their Catholic identity is grounded in deep family roots and enriched by a high level of Catholic education, with more than half having at least sixteen years of formal Catholic education. It was a liberal education in the best sense of the word, open to new ideas, tolerant, and broadminded. Their locus of authority has shifted from an external to an internal base. This formation is now reflected in what they choose to read, periodicals such as *National Catholic Reporter*, *America*, and *Commonweal*, and how they think and act. They are the embodiment of the Vatican II church.

Dillon describes VOTF Catholics as an elite group with activist experience. They stand in the tradition of an American laity seeking a church that reflects the inculturation of America's democratic impetus. Being good Catholics who attend Mass, pray, and participate in church-related organizations and movements, they reflect the tension between great commitment to church tradition and commitment to bring about change. The high levels of education of VOTF members suggest a positive correlation between knowledge of church tradition and the likelihood of being pro-change.

Generation

The pre-Vatican II and Vatican II generations of VOTF members share a collective memory, a memory spanning membership in both a strict church that shunned the modern world to becoming a mainline church that stressed openness to the world as well as a mission to it. The experiences of living through these transitional times in a church once thought unchangeable, but that could and did change in some significant respects, nurtured both a critical and a loyal spirit in these Catholics.

Many experience their Catholic heritage as a resource for critical action. Some saw their response to the scandal and participation in VOTF as flowing from their baptismal vocation. They used the language of Catholic Action to describe what they were doing. They were called to participate, to take responsibility, to act in solidarity with the vulnerable: the victim-survivors. Vatican II empowered them; they were to follow their consciences, formed by the church, to tell the truth and not collude with dishonest scenarios even if offered by some bishops.

VOTF members exercise critical fidelity. This situation points to Hirschman's assertion that in organizations it is often the most loyal who dare to speak the truth as they see it. This challenges notions that equate loyalty with blind allegiance to the agenda of organizational elites. Critical loyalty is difficult to appreciate within the system of traditional authority, which dominates the Vatican's model of Catholicism. Along these lines, Philip Jenkins, in his book on anti-Catholicism, makes a clear distinction between justified critiques of the Catholic Church, and what he calls anti-Catholic criticism.[5] As our study clearly demonstrates, VOTF Catholics direct their critiques at the sins and crimes of sexually abusive priests and at bishops who covered up their crimes. They now know enough about church history to understand that even its saints have criticized the hierarchy and challenged them to be faithful to the church's mission. Cardinal Newman, the nineteenth-century convert to Catholicism who some claim to be the "Father" of Vatican Council II, charts in history how the laity have often been the force that has kept the church faithful to the truth. It is hard to listen to VOTF Catholics without recognizing their love for this church with all its warts. Because they care about it and love it, they are no longer willing to just stand by and watch it fail to image Christ and his teachings. It is important and useful for those troubled by criticism of the church to embrace Jenkins's distinction and dare to listen to the voices of the faithful.

The experience of the post-Vatican II generation is different. When they came of age, Catholics were already in the mainstream, and they were able to take for granted the reforms the previous two generations struggled through. This generation came of age when skepticism about institutions and authority, accompanied by individualism, was at its height. As a whole this generation has a penchant to be critical and more willing to exit.

Gender

One aspect that particularly reflects the impact of change in society and the church is the variable of gender. Before the 1960s and the Second Vatican Council, Catholics typically lived out traditional patriarchal gender roles. In comparison to Protestants and Jews, they also had more children. In the 1960s they completed their move out of the ghetto, and their exposure to modern mores had an impact on gender roles. An important example is the dramatic change that has taken place in the medical profession. The percentage of medical doctors in the United States who are women has grown from 12 percent in the 1950s to more than 50 percent of all medical school graduates today. Changes in the church also enabled women to become more active in the church. These changes planted the seeds for the role of women in VOTF today.

Sixty percent of VOTF leaders are of the Vatican II generation; likewise 60 percent are women. Katzenstein identified five habitats for the development of feminist voices within the church.[6] The changes of the 1960s, that emerged through the women's movements and in the church through Vatican II, contributed to the formation of these habitats, which include academic institutions and parishes as well as church renewal and social justice organizations, liturgy groups and base communities, and women's religious orders. Our data show that the women of VOTF were amply exposed to all of these venues. As Ammerman notes, many of these women came into their progressive tendencies while attending Catholic colleges.

Dillon suggests that women may reflect these tensions of a changing church most acutely because they tend to be more highly committed, yet they also realize that for them the church is a limited opportunity structure. Ammerman observes that the women of

VOTF were those who were most willing to relinquish traditional gender roles; this can be seen in their absence from traditional gendered organizations. These women today stand in the front lines of VOTF. There are fewer gender differences among VOTF Catholics than there are in the Catholic population at large. The participation of women in VOTF at high levels has been an overwhelmingly positive influence on the attitudes and activities of the movement; they participate more actively by belonging to local affiliates, inviting others into the movement, and acting publicly, for example, by signing the Petition for Reform.

Catholic Identity

VOTF members are deeply rooted in the Catholic Church. This is demonstrated by the strength of their beliefs and practices. We have seen that they consistently participate in the sacramental life of the church. While a majority in the general Catholic population says that one can be a good Catholic without attending weekly Mass, the majority of VOTF members adhere to the traditional practice of at least weekly Mass attendance. They also reach out in service to the poor, manifesting their commitment to the works of mercy, on an equally regular basis.

VOTF is predominantly a movement of cradle Catholics, influenced by Vatican II and secure in their Catholicism. They were socialized in a Catholic culture and even were exposed to some remnants of the ghettoized immigrant church. Their families were by and large intact and regularly went to church. They learned to pray, and their faith is deeply rooted in their identities. The great majority married other Catholics in church-sanctioned marriages, though some joined religious orders.

For VOTF Catholics, the center of church life has been the parish. And it was the parish of St. John the Evangelist, in concert with several others, that made it possible for VOTF to come to life. In doing so, VOTF emerged and gradually helped Catholics throughout the Boston area to think beyond the boundaries of parish in order to confront the terrible scandal of 2002. In doing so they created a new

Catholic social movement. They have become what Eugene Kennedy, a highly respected psychologist and long-term observer of the Catholic Church, described as Culture Two Catholics, participants in the church-institution but not dominated by it. Ammerman reflected on how the social reality of VOTF Catholics impacts the way in which they participate in the life of the church. Their behaviors show that they are good and very active Catholics, though critical.

The largest portion of VOTF Catholics was raised in the turbulent culture of the 1960s and 1970s, many of whom came into their progressive tendencies while attending Catholic colleges. Few post-Vatican II Catholics have joined VOTF, but those who have are ones who share the earlier generation's deep Catholic roots and strong Catholic upbringing.

Several of the symposium scholars made the point that VOTF Catholics are different from the general Catholic population in terms of their social worlds; they resemble other elite children of modernity in terms of education, ethnicity, and culture. A significant challenge is that most of the new Catholics have little in common with them. To grow VOTF will need to identify common ground with the young and the new immigrant Catholics coming to the United States today.

VOTF as Social Movement

Frequently social movements are studied long after they have emerged, peaked, and sometimes ceased to exist. Our study has looked at VOTF as a fledgling social movement. Today VOTF in some ways is different from they way it was when we conducted our study. No matter how it develops or what its future will be, it has already been a significant movement in the history of American Catholicism.

In May of 2002, Jim Muller, then president of VOTF, was quoted in the *Boston Globe* in an article that described the movement's rapid growth from a listening session in the basement of St. John's School, to a national movement planning a convention to host forty-two hundred people on July 20, 2002. Muller recalled his words:

"If I had a dream of what this would look like three years from now, our enrollment would be half of the Catholics in the world, every parish would have a chapter, and every diocese, every nation, and the world would, too, and that our organization would be a counterbalance to the power of the hierarchy — it would have a permanent role, a bit like Congress," I continued. "My worst nightmare scenario is that the church successfully papers over the clergy sexual abuse problem and leaves intact an abusive power structure. That's why we're moving so fast, why we're meeting three times a week now. Because we know we have to seize the moment."[7]

It is now four years since Jim Muller made that statement, and neither his dream nor his worst nightmare has been realized. VOTF is still alive, with a national office, a group of elected officers, and a National Representative Council.

The pathway for new social movements is murky. How do you measure success? Is it organizational, attracting large numbers of supporters, or being recognized as a legitimate spokesperson for its particular perspective? Or is it the achievement of its goals? All these measures have been cast as the criteria of success.[8]

VOTF has entered into a tense relationship with church authorities and ultimately with the wider context in which the church is embedded. Movements challenge the taken-for-granted conceptions of order promoted by organizations and their supporting publics. Changing an institutional organization, with the reserves of legitimacy held by the church, is hard work. There is an added tension when the social movement exists within the organization, as VOTF does within the church, because it must walk the fine line of orchestrating an effective challenge while at the same time not going so far as to provoke the organization to dismiss it.

Because movements stand outside the center of power, they do not have access to the channels used by institutional insiders to address contentious issues; in comparison, they are resource poor. Organizations frequently portray them as illegitimate, and movements must time and again prove that their grievances are just. Challenger groups are frequently perceived as promoting their own special interests because they are not shrouded with institutional symbols of legitimacy. This is especially true for those challenging a hallowed institution like the church.

The power of social movements comes from the bottom up, from the ideals, solidarity, and actions of participants. Emotions and affective attachments shape the goals of collective action.[9] The emotions of ordinary mentally and emotionally healthy people drove the formation of VOTF. These were good, moral people, authentic Catholics who believed what the church taught and followed its prescriptions on sexual and social morality. They were parents who loved their children and were horrified by thoughts of molestations. They were devoted to their families and did not have a vested interest in the church as a system like the priests and bishops who participated in the cover-up.

According to Collins, emotions are "the glue of solidarity."[10] Positive feelings toward others such as victims-survivors can lead to action on their behalf.[11] VOTF's first goal was to support victim-survivors of the sexual abuse crisis in the church. Anger at perceived injustices can lead to outrage and indignation. The central emotion in VOTF is moral outrage and righteous indignation about an injustice. "Moral shock" is the first step to recruitment to the movement; outrage can generate action.

This was indeed the case for VOTF. Its founders were people used to acting and getting things done. They were professionals involved in leadership in the workplace as well as the community. These were "can do" people who came forward when things needed to be done. They had strong personal networks made up of family, friends, and neighbors. They also were connected to collective networks like the parish and other voluntary associations. Unlike the isolated priests who molested vulnerable children and could depend on a bishop to protect them, these were adults who could look people in the eye, ask for what they needed, and follow through to accomplish a task.

It is evident today that the laity has a great deal of knowledge about how to organize itself. In many parishes, the priest no longer stands in the midst of a room full of immigrant Catholics as the wisest and most educated figure. The laity is educated, both in a civil and Catholic sense; it has the intellectual resources and commitment to initiate a challenge to the status quo. This is the essence of social movement work. Yet, while VOTF is a social movement within the Catholic Church organization, it is by no means the first; other reformist movements have preceded it; some, such as Call to Action, have sustained a challenge for over a quarter of a century while others are hardly remembered.

The story of VOTF points to the importance of pastoral leadership in mounting this challenge to bishops who engaged in cover-ups and the institution that seemed to be shielding them. Good pastoral leadership helped parishioners to effectively respond to the scandal, and VOTF membership was a dimension of this response. But in situations where the pastor sought to minimize or deny the significance of the scandal, VOTF members became a protest group.

This tension between the church with its hierarchical organizational culture and the American democratic culture continues as a chronic culture clash. According to Gamson, many in the hierarchy view the suggestions of VOTF like a camel's nose pushing itself under a tent, one big movement and the tent could be toppled. Change in the church is not simple, and it is the hierarchy that officially makes the choices. At Vatican II they opted for change. Will they do so now?

"Keep the faith. Change the Church." Such words would never have been heard before the Second Vatican Council when the faith and the church were assumed to be inseparable. This saying reflects modern distinctions and the models of church proposed by theologians like Cardinal Avery Dulles. From this perspective, "Keep the faith" can mean hold on to the Sacred Scriptures, be the community of Jesus Christ, spread the faith; this is what it means to be Catholic. How effectively the institution supports the mission of the church is the measure of its success. When it is ineffective in this end, change it so that it responds to its constitutional mandate. The church is always in need of reform, and as Cardinal Newman observed, "In a higher world it is otherwise, but here below, to live is to change and to be perfect is to have changed often." VOTF stands in continuity with the host of reformers who have demanded that the church as an institution be faithful to its mission.

This fledgling social movement also faces limitations. Many VOTF members are Catholics who were comfortable in the pews and who participated in parish life. Yet none were in the inner circle of the church, aware of the modus operandi of the hierarchy; revelations of the underbelly of the church were a surprise to them. They were not in possession of the "cynical knowledge" of insiders who knew the church bureaucracy and of what it was capable. They did not have the generation of Catholic insiders like Msgr. Jack Egan or Msgr. George Higgins to advise them. But they were alert to the need for help, and sought out canon lawyers such as Ladislas Orsy and theologians from Boston College such as Stephen Pope, Lisa Sowell Cahill, and Tom Groome for guidance. One immediate outcome was their immersion in the documents of Vatican II, assuring them that they enjoy a fundamental equality arising from baptism in Christ (*Lumen Gentium,* 32) and that they have been called, each according to his or her own particular gifts, to exercise the mission God has entrusted to the church to carry out in the world (*Lumen Gentium,* 30, 32). As a result, while they have not had success in gaining recognition from the hierarchy, they have gained confidence in their own sense of legitimacy.

The good news for VOTF is that its leaders (and members) have the resources of the successful middle-aged American population. The bad news is that they do not have the energy of the young, nor is there any easy or obvious way to attract them to their ranks.

As a group, VOTF Catholics are elites; their networks do not cover the broad base of American Catholics. The new immigrants live in other places, move in different circles, and have other interests. Another missing piece of VOTF as well as for the bishops challenged by VOTF is the generation gap among Catholics. Vast numbers of the young are not there for anything.

VOTF and the Church: Theological Considerations

The story of Voice of the Faithful is part of the larger story of the Catholic Church in the United States. This story has been consistently marked by tension between the forms of democracy and monarchy. Both have had an impact on the organization of the Catholic Church.

The first bishop of the United States, John Carroll, believed the religion in the new nation had "undergone a revolution more extraordinary than our political one." He advocated an inculturated church with Mass in English, and priests electing bishops. Yet he opposed parishioners electing lay trustees and choosing parish priests. As time went on he became more Roman in his perspective. Fast forward 160 years to the 1940s when Jesuit Father John Courtney Murray wrote about church-state relations and the value of human rights, freedom, and respect for diversity. Once censured for his views, he was invited to Vatican II, which produced the Declaration on Religious Freedom. History demonstrates that the Catholic Church has both rebuffed and embraced the particular gifts offered by the American experience. A major challenge for VOTF is how to effectively balance the tension of being members of an organization and challengers to it. Theologians Mary Hines and Robert Imbelli reflect on this element of VOTF's existence. Hines affirms that VOTF is an important movement in the U.S. church and that its existence is provided for in canon law, which allows the laity to form organizations, albeit with limitations (canon 215).

Hines notes that in one respect the scandal was an institutional crisis centered in the action of the hierarchy. It exposed serious institutional problems of the church, such as conflicts about the interpretation of Vatican II, already aggravated since the Synod in 1985 that marked the twentieth anniversary of Vatican II.

VOTF responded to this institutional crisis with an institutional response. VOTF began with a narrow focus on the scandal of 2002. In contrast, many earlier movements in the church from the Franciscan movement in the thirteenth century to the more recent Call to Action emerged because they had broader concerns. However, VOTF is not alone in compartmentalizing the church; even *Lumen Gentium* attempted this when it relegated the laity to the external mission to build the Kingdom of God in the world and the clergy and hierarchy to the internal life of the church. This was seen to be inadequate.

Hines counsels VOTF not to divorce the institution from other dimensions of the church, especially mission. When you divorce structure from mission and doctrine the result is ecclesiologically deficient and risks absolutizing the institutional.

VOTF seeks to extend justice and transparency in the church through the broader participation of the laity. Many VOTF Catholics are unreflectively American, piqued by the tension between the American penchant for legal rational authority and the Vatican's traditionalist authority. Many of them are not fully aware of how well trodden this path of tension is.

Hines affirms that in the early church there were what we would today describe as democratic practices, yet their basis was a theological vision of a spirit-filled community. Vatican II embraces this early vision of church, and in *Lumen Gentium* 12, asserts that articulations of faith and morals without the participation of the faithful are deficient. VOTF members would do well to become familiar with others who have held such thoughts. One example is laid out in Cardinal Newman's *On Consulting the Faithful in Matters of Doctrine*. VOTF needs to keep its momentum, broaden its vision, and continue responding to the call of the laity to contribute to the faith of the church and its faithfulness to its mission.

In her analysis, Hines proposes that the model of the church from which VOTF operates may be called an ecclesiology from below, because it embraces the People of God image used by Vatican II and stresses that the Holy Spirit can work from the grass roots up. There is a tension between ecclesiologies that emanate from above, centered on Christ's action through the hierarchy, and from below, centered in the action of the spirit through the Body of Christ. Hines advises that all parties, including VOTF, need to realize that no one model captures the totality of the church. She reminds both hierarchy and laity of the important passage in chapter 12 of *Lumen Gentium*:

> The body of the faithful as a whole, anointed as they are by the Holy One...cannot err in matters of belief. Thanks to a supernatural sense of the faith which characterizes the People as a whole, it manifests this unerring quality when, "from the

bishops down to the last member of the laity," it shows universal agreement in matters of faith and morals.

She goes further to urge VOTF not to excuse itself from matters of faith and morals. For chapter 12 of *Lumen Gentium* surely suggests that "decisions on faith and morals arrived at without participation of the faithful are significantly deficient." Theologians Hines and Imbelli both stress that the laity and the hierarchy must take each other seriously. This is essential for the working of the church in the modern world.

Likewise both Hines and Dillon urge VOTF not to divorce its focus on church structure from mission and doctrine. Laity must learn to link their ecclesiology from below with the ecclesiology from above so that in the spirit of *Lumen Gentium* the whole church — laity, priests, and bishops — is included.

Growing VOTF?

As VOTF gets further away from its initial impetus to confront the scandal of the sexual abuse of minors and its cover-up, the passion of interests and commitment will wane unless VOTF can articulate a vision of its place in the church in light of its mission. This might help it to achieve greater success in attracting a wider variety of Catholics, including the young and Catholics not of European ancestry.

Robert Imbelli affirms VOTF as a movement that advocates gospel values, including transparency and participation. He views it as both a local movement and a large tent and encourages it to clarify its mission and goals. Imbelli proposes an ecclesial spirituality that might help VOTF in this effort; he refers to it as a Catholic grammar.

First he proposes some images that express both the breadth and the tensions of the Catholic Church: head and body, institutional and spiritual-mystical, People of God and Body of Christ. There is no disunity between Christ and the spirit; the spirit is of Christ. The active participation of the laity in the church is more than managerial sharing. Likewise the church is hierarchical, not so that one part can dominate another. What makes the church unique is that ultimately both the laity and the hierarchy are accountable to Christ. The ultimate goal for both is transformation through conversion in the church; the goal is growth in holiness: *communio*, which can only be achieved through an ongoing process.

Imbelli suggests that true dialogue between VOTF and the hierarchy would benefit from an "asceticism of language," avoiding the rhetorical inflation and generalizations that are so much a part of American parlance today. He cites the Common Ground Project, where the late Cardinal Joseph Bernardin called for dialogue not as an end in itself, but as a step toward discernment, which was meant to energize discipleship and mission. Imbelli encouraged VOTF to be an agent of renewal by keeping its eye on Christ and embracing a comprehensive, integral Catholic vision.

VOTF and the Future

What does VOTF need to do to become a more effective movement? This study has generated proposals to assist VOTF in accomplishing its goals. Social movement successes are the product of a favorable interaction between the group's resources and the wider environment.

Environments are changing, and the changes usually give one party over another an advantage. When the larger environment is favorable to change, social movements have an advantage. Likewise, instability within an organization can increase the leverage of challengers. When forces supporting the power structure are undermined, the power differential between organizational elites and challengers is narrowed, and it becomes more costly for elites to repress challengers.

From the theoretical perspective of social movement research, John McCarthy offers some prescriptions. He calls for VOTF to define and act on the opportunity structures available to it. For example, even though some bishops have sought to repress VOTF, there is a body of supportive pastors. VOTF should look to them for active support. Likewise VOTF members have social capital with pastors because they are active Catholics who have held responsible positions in parishes, for example, on the parish or finance councils. Second,

VOTF needs to strategically frame its goals, means, and initiatives. This must be done effectively and convincingly. It must clearly present its strengths and limitations, determine what needs to be done, and convincingly articulate why supporters should get more involved.

VOTF's organizational style is a common type known as a federated local group. It needs to adapt its organizational and tactical repertoires to more actively engage its supporters. Currently, only a minority are linked to local groups through active participation or financial support. Such isolated members are hard to retain, and as a result an organization spends much time searching for new members to keep its size stable. This is a drain on resources.

VOTF needs to turn passive supporters into active members. It can do this by drawing on existing social networks. Being asked to join is the best predictor of someone joining a group. It needs to turn members into activists. Current members have many resources. This is the advantage of the age and experience level of members. The questions on salience indicate that VOTF has access to 1 million dollars a year and fifty thousand work hours a month. They need to turn that potential in resources into reality. But how?

To intensify commitment to the organization they need to find things for people to do. These things have to have substance. To tap the financial potential, they need to have programs that attract. Both national political parties and special-interest groups have learned how to raise money on the Internet by framing issues with key phrases, and by asking for money without fear of being ignored. VOTF Catholics have the money; the national office needs to frame the issues so as to attract a response.

On the other hand as local groups grow there will be pressure for them to become independent; there is likely to be ongoing conflict about goals, means, and decisions as well as the potential for tension with the larger organization. How well it will contain these tendencies will depend largely on how well its new National Representative Council is able to function.

Finally, VOTF must mobilize to sustain supporters and resources. Currently it has used both insider tactics such as meetings with bishops and petitions, and outsider tactics (such as a donation strike). The danger of using outsider tactics is alienation.

VOTF needs to be more reflective. It needs to understand the histories of similar groups and look at how these groups addressed the problems VOTF is facing. VOTF needs to consider long-term strategies, build momentum, take advantage of new knowledge, and use the resources of its present membership. In terms of framing in the future, the issues it addresses must be less tightly coupled to the 2002 scandal; from an ecclesiological perspective, Hines and Imbelli make similar suggestions. VOTF needs to incorporate new substantive issues that are related to their goals. New membership needs to be involved in this. As the members face its own organizational conflicts, they must be transparent. They need to determine whether the cost of trying to recruit younger members is worth the benefit. One possible target is campus ministries; VOTF could develop and link with social justice projects that have strong appeal to young Catholics.

It is doubtful that VOTF will grow among Hispanic Catholics or college Catholics, unless it is able to expand its meaning of "change the church." The 2005 survey indicates that young Catholics especially state that their number-one belief as a Catholic (as central as their belief in the life, death, and resurrection of Jesus) is their concern for the poor and disadvantaged. To reach out to them requires VOTF to expand its sense of vision and mission. VOTF needs to interpret the signs of the times and to realize that doing so is a part of its participation in a dynamic and changing church.

As we write this concluding chapter, the immigration question is a vital social justice issue of national importance to church and civil society. With 12 million illegal immigrants in the United States it will be an issue for years to come. The immediate challenge for VOTF is how to refocus its goals to incorporate Catholic social teaching so it can share common ground with the new immigrants, successors to the earlier immigrants who built the foundation on which VOTF Catholics stand.

VOTF Catholics need to be agents of dialogue. They would truly help the church by fostering dialogue among lay Catholics on social and ecclesiastical issues. By means of such a process, they may well help the bishops understand the reasons for the range of lay Catholic views on a range of topics, including immigration. There are many pressing issues linking the church and civil society. VOTF Catholics can be in a position to address them, and in the process stake a claim for participation in the national dialogue. By so doing perhaps VOTF could become a mediator between lay Catholics of different perspectives.

VOTF should not go about the business of church reform alone. It needs to build relationships with other Catholic groups. To successfully forge these relationships, VOTF leaders need to show thought and foresight in the way the organization conducts itself. The National Center for Pastoral Life, founded by the late Msgr. Philip Murnion, focuses on pastoral ministry in the United States. It has conducted research on how and to what degree the growing number of laypersons working in paid employment in parish and diocesan offices is providing new leadership for this church. The National Association for Lay Ministry (NALM) connects laity in professional ministry, many of whom are serving in the three thousand parishes without resident priests. VOTF should also build a relationship with the Leadership Roundtable, a group of Catholics with roots in the business community. They have sponsored meetings with the members of the hierarchy and academic community to consider what can be done to bring more financial transparency and accountability in the church. The Catholic Theological Society of America (CTSA), the largest and oldest association of theologians in the United States, and the Canon Law Society are scholarly organizations that would be able to collaborate with VOTF toward the goal of using doctrine to advance its mission. Likewise collaboration with the organizations of religious orders such as the Congregation of Major Superiors of Men (CMSM) and the Leadership Conference of Women Religious (LCWR) — whose members have a strong penchant for supporting community and social justice efforts, as well as having a presence among marginalized Catholics such as recent immigrants — could open up new and broader connections with the members of the church. In effect, there are significant opportunities for VOTF to add its voice in support of social and church reform issues.

A final thought: our research shows that VOTF Catholics have contributed to reform of the church by their thoughtful and consistent participation in the life of the church. The six distinguished scholars who have critically read our findings have confirmed this. They have stressed that VOTF Catholics are "very good Catholics" who are "the successful products of the impressive Catholic educational and social subculture." They are Catholics who are loyal, exercise voice, and do not want to exit the Catholic community. The scholars' discussion of VOTF's strengths and weaknesses from a variety of perspectives provide a basis to assist VOTF, its leaders and supporters, to continue to grow and to influence the process and direction of change within the church.

It is our hope that they will find this critical narrative of the first three years of VOTF's existence useful in planning for their future. Finally, we dare to hope that at least some bishops and priests will come to recognize VOTF Catholics as vital partners in the church's mission to the modern world.

Appendix A

Advisory Committee for
Voice of the Faithful Project

Most Reverend William B. Friend, DD
Bishop of Shreveport
The Catholic Center
3500 Fairfield Ave.
Shreveport, LA 71104

Reverend Ted Keating, SM
Executive Director
Conference of Major Superiors of Men's Institutes
8808 Cameron St.
Silver Spring, MD 20910

Reverend James Coriden
Professor of Church Law
Washington Theological Union
6896 Laurel St. NW
Washington, DC 20012-2016

Dr. Ruth Wallace
4908 41st St. NW
Washington, DC 20016

Dr. Kathleen Mass Weigert
Center for Social Justice: Research, Teaching and Service
Georgetown University
Washington, DC 20057

Dr. Dean Hoge
Life Cycle Institute
Catholic University of America
Washington, DC 20064

Reverend Raymond Kemp
Woodstock Theological Center
Georgetown University
Washington, DC 20057-1137

Reverend William Byron, SJ
Sellinger School of Business
Loyola College of Maryland
4603 Milbrook Rd.
Baltimore, MD 21212

Hector Rodriguez
Catholic Migrant Farm Workers Network
6960 Sunfleck Row
Columbia, MD 21045

Appendix B

Questionnaire for VOTF Founders and Leaders

BACKGROUND INFORMATION

Please place an "X" in the bracket by the appropriate item. If the items require an extended response, please type within the brackets.

1. Name [ ] M [ ] F [ ]
2. Date of birth [ ]
3. Place of birth [ ]

Religious History

Self

4. Infant baptism as Catholic? Yes [ ] No [ ] Other [ ] Please specify [ ]
5. Became Catholic as Adult? Yes [ ] No [ ] Other [ ]
6. If so, Participated in RCIA? Yes [ ] No [ ] Other [ ]
7. Attended seminary or religious formation? Yes [ ] No [ ] Diocese/Order [ ]
8. Ordained? Yes [ ] No [ ] Number of years of service [ ]
9. Professed? Yes [ ] No [ ] Number of years of service [ ]

Parents

10. Father: Baptized Catholic? Yes [ ] No [ ] If so, infant baptism [ ] Adult Convert [ ]
11. Mother: Baptized Catholic? Yes [ ] No [ ] If so, infant baptism [ ] Adult Convert [ ]

Education

Self

12. High school [ ] Some college [ ] B.A./B.S. [ ] M.A./M.S. [ ] Ph.D. [ ]

13. Professional degree (Please Specify) [ ]

14. Catholic education: Grade school? Yes [ ] No [ ] Number of years [ ]

15. Catholic high school ? Yes [ ] No [ ] Number of years [ ]

16. Catholic college? Yes [ ] No [ ]

Parents

17. Father's Education

    a. High school [ ] Some college [ ] B.A./B.S. [ ] M.A./M.S. [ ] Ph.D. [ ] Professional degree (Please specify) [ ]

    b. Catholic education: Grade school? Yes [ ] No [ ] High school ? Yes [ ] No [ ] College? Yes [ ] No [ ]

18. Mother's Education

    a. High school [ ] Some college [ ] B.A./B.S. [ ] M.A./M.S. [ ] Ph.D. [ ] Professional degree (Please specify) [ ]

    b. Catholic education: Grade school? Yes [ ] No [ ] High school ? Yes [ ] No [ ] College? Yes [ ] No [ ]

Family Life

19. Are you married? Yes [ ] No [ ]

20. Is your marriage recognized by the Catholic Church? Yes [ ] No [ ]

21. Is your spouse Catholic? Yes [ ] No [ ]

22. Do you have children? Yes [ ] No [ ] How many? [ ] List their ages [ ]

23. How many go or have gone to Catholic schools? [ ]

24. As far as you know, how many of your adult children attend church regularly? [ ]

25. How many siblings do you have? [ ]

What is your ethnic ancestry? ("X" all that may apply)

26. Irish [ ] Italian [ ] French [ ] English [ ] Latino [ ] Afro-American [ ] Eastern European [ ] (please specify) [ ] Other [ ] (please specify) [ ]

Are you employed?

27. full-time [ ] part-time [ ] house wife/husband [ ] unemployed [ ] retired? [ ]

28. Nature of employment [ ]

Professional Career

29. What kind of work you do?

> Academic [ ] specify discipline [ ]
>
> Professional worker [ ]
>
> Manager, executive, or official [ ]
>
> Business owner [ ]
>
> Clerical [ ]
>
> Service [ ]
>
> Skilled tradesman [ ]
>
> Semi-skilled [ ]
>
> Laborer [ ]
>
> Full-time student [ ]
>
> Retired [ ]
>
> Housewife [ ]
>
> Other/no answer [ ]

30. Is your annual *household* income before taxes:

a. Under $10,000 (under $192 per week) [ ]

b. $10,000 to $19,999 ($193 to $384 per week) [ ]

c. $20,000 to $29,999 ($385 to $576 per week) [ ]

d. $30,000 to $39,999 ($577 to $769 per week) [ ]

e. $40,000 to $49,999 ($770 to $960 per week) [ ]

f. $50,000 to $74,999 ($961 to $1,442 per week) [ ]

g. $75,000 to $99,999 ($1,443 to 1,923 per week) [ ]

g. $100,000 and over [ ]

h. Don't know [ ]

i. No response [ ]

Religious Beliefs and Practices

31. How often do you attend Mass?

a. daily [ ]

b. at least once a week [ ]

c. almost every week [ ]

d. about once a month [ ]

e. seldom [ ]

f. never [ ]

g. no answer [ ]

32. How regularly do you pray, apart from Mass?

a. more than once a day [ ]

b. daily [ ]

c. at least once a week [ ]

d. occasionally [ ]

e. seldom [ ]

f. never [ ]

g. no answer [ ]

33. How important is the Catholic Church to you personally?

    a. the most important part of my life [ ]

    b. among the most important parts of my life [ ]

    c. quite important to me, but so are many other areas of my life [ ]

    d. not terribly important to me [ ]

    e. not very important to me at all [ ]

    f. not sure [ ]

34. Imagine a scale from 1 to 7. At point 1 is the statement, "I would never leave the Catholic Church." At point 7 is the statement, "Yes, I might leave the Catholic Church."

    Points 1 2 3 4 5 6 7   Don't know

    Please indicate the number that best represents you [ ]

35. Are you a registered member of a parish? Yes [ ] No [ ]

36. Are you or have you been a member of any parish committees or organizations? Yes [ ] No [ ] (Please specify) [ ]

37. Are you or have you been a liturgical minister (e.g., lector, etc.)? Yes [ ] No [ ]

    a. Lector [ ]

    b. Eucharistic minister [ ]

    c. Greeter/usher [ ]

    d. Mass server [ ]

    e. Music ministry [ ]

38. Are you now or have you been any of the following:

    a. teacher in any of the following: RCIA [ ] CCD [ ] Religious Education [ ]

    b. teacher in Catholic grade or high school? Yes [ ] No [ ]

39. Did your parish participate in RENEW? Yes [ ] No [ ]

40. Did you participate in RENEW activities? Yes [ ] No [ ]

41a. Does your parish now have or has it ever had a Small Christian Community Program? Yes [ ] No [ ] Don't Know [ ]

41b. Are you now or have you been a member of a Small Christian Community? Yes [ ] No [ ]

42. Do you now or have you participated in Catholic social movements (e.g., Catholic Worker, Christian Family Movement, Call to Action, etc.), Yes [ ] No [ ]

43. Indicate if you now or you have participated in these or other Catholic Organizations by placing an X in the appropriate bracket:

    a. Knights of Columbus [ ]

    b. Daughters of Isabella [ ]

    c. National Conference of Catholic Women [ ]

    d. Catholic League [ ]

    e. Holy Name Society [ ]

    f. Other: (please specify) [ ]

Participation in Diocesan Life

44. Are you or have you been a member of any diocesan committees or organizations? Yes [ ] No [ ] (Please specify) [ ]

45. Are you or have you been a member of any national committees or organizations under the sponsorship of the U.S. Bishops' Conference? (E.g., CHD) Yes [ ] No [ ] (Please specify) [ ]

46. Are you or have you been a member of any national organizations that promote social justice? (E.g., Pax Christi, Bread for the World, Habitat for Humanity, etc.) Yes [ ] No [ ] (Please specify) [ ]

47. Do you or your family subscribe to any of the following:

    a. *America* [ ]

    b. *Commonweal* [ ]

    c. *National Catholic Reporter* [ ]

    d. *St. Anthony Messenger* [ ]

    e. *U.S. Catholic* [ ]

    f. *The Wanderer* [ ]

    g. *First Things* [ ]

    h. Local diocesan paper [ ]

48. Politically, would you identify yourself as:

    a. Conservative [ ]

    b. Moderate [ ]

    c. Liberal [ ]

49. Do you identify with one of the following political parties?

    a. Republican [ ]

    b. Democratic [ ]

    c. Green [ ]

    d. Other [ ] (Please specify)

Appendix C

Interview Schedule for VOTF Founders-Leaders

1. When did you become aware of the Boston hierarchy's cover-up of the clergy's sexual abuse of minors?

2. How did you become aware of the scandal?

3. What were your primary emotional reactions?

4. What was your first behavioral response?

5. Who was the first person that you talked to about the scandal?

6. Did you call anyone by phone? Or send out one or more emails? If yes, when? Right away? Later that day? During the week? And to whom? Friends? Relatives?

7. Did you participate in any meetings? When? Where? How many participated?

8. Where did your initial meeting with others take place? In someone's home? Church property? Other?

9. Who called the first meeting? How many attended?

10. Did your pastor offer a public response to the scandal? During Mass? After Mass? The first day? Or later?

11. Were there any other actions taken by your pastor that aided or hindered discussion of the scandal and/or action responses?

12. Was the pastor's public response to the scandal the same as his private response? Or was it different? Explain how.

13. Who was involved in generating the idea of developing an organization to respond to the scandal?

14. Was this organization always referred to as VOTF? How did the name develop?

15. Who invited you to participate in the organization? Did you invite others to participate in VOTF? Explain.

16. Do you consider yourself a founding member of VOTF [if not already clear]?

17. What motivated you to take an active response to the scandal?

18. Do you see a connection between your formal education and the way that you perceived this scandal? And your response to it? Explain.

19. Do you think your knowledge of Catholicism (Scripture, Theology, Canon Law, Ethics, Catechetics, Vatican II) influenced your response to the scandal? How so?

20. Do you see a connection between your professional experience and the way you perceived this scandal? And your response to it? Explain.

21. Do you see a connection between your previous participation in the church and the way that you perceived this scandal? And your response?

22. Have you been active in non-religious voluntary associations? If so, did this background experience influence the way you responded to this scandal?

23. Have you had any experience with social movement organizations that might have influenced you in deciding to become active in response to this scandal? Like Call to Action? WOC? Future Church? Catholic League?

24. Any experience with civic organizations that might have been influential in how you saw this scandal?

25. Prior experience as a leader? Have you played leadership roles in any social organizations prior to VOTF? Cite them and elaborate as relevant.

26. What features of American cultural beliefs and values have influenced the way you think about the Catholic Church?

27. How do these factors affect the way you function as a Catholic?

28. What features of your identity as a Catholic are most salient to you?

29. Is your being Catholic visible to others?

30. What aspects of the scandal were most offensive to you personally?

31. Was the feeling of being offended, and hurt, shared with your significant others?

32. In sum, what factors led you to become active in VOTF [if not already clear]?

33. In your own words, what is the central mission of VOTF?

34. How do you understand VOTF's mission statement? How do you feel about it?

35. What resources are available to help VOTF achieve its goals?

36. Are ethnic-related factors a focus of VOTF's mission and goals at this time? How?

37. Do you have a sense of any ethnic-racial participation in VOTF groups?

38. Are age and gender variables of concern to VOTF leaders at this time? In what ways? And what if anything is being done to address it or them?

39. Any final comments? Anything we missed that we should have asked?

Appendix D

Email Correspondence with Founders of Voice of the Faithful

The following email correspondence with founders of VOTF traces the beginnings of the history of the relationship between VOTF and the authors. Among other things, it shows how the Internet has changed the nature of such relationships.

From: PaulBaierVOTF@aol.com
To: Dantonio@cua.edu
Sent: Thursday, March 6, 2003

Hi Bill,

I am excited about your potential research project to study VOTF and would be more than happy to make myself and others available to assist in your work.

The birth of VOTF, the conference, and the growth last year was, I truly believe, a Spirit-led initiative to which many people contributed.

Importantly, we used many Internet tools (emails, message boards, etc.) which have redefined how nonprofits deliver their message and organize. Many other nonprofits are also learning from this as well.

Feel free to call or write when I can be of help.

Paul Baier
Co-founder of VOTF
paulbaierVOTF@aol.com
781 910 5467

From: William V. D'Antonio
To: PaulbaierVOTF@aol.com; Jim_Post@votf.org
Sent: Wednesday, August 27, 2003

Dear Jim and Paul,

I am happy to report that we have received a grant to carry out a two-year study of VOTF. My colleague, Father Tony Pogorelc, a Ph.D. sociologist from Purdue, who also has a Master's of Divinity, will be associate director of the project. Our goals will be to understand the social forces that enabled the leaders of VOTF to form a social movement organization (SMO) in response to the sexual abuse crisis in the archdiocese of Boston. We also want to understand the development of this SMO, the role of the July 2002 conference, and the role of the Internet in facilitating the rapid growth of VOTF locally as well as nationally.

May we quote from the abstract of our proposal to offer a more specific summary of our purpose: "The purpose of this research is to study the emergence and growth of... Voice of the Faithful. This movement is unique because it emerged from the resolution of lay Catholics in response to unethical and even criminal behavior by the clergy.... American Catholics have long insisted that they have the right to participate in church governance in matters ranging from church finances to parish councils. Our study will focus on VOTF's potential to be an agent to help bring about such change."

We are in the process of digesting the information VOTF communicated via the Internet so that we have a foundational understanding of VOTF in preparation for our initial meeting with Boston VOTF leaders. We want to introduce ourselves to you with two very brief bios that will enable you to become more familiar with us and our work. In the end we want to provide VOTF with a social history of its origins, its grounding in the social ideals of the United States, and in the beliefs, teachings and values of the Catholic Church.

Brief bios: William V. D'Antonio, Ph.D.; taught at Michigan State U (1957–59); Notre Dame (1959–71); University of Connecticut (1971–82); American Sociological Association-Executive Officer (1982–91); Catholic University — Visiting Research Professor (1993–); publications include: Religion, Revolution, and Reform: New Forces for Change in Latin America; Families and Religions: Conflict and Change in Modern Society; American Catholic Laity in a Changing Church; Laity, American and Catholic, Transforming the Church; American Catholics: Gender, Generation, and Commitment; and The Catholic Experience of Small Christian Communities.

Anthony J. Pogorelc, M.Div. (1987, St. Michael's College of the University of Toronto); Ph.D. (2002 Purdue University), taught at Purdue University (1997–2001); Catholic University (2003–); Ordained 1988. Pastoral work in Archdiocese of San Antonio (1988–94), and in Diocese of Lafayette in Indiana (1994–2001). Director of Pastoral Formation at Theological College: Seminary of Catholic University (2002–); Dean of Men (2003–). Publications include American Catholics: One Church, Two Cultures? (2000 RRR). Dissertation: "Social Movements within Organizations: The Case of Call to Action and U.S. Bishops."

From: William V. D'Antonio
To: Jim_Post@votf.org
Sent: October 7, 2003

Jim —

It was great to meet and listen to you last evening. I mentioned briefly that a colleague, Rev. Dr. Tony Pogorelc, and I have received a grant to carry out a two year study of VOTF. It is social history in one part, and an effort to find out how closely those who belong to VOTF groups are in sync with the national leadership.

I won't try to spell out our ideas in detail here, but we are for the time being seeing VOTF as a social movement within the larger social organization of the Roman Catholic Church. How well that general framework holds up is for us to find out over the next two years.

We hope to interview as many of the founding members of VOTF as possible. Last night's talk was a great introduction to our interview with you. One of our interests is to learn more about how the founders' and leaders' personal histories as Catholics and as citizens have provided them with values and beliefs that made possible the growth and now development of what has become an international movement in less than two years.

I hope to get to Boston before the end of October, to meet as many of the leaders as possible and set forth in more detail our goals. We are in the first place sociologists deeply committed to our discipline as well as to the church. We hope our study will be more than knowledge for its own sake. We hope it will be found worthwhile both to the officers and members of VOTF and to at least some of the clergy.

I look forward to seeing you again soon, and will be mailing you a cc of our book *American Catholics: Gender, Generation, and Commitment*.

Cordially, Bill D'Antonio

From: James Post
To: William V. D'Antonio
Sent: October 8, 2003

Dear Bill,

Thank you for your note. It was a pleasure to meet you and I look forward to discussing your project. We have received a number of requests for cooperation and are trying to be even-handed in the way we work with journalists and scholars re: books and articles. Let's plan to talk before you travel to Boston. I look forward to reading your book, *American Catholics: Gender, Generation, and Commitment,* and talking in the near future.

Regards, Jim

P.S. I am copying Luise Cahill Dittrich, VOTF's communications director. Luise helps to keep all these projects in order and does her best to prevent me from getting too confused!

From: James Post
To: William V. D'Antonio
Sent: October 18, 2003

Dear Bill,

I will mention the project to the board of trustees at the next regularly scheduled meeting.

It would be helpful to have a one page description of what you propose to do, and the type of assistance you will need. We have had a number of such requests and try to deal in an even-handed way with scholars and journalists.

Regards,

Jim

P.S. Thanks for sending me a copy of *American Catholics,* which arrived this past week. I hope to read it soon.

From: D'Antonio, William V.
To: James Post
Sent: October 18, 2003

Jim — thanks for the quick response. We have attached a one page summary of what we hope to accomplish in the next two years. What we hope for from you all is simply a list as complete as you can make it of all the people who helped bring VOTF into being, and then a list of its current officers and committee members.

We want to interview all who are willing to be interviewed, using a standard interview schedule. Social movements like VOTF just don't pop up anyplace; they need events like the discovery of the abuse and cover-up, and then they need people with vision and the skills to make things happen. And resources beyond intellectual, spiritual, and organizational skills. My interest in change in the church goes back to my Notre Dame days as a young sociologist working with scholars from various disciplines trying to make sense of Vatican II, in our personal and in our academic lives. Father Tony just completed his Ph.D at Purdue in sociology, with his dissertation on Call to Action as a social movement.

You will probably have received the cc of our latest book by now, so have some sense of what I have been doing in recent years.

I am attaching the statement.

—

VOTF — a summary description of the goals of our study

The Louisville Institute has provided a grant for a two-year study entitled *Voice of the Faithful: A Sociological Study of a Lay Catholic Social Movement.* The purpose of our research is to study the emergence and growth of this social movement within the Catholic Church, which is unique because it was brought into being mainly through the resources of lay Catholics. It emerged as a lay response to the cover-up by the Boston hierarchy of the abuse of minors by some members of the Boston clergy.

Our objectives are to study the leaders and members of VOTF to understand what personal and professional resources enabled them to create a social movement organization in Boston. We hope to conduct in-depth interviews with the founders and leaders of VOTF. These interviews would cover such areas as personal and professional resources including their family background, education, professional life, commitment to Catholic beliefs and teachings as well as the influence of American values such as equality and democracy, their prior participation in voluntary associations and parish life. We also plan to survey a sample of VOTF members and draw comparisons with other parts of the Catholic populace in the United States. Though VOTF is becoming a national movement, this initial part of our research will concentrate on Boston, because that is its place of origin and current national leadership.

From: Jepostl@aol.com
To: VOTF Board of Trustees
Sent: December 1, 2003

Friends,

VOTF has been the subject of various newspaper and magazine articles. Now a number of new books regarding the Catholic Church refer to VOTF (e.g., Peter Steinfels, *A People Adrift*) and one or two have lengthy descriptions of VOTF (e.g., David Gibson, *The Coming Catholic Church,* chapter 6, "Revolution from Below"). In 2004, a book by Jim Miller and Charlie Kenney (to be published by Rodale Press) will recount more of a history of VOTF.

We recently received a request from William (Bill) D'Antonio — a well-known scholar from Catholic University — and an associate to cooperate with their study of VOTF. They view VOTF as "a social movement within a social organization (church)." Bill and his coauthor are sociologists trying to understand why VOTF emerged as it did, the people who have provided leadership over two years and the evolution of VOTF as an organization.

Bill will be in Boston from Tuesday December 16 through Thursday December 18 and is hoping to meet and talk with you.

Earlier this year, the VOTF board of trustees adopted a policy of providing appropriate cooperation to journalists, students, and scholars who wish to study the VOTF movement. We know that many of you feel an obligation to help others understand the formation and focus of VOTF. I believe these studies/publications enable others to better understand the meaning of VOTF to the life of the Catholic Church.

You have NO OBLIGATIONS to speak with any interviewer. Participation in any research project is strictly voluntary. (We do hope you will tell us about projects however, in order that we may follow their development.)

Please respond by letting me know if...

(a) you are willing to meet with Bill, and

(b) whether you can do so on December 16, 17, or 18.

If you are willing to do so, I will have Bill contact you directly via email to set a specific time. Thanks.

Best wishes,

Jim

Appendix E

Eighty-five Item Questionnaire for VOTF Members

Please respond to the following questions. If an item requires an extended response, please type in the space below the question.

1. Password

2. Year of birth

3. Sex: Female Male

4. Zip Code

5. Diocese

6. What is your ethnic ancestry? Check all that may apply.

   Irish

   Italian

   French

   English

   Latino

   African American

   Eastern European

   Other (please specify)

7. Religious background

   Cradle Catholic

   Convert

8. Are you a registered member of a parish? Yes No

9. Education

   High school

   Some college

   College degree

   Graduate degree

10. Catholic education: Yes No

    a. Catholic grade school?

    b. Catholic high school?

    c. Catholic college?

11. Have you studied theology, scripture, or canon law?

    a. Yes, I have a university degree.

    b. I have completed a certificate program.

    c. I have taken theology courses in a university.

    d. I have taken diocesan/parish sponsored courses.

    e. I have taken VOTF sponsored study sessions.

    f. Other (please specify)

12. Did you attend a seminary or religious formation program?

    Yes No

13. If Yes,

    a. Were you ordained?

    b. Were you professed?

Parents:

14. Father: Catholic?   Yes No

15. Mother: Catholic?   Yes No

16. Father's education:

> Did not complete high school
>
> High school graduate
>
> College graduate

17. Mother's education

> Did not complete high school
>
> High school graduate
>
> College graduate
>
> Family life

18. Your marital status:

> Single
>
> Married
>
> Divorced
>
> Other (please specify)

19. If you are married:

> a. Does the Catholic Church recognize your marriage?
>
> b. Is your spouse Catholic?

20. Do you have children?   Yes No

21. If so, how many?

22. Do (did) they attend Catholic schools?   Yes No

23. How many attended Catholic school?

24. If you have adult children, as far as you know, do most of them attend church regularly?   Yes No

Clerical Sexual Abuse of Minors and Its Cover-up

25. In regard to your first attendance at a VOTF meeting:

    a. I went on my own.

    b. I went with another person

    c. I was invited by another person to attend.

26. Did you invite others to attend VOTF meetings?   Yes No

27. Did your pastor offer a public response to the scandal?   Yes No

28. If you feel any item requires an extended response, please use the space provided below:

29. Did your pastor's response to the scandal or lack of it influence your decision to participate in VOTF?   Yes No
    Please explain:

30. My pastor is supportive of VOTF.

    a. strongly agree

    b. agree

    c. neutral

    d. disagree

    e. strongly disagree

Socio-economic status

31. Are you employed?

    full-time

    part-time

    house wife/husband

    unemployed

    retired

32. If you are or have been employed, describe the nature of your employment.

    a. Academic

    b. Professional worker

    c. Manager, executive, or official

    d. Business owner

    e. Clerical

    f. Service

    g. Skilled trade

    h. Semi-skilled

    i. Laborer

    j. Full-time student

    k. No answer

    l. Other (please specify)

33. Academic (Specify discipline if you checked "a" in question above.)

34. Your annual household income before taxes:

    a. Under $10,000 (under $192 per week)

    b. $10,000 to $19,999 ($193 to 384 per week)

    c. $20,000 to $29,999 ($385 to 576 per week)

    d. $30,000 to $39,999 ($577 to 769 per week)

    e. $40,000 to $49,999 ($770 to 960 per week)

    f. $50,000 to $74,999 ($961 to 1,442 per week)

    g. $75,000 to $99,999 ($1,443 to 1,923 per week) [ ]

    h. $100,000 and over:

    i. Don't know

    j. No response

35. If you feel any item requires an extended response, please use the space provided below:

Religious Beliefs and Practices

36. How often do you attend Mass?

    a. daily

    b. at least once a week

    c. almost every week

    d. about once a month

    e. seldom

    f. never

    g. no answer

37. How regularly do you pray, apart from Mass?

    a. more than once a day

    b. daily

    c. at least once a week

    d. occasionally

    e. seldom

    f. never

    g. no answer

38. How regularly do you perform activities to serve the needy (serve in soup kitchens, tutoring programs, etc.)?

    a. at least once a week

    b. more than once a month

    c. monthly

    d. occasionally

     e. seldom

     f. never

     g. no answer

39. Please indicate the level of your knowledge of the documents of the Second Vatican Council (Vatican II). Check all that apply.

     a. I have read all of them

     b. I have not read any of them

     c. In the past I have participated in seminars and lectures on Vatican II

     d. VOTF study sessions have been my main source of knowledge about Vatican II

     e. I have read some of them (please specify)

40. How important is the Catholic Church to you personally?

     a. the most important part of my life

     b. among the most important parts of my life

     c. quite important to me, but so are many other areas of my life

     d. not terribly important to me

     e. not very important to me at all

     f. not sure

41. If you feel any item requires an extended response, please use the space provided below:

42. Now I would like you to imagine a scale from 1 to 7. At point 1 is the statement, "I would never leave the Catholic Church." At point 7 is the statement, "Yes, I might leave the Catholic Church." Please indicate the number that best represents you:

     1 2 3 4 5 6 7   Don't Know

43. Indicate if you are or have been a member of the following committees. Check as many as apply.

    a. Member of parish council

    b. Member of finance council

    c. Member of liturgy committee

    d. Member of parish school board

    e. Member of other parish committees (Please specify below)

44. If you answered "Member of other parish committees," please specify here:

45. Indicate if you now or have participated in the following liturgical ministries. Check as many as apply.

    a. Lector

    b. Eucharistic Minister

    c. Greeter/Usher

    d. Mass server

    e. Music ministry

    f. Other (please specify)

46. Indicate if you now or have been a teacher in any of the following. Check as many as apply.

    a. Religious Education for children or teens (CCD or PSR)

    b. Catholic grade school

    c. Catholic high school

    d. RCIA

    e. None of the above

    f. Other (please specify)

47. Indicate if you now or have participated in the following groups. Check all that apply.

    a. RENEW

    b. Small Christian Community (Faith sharing group)

    c. Intentional Eucharist Centered Community

    d. Hispanic-Latino Community

    e. Other (please specify)

48. If you feel any item requires an extended response, please use the space provided below:

49. Indicate if you now or have participated in these or other Catholic social movements. Check all that apply.

    a. Christian Family Movement

    b. Young Christian Students

    c. Young Christian Workers

    d. Catholic Worker Movement

    e. Focolare

    f. Neocatechumenate

    g. Call to Action

    h. Marriage Encounter

    i. Cursillo

    j. Charismatic Movement

    k. Dignity

    l. Right to Life

    m. Catholics for a Free Choice

    n. Other (please specify)

50. Indicate if you now or have participated in these or other Catholic organizations. Check all that apply.

    a. Daughters of Isabella

    b. Knights of Columbus

    c. National Conference of Catholic Women

    d. Catholic League

    e. Holy Name Society

    f. Christian Mothers

    g. St. Vincent de Paul Society

    h. Jesuit Volunteers

    i. Other (please specify)

51. Indicate if you now or have participated in these or other Catholic committees or organizations. Check all that apply.

    a. Diocesan pastoral council

    b. Diocesan finance committee

    c. Other diocesan committees or organizations
       (Please specify)

52. Are you or have you been a member of any national committees or organizations under the sponsorship of the U.S. Bishops' Conference? (E.g., CCHD)

    No

    Yes (please specify)

53. Are you or have you been a member of any national organizations that promote social justice? (E.g., Habitat for Humanity, Pax Christi, Bread for the World, etc.)

    No

    Yes (please specify)

54. If you feel any item requires an extended response, please use the text box provided below.

55. Please indicate whether you strongly agree, somewhat agree, somewhat disagree, or strongly disagree with the following statements:

   a. Most priests expect the members of the laity to be followers not leaders in the parish.

   b. Catholic parishes are too big and impersonal.

   c. The Catholic hierarchy is out of touch with the laity.

   d. On the whole parish priests do a good job.

   e. When the hierarchy is unresponsive to the views of the laity on matters which concern the good of the church, withholding financial contributions is an appropriate means for getting their attention.

56. Decision-making in the Catholic Church regarding issues that do not involve the doctrine of the faith should allow for wider participation by the laity. Do you favor or oppose this idea or are you not sure?

   a. at the local parish level

   b. at the diocesan level

   c. at the national level

   d. at the international (Vatican) level

57. Do you favor or oppose the idea that the Catholic laity have a right to participate in the following areas of church life, or are you not sure?

   a. Deciding how parish income should be spent

   b. Selecting priests for their parish

   c. Selecting bishops for their dioceses

58. How much of your time are you willing to devote to promote meaningful participation by the laity in church decision-making?

    a. None

    b. One hour per week

    c. Two to five hours per week

    d. Six to ten hours per week

    e. More than ten hours per week

59. How much of your financial resources per year are you willing to give to VOTF to promote meaningful participation by the laity in church decision-making?

    a. None

    b. $50 or less

    c. $51–$100

    d. $101–$300

    e. $301–$500

    f. More than $500

60. If you feel any item requires an extended response, please use the space provided below:

61. Does your household subscribe to any of the following? Check all that apply.

    a. *America*

    b. *Commonweal*

    c. *Crisis*

    d. *National Catholic Reporter*

    e. *St. Anthony Messenger*

    f. *U.S. Catholic*

    g. *In the Vineyard*

h. *Our Sunday Visitor*

i. *The Wanderer*

j. *First Things*

k. Local diocesan paper

l. Other (please specify)

62. How familiar are you with the National Review Board for the Protection of Children and Young People?

    a. Not familiar

    b. I have heard of it

    c. I have some knowledge about the board and its functions

    d. I have a great deal of knowledge about the board and its functions

63. How familiar are you with the report produced by the National Review Board for the Protection of Children and Young People (called the Bennett Report)?

    a. Not familiar

    b. I have heard of it

    c. I have some knowledge of its contents and conclusions

    d. I have a great deal of knowledge about its contents and conclusions

64. How familiar are you with the study produced by the John Jay College on the sexual abuse of children by priests?

    a. Not familiar

    b. I have heard of it

    c. I have some knowledge of its contents and conclusions

    d. I have a great deal of knowledge about its contents and conclusions

65. I am a(n):   Conservative Moderate Liberal   No Answer

    a. Political

    b. Economic

    c. Social-Cultural

66. Do you identify with one of the following political parties?

    Republican

    Democratic

    Green

    Other (please specify)

67. If you feel any item requires an extended response, please use the space provided below:

68. How closely do you identify with the stated goals of VOTF? strongly? somewhat? to a small degree? not at all?

    a. To support victims of clerical sexual abuse

    b. To support priests of integrity

    c. To shape structural change in the church

69. Are you a member of a VOTF affiliate? Yes No

70. In the last twelve months have you: (Check all that apply.)

    a. Donated money to the VOTF national office

    b. Donated money to a VOTF local affiliate

    c. Attended VOTF meetings (please specify number)

    d. Attended a regional conference

    e. Signed the VOTF Petition for Reform

Open-ended questions

71. What does the third goal of VOTF "to shape structural change in the church" mean to you? Please explain.

72. Do you think that in the future VOTF will be an important force promoting the participation of the laity in the decision-making in the Catholic Church? Why or Why not?

73. What are the strengths of your local VOTF affiliates? In what ways does it need to improve?

74. Are you content with the diversity of VOTF regarding the representation of ethnic groups and age groups? Please elaborate.

75. Do you experience any tensions between being a Catholic and being an American? (For example, does the Catholic stress on hierarchy and tradition, in contrast to the American stress on democracy and innovation, cause conflict for you?) If so, can you discuss these tensions?

76. What factors were most important in influencing your decision to participate in VOTF?

77. Is the Executive Office of the National VOTF providing effective day-to-day leadership that will enable VOTF to persist and fulfill its mission? Yes No

78. What do you perceive to be the Executive Office's strengths?

79. What do you perceive to be its weaknesses?

80. Are the elected officers and the appointed Board of Trustees of VOTF charting an effective direction that will enable VOTF to persist and fulfill its mission?   Yes No

81. What do you perceive to be the officers'/trustees' strengths?

82. What do you perceive to be the officers'/trustees' weaknesses?

83. Is Voice of the Faithful's Representative Council providing effective guidance and direction that will enable VOTF to persist and fulfill its mission? Yes No

84. What do you consider the Representative Council's strengths?

85. What do you consider the Representative Council's weaknesses?

Appendix F

Additional Tables

Table A. VOTF Leaders and Members
Compared to 2005 National Survey

	VOTF Leaders N=35	VOTF Members N=1273	2005 National Survey N=875
Sex			
Male	40	41	46
Female	60	59	54
Year of birth			
Pre-Vatican II	31	41	17
Vatican II	60	48	35
Post-Vatican II	9	11	49
Educational level			
High school or less	–	2	32
Some college/technical training	–	10	35
College graduate	34	27	19
Graduate degree	66	60	14
Catholic education			
Elementary	74	70	49
High school	59	62	29
College/university	52	57	12
Married			
Yes	82	67	70
Marriage recognized by Catholic Church			
Yes	86	92	73
Mass attendance			
Weekly	63	65	34
At least monthly	26	24	30
Never/seldom	11	11	36
How often pray			
Daily	69	79	63
Occasionally	25	18	32
Never/seldom	6	2	5
Importance of Catholic Church			
Among most important	58	62	44
Quite important	42	28	37
Not very important/not sure/no answer	–	11	19
Possibility of leaving church			
"1" and "2" – would never leave	48	50	56
"3," "4" and "5" – probably not	20	27	31
"6" and "7" – might leave	32	33	14
Registered member of parish			
Yes	84	85	68
Political party identification			
Republican	14	18	39
Democrat	55	63	42
Independent/other	31	18	19

Note: Percentages may not add up to or might be slightly higher than 100% because of rounding.

Table 4.2. Religious Beliefs and Practices of VOTF Members, by Gender (in percentages)

	Total (%)	Female (%)	Male (%)
Cradle Catholic? – Yes	93	94	93
Catholic education			
Grade school	70	70	70
High school	61	61	61
College	58	56	59
Father Catholic? – yes	86	86	86
Mother Catholic? – yes	92	92	92
Marriage recognized by church? – yes	91	92	91
Spouse Catholic? – yes	83	79	87
Attend Mass			
Daily/weekly	66	65	67
Almost every week/monthly	23	24	23
Seldom/never	11	11	10
Pray, apart from Mass			
Daily, and more	80	83	76
Weekly, occasionally	18	16	21
Seldom/never	2	1	3
Help the needy			
Weekly, or more	29	31	26
Monthly, or more	51	54	47
Seldom/never	20	15	26
Importance of Catholic Church to you personally			
The most or among the most important parts of my life	65	65	66
Quite important to me	29	31	26
Not very important	6	4	8
Possibility of Leaving the Church			
1–2. Would never leave	50	47	55
3–5.	27	29	25
6–7. Might leave	23	24	21

Table 4.3. Participation of VOTF Members' in Church Life, by Gender (in percentages)

	Total (%)	Female (%)	Male (%)
Are or have been member of – yes			
Parish council	37	34	43
Finance council	21	13	32
Liturgy committee	45	47	42
Parish school board	23	19	28
Other parish committees	61	64	55
Now or have participated in – yes			
Lector	43	43	47
Eucharistic minister	43	48	41
Usher/greeter	19	16	24
Mass server	19	7	38
Music ministry	22	25	19
Now or ever a teacher in – yes			
CCD/PSR	53	58	45
Catholic grade school	14	18	8
Catholic high school	12	12	12
RCIA	17	15	20
Now or ever participated in – yes			
RENEW	24	24	25
Small Christian Community	35	36	33
Are or have participated in Catholic social movements – yes			
Call to Action	22	22	21
Marriage Encounter	19	17	23
Cursillo	17	15	20
Charismatic Movement	12	12	13
Right to Life	10	9	12
Christian Family Movement	8	5	11
Catholic Worker Movement	8	7	9
Member of social justice organizations – yes	47	50	42

Table 4.4. VOTF Members' Behavior and Attitudes toward Church Policies, by Gender (in percentages)

	Total (%)	Female (%)	Male (%)
Strongly Agree that			
Hierarchy out of touch	85	86	83
Priests expect laity to be followers	44	45	42
Parishes are too big	29	29	28
Priests do a good job	18	17	20
Can withhold contributions	66	65	67
Laity has right to participate – yes			
Decide parish spending	98	98	99
Selecting priests for parish	84	86	81
Selecting bishops	85	85	83
Amount of time willing to devote to church governance			
An hour per week or less	46	49	41
2–5 hours per week	47	46	49
6–10 hours per week	7	5	10
Money per year willing to give to VOTF			
None	16	14	19
$50 or less	37	40	31
$51–100	30	30	29
More than $100	17	16	21
Ideological Orientations			
I am a political			
Conservative	13	10	19
Moderate	38	38	37
Liberal	49	52	44
I am an economic			
Conservative	19	14	27
Moderate	50	56	43
Liberal	30	30	30
I am a socio-cultural			
Conservative	9	6	12
Moderate	37	38	37
Liberal	54	56	50
I am a			
Republican	18	15	22
Democrat	64	66	60
Independent/Green	18	19	18

Table 4.11. VOTF Members Participation in Church Life, by Generation (in percentages)

	Total	Pre-Vat II	Vat II	Post-Vat II
Are or was member of				
Parish council	37	41	39	17
Finance council	21	21	24	8
Liturgy committee	44	41	51	23
Parish school board	23	24	24	13
Liturgical Ministries – yes				
Lector	45	47	45	42
Eucharistic minister	45	44	48	36
Mass server	20	21	20	18
Music ministry	22	17	28	20
Teacher in Religious Education – yes				
CCD/PSR	53	54	54	45
Catholic grade school	13	17	13	6
Catholic high school	12	14	10	9
RCIA	16	15	20	9
RENEW	23	25	25	13
Small Christian Community	34	37	35	23
Call to Action	22	25	21	13
Marriage Encounter	19	18	22	13
Charismatic Movement	12	9	16	6
Right to Life	10	9	11	10
Member of social justice organizations	40	41	40	36

Table 4.14. Demographic Profile of VOTF Members by Region of the Country (in percentages)

N=	Total 1200	MA 281	East 443	South 158	Midwest 195	West 123
Pre-Vatican II	41	37	48	38	36	38
Vatican II	48	53	42	48	52	50
Post-Vatican II	11	10	10	14	12	12
Ethnic Ancestry						
Irish	63	72	64	59	53	60
English	21	21	18	26	23	23
Italian	12	19	17	11	2	3
French	11	15	9	15	11	7
Other European	9	8	7	10	18	6
Latino	2	1	2	3	1	7
All Others (includes African Americans)	32	21	28	35	50	46

Note: Respondents were allowed to select more than one ancestry.

	Total	MA	East	South	Midwest	West
Education						
High school/some college	12	12	11	14	15	15
College degree	27	31	23	31	32	26
Graduate degree	60	57	66	55	53	59
Nature of employment						
Academic	20	18	22	20	21	15
Professional	30	35	28	30	27	31
Mgrl., Exec., Bus.	22	19	22	23	28	19
Annual household income						
Under $49,999	25	25	21	25	30	24
$50,000–99,999	34	36	33	33	35	34
$100,000 or more	29	26	30	35	28	26
I am a political conservative	12	15	18	24	23	17
I am a political moderate	34	39	34	28	35	30
I am a political liberal	43	40	47	37	43	53
I am an economic conservative	17	15	17	19	21	16
I am an economic moderate	43	45	44	39	42	48
I am an economic liberal	26	25	28	23	24	28
I am a socio-cultural moderate	33	34	33	29	34	30
I am a socio-cultural conservative	8	8	9	10	5	6
I am a socio-cultural liberal	46	45	48	42	49	55
I am a Republican	18	15	18	24	23	17
I am a Democrat	63	62	65	54	61	71
I am an Independent	19	23	17	22	16	12

Table 4.15. Religious Practices and Attitudes of VOTF Members, by Region (in percentages)

	Total	MA	East	South	Midwest	West
N=	1200	281	443	158	195	123
Catholic education						
Grade school	70	61	73	63	82	70
High school	61	59	66	54	63	59
College	57	58	61	49	55	59
Marriage recognized by church? Yes	92	90	94	93	91	86
Attend Mass						
Daily/weekly	65	64	70	69	63	60
Monthly or more	24	26	21	17	28	25
Pray, apart from Mass						
Daily or more often	81	77	79	84	86	78
Help the needy						
Weekly	29	22	30	36	28	34
Monthly or more	51	55	50	50	57	48
Importance of Catholic Church						
Most or among most important						
parts of my life	65	65	70	66	62	60
Possibility of leaving the church*						
Never leave	50	48	45	54	45	45
Might leave	32	34	27	32	34	38

*We used a seven-point scale, with point 1 being "I would never leave," and point 7, "Yes, I might leave." The percentages here are to be read as follows: Never Leave=points 1 and 2; Might Leave=points 5, 6, and 7. If we used only points 6 and 7 as indicators of "Might Leave," the average percentage would then=23%, with a range from a low of 17% in the eastern region to a high of 30% in the West.

Table 4.17. Participation of VOTF Members in Church Life, by Region (in percentages)

	Total	MA	East	South	Midwest	West
N=	1200	281	443	158	195	123
Have you been member of committees – yes						
Parish council	36	30	39	35	44	42
Finance council	21	10	23	25	25	34
Liturgy council	44	36	47	39	47	55
Parish school board	23	16	25	20	29	30
Other Parish committee	61	54	62	58	70	71
Now or have you participated in liturgical ministries – yes						
Lector	44	44	42	46	49	51
Eucharistic minister	44	41	42	48	56	50
Usher/Greeter	19	16	17	23	27	22
Mass Server	20	14	17	23	27	25
Music Ministry	22	26	19	22	23	26
Now or ever a teacher in Religious Education – yes						
CCD/PSR	52	61	53	49	50	46
Catholic grade school	14	12	13	13	19	15
Catholic high school	12	10	11	9	14	16
RCIA	17	13	16	20	19	24
Now or have participated in Parish groups – yes						
RENEW	24	9	27	27	36	29
Small Christian community	34	20	37	36	44	47
Are or have participated in Catholic social movement – yes						
Call to Action	21	12	23	23	33	24
Marriage Encounter	19	17	20	18	21	25
Cursillo	17	20	15	20	21	15
Charismatic Movement	12	12	12	10	15	12
Right to Life	10	9	8	14	14	
Are or have been a member of social justice organization – yes	46	42	49	47	54	34

Table 4.18. Knowledge of Vatican II and Other Documents, by Region (in percentages)

	Total	MA	East	South	Midwest	West
N=	1200	281	443	158	195	123
Knowledge of documents of Vatican II						
Read all	15	11	18	18	17	15
Read none	23	26	21	22	20	16
Participated in seminars on Vatican II	46	50	45	46	47	48
Knowledge of National Review Board on Protection of Children and Young People						
Not familiar	24	28	20	26	19	30
Great deal of knowledge	10	8	12	13	12	10
Familiarity of Report on National Review Board (Bennett Report)						
Not familiar	24	28	21	29	20	24
Great deal of knowledge	10	8	10	11	11	11
Familiarity with John Jay College Study						
Not familiar	24	32	19	27	22	24
Great deal of knowledge	10	6	11	12	11	11
Household subscribes to:						
Local diocesan paper	39	20	44	57	50	42
National Catholic Reporter	32	21	40	32	35	37
America	22	15	30	17	24	24
Commonweal	13	9	18	9	13	19
St. Anthony Messenger	9	8	9	6	13	8
U.S. Catholic	8	5	7	8	11	11

Note: *The Wanderer* was removed from table; no one subscribes to it

Table 4.19. Behavior and Attitudes toward Church Policy, by Region (in percentages)

	Total	MA	East	South	Midwest	West
N=	1200	281	443	158	195	123
Strongly agree with these statements:						
Priests expect laity to be followers	44	36	49	47	38	46
Catholic parishes too big and impersonal	28	22	29	31	28	37
Hierarchy out of touch	84	85	84	86	82	84
Priests do good job	18	20	19	18	17	14
Wider participation by laity – favor						
Local level	98	99	98	98	98	98
Diocesan level	96	97	97	97	96	93
National level	94	94	95	94	93	92
International level	90	90	90	88	89	89
Laity right to participate – favor						
Decide about parish spending	98	97	99	99	99	98
Select priests	83	83	83	79	83	86
Select bishops	84	81	85	84	86	86
Amount of time willing to devote to church decision-making						
An hour per week or less	45	50	41	41	47	48
2–5 hours	48	46	52	49	48	40
6–10 hours a week or more per week	7	4	7	10	5	12
Money per year willing to give to VOTF to promote laity's role in church decision making						
None	16	12	13	15	23	22
$50 or less	36	39	35	33	40	38
$51–$100	30	32	32	36	21	23
More than $100	18	16	20	16	16	17

Notes

Introduction / Voice of the Faithful: A Sociological Study

1. James E. Muller and Charles Kenney, *Keep the Faith, Change the Church* (Emmaus, PA: Rodale Books, 2004).

Chapter 2 / VOTF's Founding Leaders

1. We constructed our list of interviewees by making contact with the then president, Jim Post, and through him, the executive director, Steve Krueger. They provided us with the names of founding members, who in turn provided us with other names. They made clear that a key person to the emergence of VOTF was Dr. James Muller, a cardiologist, who had earlier in his life organized an international movement of doctors against nuclear war. They pointed out that Dr. Muller was even at this time completing a book on VOTF, in conjunction with a writer: James E. Muller and Charles Kenney, *Keep the Faith, Change the Church* (Emmaus, PA: Rodale Books, 2004). The book itself was published during the course of our study. In his book Jim Muller recognized forty-six persons as founders; of these we interviewed twenty-seven. At the time of our study only a handful of the others on his list had been recommended as interviewees because of their contributions to VOTF's founding. Some of those we contacted did not feel they had a contribution to make, while others could not be located. Two had to cancel appointments. Most of the other interviewees had become part of the leadership structure by late 2003 or early 2004.

2. Boston Population and Demographics, *Boston.areaconnect.com/statistics.htm*. Based on 2000 U.S. Census data, 1–3.

Chapter 3 / VOTF Members: Who They Are and Why They Stay

1. The earliest roots of Call to Action can be found in the lay movements founded by Msgr. Reynold Hillenbrand in Chicago, which were called Catholic Action. In movements such as Young Christian Students, Young Christian Workers, and the Christian Family Movement, lay Catholics were able to support one another as they sought to live their faith in daily life. In the early 1970s the U.S. bishops sponsored a consultation and conference that came to be known as Call to Action. Led by the president of the Bishops' Conference (NCCB), Cardinal John Dearden, and inspired by Vatican II, Call to Action sought to mobilize the laity to promote social justice. When due to a conflict between delegates and the NCCB following the conference the latter withdrew its support, the Chicago movements adopted it and it became first a Chicago-based and finally a national organization. See Anthony Pogorelc, "Social Movements within Organizations: The Case of Call to Action and U.S. Catholic Bishops," diss., Purdue University, 2002.

2. Mary Jo Bane, "Bishop Accountability: A Challenge to Lay Catholics," *Boston Globe*, February 3, 2002.

3. VOTF has been banned in approximately eight dioceses, and this is likely to have had an effect on a pastor's attitudes.

4. Albert O. Hirschman, *Exit, Voice, and Loyalty: Responses to Decline in Firms, Organizations, and States* (Cambridge, MA: Harvard University Press, 1970).

5. Edward C. Banfield, *Political Influence* (New York: Free Press of Glencoe, 1961).

6. Hirschman, *Exit, Voice, and Loyalty*, 27.

7. Paul Philibert, O.P., *The Priesthood of the Faithful* (Collegeville, MN: Liturgical Press, 2005), 17.

Chapter 4 / VOTF Members: Gender, Generation, and Region

1. Other variables like membership in a parish often are predictive, but in the case of VOTF members, with 85 percent registered, there is little to vary.

2. Ruth A. Wallace, *They Call Her Pastor: A New Role for Catholic Women* (Albany: State University of New York Press, 1992).

3. Ruth A. Wallace, *They Call Him Pastor: Married Men in Charge of Catholic Parishes* (New York: Paulist, 2003).

4. Karl Mannheim, "The Problem of Generations," in *Mannheim's Collected Essays on the Sociology of Knowledge*, ed. P. Kecskemeti (London: Routledge & Kegan Paul, 1952); Douglas A. Walrath, *Frameworks: Patterns for Living and Believing Today* (New York: The Pilgrim Press, 1987).

5. William V. D'Antonio, James D. Davidson, Dean R. Hoge, and Ruth Wallace, *American Catholic Laity in a Changing Church* (Kansas City: Sheed and Ward, 1989); William V. D'Antonio, James D. Davidson, Dean R. Hoge, and Ruth Wallace, *American Catholic Laity: Transforming the Church* (Kansas City: Sheed and Ward, 1996); William V. D'Antonio, Dean R. Hoge, James D. Davidson, and Katherine Meyer, *American Catholics: Gender, Generation, and Commitment* (Lanham, MD: AltaMira Press, 2001); James D. Davidson et al., *The Search for Common Ground* (Huntington, IN: Our Sunday Visitor, 1997).

6. Jay Dolan, *The American Catholic Experience: A History from Colonial Times to the Present* (Garden City, NY: Doubleday, 1985); John Cogley and Rodger Van Allen, *Catholic America* (Kansas City: Sheed and Ward, 1986).

7. Dolan, *The American Catholic Experience*.

8. Gerhard Lenski, *The Religious Factor* (Garden City, NY: Doubleday Anchor Books, 1963); Melvin L. Kohn, *Class and Conformity: A Study in Values* (Chicago: University of Chicago Press, 1977).

9. Dolan, *The American Catholic Experience*; Andrea Williams and James D. Davidson, "Catholic Conceptions of Faith: A Generational Analysis," *Sociology of Religion* 57 (1996): 273–89; Andrew M. Greeley, "The Revolutionary Event of Vatican II," *Commonweal* 125 (September 11, 1998): 14–20.

10. Duane F. Alwin, "Religion and Parental Child Rearing Orientations: Evidence of a Catholic-Protestant Convergence," *American Journal of Sociology* 92 (1986): 412–40; D'Antonio et al., *American Catholic Laity in a Changing Church*; D'Antonio et al., *American Catholic Laity*; D'Antonio et al., *American Catholics: Gender, Generation, and Commitment* (Lanham, MD: AltaMira Press, 2001); Christopher G. Ellison and Darren E. Sherkat, "Obedience and Autonomy: Religion

and Parental Values Reconsidered," *Journal for the Scientific Study of Religion* 32, no. 4 (1993): 313–329.

11. Robert Putnam, *Bowling Alone: The Collapse and Revival of American Community* (New York: Simon & Schuster, 2000).

12. Bryan T. Froehle and Mary L. Gautier, *Catholicism USA* (Maryknoll, NY: Orbis Books, 2000).

13. Charles Morris, *American Catholic: The Saints and Sinners Who Built America's Most Powerful Church* (New York: Random House, 1997).

14. Ibid.

15. Saul E. Bronder, *Social Justice and Church Authority: The Public Life of Archbishop Robert E. Lucey* (Philadelphia: Temple University Press, 1982).

Chapter 5 / The Social Sources of Dissent / Nancy T. Ammerman

1. H. Richard Niebuhr, *The Social Sources of Denominationalism* (New York: World Publishing, 1929).

2. Nancy Tatom Ammerman, *Baptist Battles: Social Change and Religious Conflict in the Southern Baptist Convention* (New Brunswick, NJ: Rutgers University Press, 1990).

3. Eighty-five percent of American adults attended public or non-religious private schools. This figure calculated from the General Social Survey. See NORC (National Opinion Research Center), *GSSDIRS General Social Survey: 1972–2000 Cumulative Codebook* [Internet], National Opinion Research Center at the University of Chicago 2001 (cited January 5, 2006); available from *www.webapp.icpsr.umich.edu/GSS/*. Figures for Voice of the Faithful members throughout the text are taken from research reports supplied to the author. Figures for the American Catholic laity are taken from the set of reports introduced by D'Antonio in the September 30, 2005, *National Catholic Reporter*, available at *www.natcath.com/NCR_Online/archives2/2005c/093005/093005a.php*.

4. It should be noted that at least a few of the respondents indicated that joining Voice of the Faithful was a cause of renewed Catholic commitment. Some people who had become disaffected found in VOTF a new way to become connected again.

5. Robert D. Putnam notes these generational differences in "social capital" (*Bowling Alone: The Collapse and Revival of American Community* [New York: Simon & Schuster, 2000]). Robert Wuthnow also documents the way styles of belonging have changed (*Loose Connections: Joining Together in America's Fragmented Communities* [Cambridge, MA: Harvard University Press, 1998]).

6. Author's calculations from General Social Survey data (NORC 2001).

7. Paul DiMaggio and John Mohr, "Cultural Capital, Educational Attainment, and Marital Selection," *American Journal of Sociology* 90, no. 6 (1985): 1231–57.

8. See, for example, John T. McGreevy, *Parish Boundaries: The Catholic Encounter with Race in the Twentieth-Century Urban North* (Chicago: University of Chicago Press, 1996); Robert A. Orsi, *The Madonna of 115th Street: Faith and Community in Italian Harlem, 1880–1950* (New Haven, CT: Yale University Press, 1985); and Robert A. Orsi, *Thank You, St. Jude* (New Haven, CT: Yale University Press, 1996).

9. Jeffrey Hadden, *The Gathering Storm in the Churches* (Garden City, NY: Doubleday, 1969).

10. Joanna Gillespie provides a fascinating portrait of generational differences among Episcopal women. See Joanna B. Gillespie, "Gender and Generations in Congregations," in *Episcopal Women,* ed. C. Prelinger (New York: Oxford University Press, 1993).

11. Michele Dillon, *Catholic Identity: Balancing Reason, Faith, and Power* (New York: Cambridge University Press, 1999).

12. On these class-related differences in "taste" in church music, see Tex Sample, *White Soul: Country Music, the Church, and Working Americans* (Nashville: Abingdon, 1996), who is, of course, building on Pierre Bourdieu (*Language and Symbolic Power* [Cambridge, MA: Harvard University Press, 1991]) and others who have written about cultural capital (DiMaggio and Mohr, "Cultural Capital, Educational Attainment, and Marital Selection").

Chapter 6 / Bringing Doctrine Back into Action/ Michele Dillon

1. Patrick Carey, *Catholics in America: A History* (Westport, CT: Praeger, 2004).

2. Nathan Hatch, *The Democratization of American Christianity* (New Haven, CT: Yale University Press, 1989).

3. Jay Dolan, *The American Catholic Experience: A History from the Colonial Times to the Present* (Garden City, NY: Doubleday, 1985).

4. Carey, *Catholics in America,* 28.

5. Ibid., 28–29.

6. For a summary of Americanism and Modernism see Michele Dillon, *Catholic Identity: Balancing Reason, Faith, and Power* (New York: Cambridge University Press, 1999), 45–46.

7. John O'Malley, *Tradition and Transition: Historical Perspectives on Vatican II* (Wilmington, DE: Michael Glazier, 1989).

8. John Seidler and Katherine Meyer, *Conflict and Change in the Catholic Church* (New Brunswick, NJ: Rutgers University Press, 1989).

9. Dillon, *Catholic Identity,* 49–53.

10. Anthony Pogorelc, "Social Movements within Organizations: The Case of Call to Action and U.S. Catholic Bishops." diss., Purdue University, 2002.

11. Because the question responses of VOTF founders/leaders (N=35) are very similar to the answers provided by VOTF members (N=1273), and because of the members' much larger sample size, I focus here on the percentage distributions in the results from the survey of VOTF members.

12. Eighty-nine percent of VOTF leaders report weekly or almost weekly Mass attendance, and 69 percent pray daily.

13. Dillon, *Catholic Identity.*

14. Andrew Greeley, *Priests: A Calling in Crisis* (Chicago: University of Chicago Press, 2004); Larry Witham, *Who Shall Lead Them? The Future of Ministry in America* (New York: Oxford University Press, 2005).

15. Greeley, *Priests,* 92–95.

16. Ibid., 94.

17. Ibid.

18. Forty-three percent of men compared to 34 percent of women have served on the parish council, and 32 percent of men compared to 13 percent of women have served on the finance council.

19. Despite the slogan that the "church never changes," the church's history is replete with examples of changes in doctrine and church practices. Most recently, Vatican II changed doctrine when, for example, it moved to a new understanding of religious freedom and its implications for personal conscience and church-state relations. Similarly, the shift from Latin to a vernacular liturgy was not simply a change in a church practice but also reflects the doctrinal shift toward an emphasis on realizing the church as the People of God and thus participating communally in Catholicism's core sacraments. The dogma of Jesus is immutable, but what Jesus means for Catholics in their particular context is clearly open to adaptation and revision while still being in continuity with Revelation and the church's living Tradition. See David Tracy, *Plurality and Ambiguity* (San Francisco: Harper & Row, 1987).

Chapter 7 / Voice of the Faithful Survey / Mary E. Hines

1. James E. Muller and Charles Kenney, *Keep the Faith, Change the Church* (New York: Rodale, 2004), 243–45.

2. Synod of Bishops, "The Final Report," *Origins* 15 (December 19, 1985): 444–53.

3. Edward Schillebeeckx, *The Church with a Human Face* (New York: Crossroad, 1985), 74–75.

4. Muller and Kenney, *Keep the Faith*, 137.

5. Avery Dulles's book *Models of the Church* (New York: Doubleday, 1974), written shortly after the council, describes several models or images of the church: institution, herald, servant, sacrament, and mystical communion. People of God is the more historical of the two examples of mystical communion that Dulles offers, the other being Body of Christ, a more Christomonistic image.

6. Johannes Metz, *Followers of Christ*, trans. Thomas Linton (New York: Paulist, 1978), 11–12.

7. I recognize that there is in fact some overlap in membership. The survey reports that one in four members of VOTF are members of CTA or another group.

8. Muller and Kenney, *Keep the Faith*, 127–28.

9. See the discussion of Call to Action in Mary E. Hines, "Ecclesiology for a Public Church: The United States Context," *Catholic Theological Society of America Proceedings* 55 (2000): 40–43.

10. VOTF leaders were told by Bishop Edyvean that they had an image problem of being too liberal (Muller and Kenney, *Keep the Faith*, 138).

11. The Community of Sant'Egidio is a lay movement that began in Rome in 1968 following Vatican II. For further information see its website: *www.santegidio.org/en*.

12. When asked what is most important to them about the church, respondents often mentioned the liturgy, certainly also central to the church's self-understanding. The relationship of the liturgy to the church's mission in the world was not often cited.

13. Chapter 2 of *Lumen Gentium* entitled "The People of God," of course refers to all the members of the church, lay and clergy, but it was a new and heady experience for laity of the time, accustomed to equating the church with the clergy, to find themselves included and given active roles in the church.

14. See "Organizational Structures of the Catholic Church: A Primer," VOTF, 2005.

15. Michael J. Buckley, "Resources for Reform for the First Millennium," in *Common Calling: The Laity and Governance of the Catholic Church,* ed. Stephen J. Pope (Washington, DC: Georgetown University Press, 2004), 71–86.

16. Francine Cardman, "Laity and the Development of Doctrine," in *Common Calling,* 51–69.

17. See John Henry Newman, "On Consulting the Faithful in Matters of Doctrine," *The Rambler* (July 1859).

18. Joseph Ratzinger, "Free Expression and Obedience in the Church," in *The Church: Readings in Theology,* ed. Hugo Rahner (New York: P. J. Kenedy and Sons, 1963), 214.

Chapter 8 / "The Faith We Are Called to Keep ... and to Spread" / Robert Imbelli

1. "Building a Church of Communion" (New York: National Pastoral Life Conference, 2005), 14.

2. Ibid.

3. Ibid., 18.

4. Richard John Neuhaus, *First Things,* November 2005, 64.

5. See *www.votf.org/Who_We_Are/statementofbelief.html.*

6. Ibid.

7. Peter Steinfels, *A People Adrift: The Crisis of the Roman Catholic Church in America* (New York: Simon and Schuster, 2003), 1.

8. Ibid., 39.

9. "Dogmatic Constitution on the Church" (*Lumen Gentium*), no. 8.

10. Karl Rahner, "Christian Living Formerly and Today," in *Theological Investigations,* vol. 7 (New York: Herder, 1971), 41. For a provocative and relevant treatment of this rich theme, see Frans Jozef van Beeck, *Catholic Identity after Vatican II* (Chicago: Loyola University Press, 1985).

11. See Luke Timothy Johnson, *Living Jesus: Learning the Heart of the Gospel* (San Francisco: Harper, 1999).

12. John Paul II, *Novo Millennio Ineunte* (Boston: Pauline Books and Media, 2001), no. 29. See also the illuminating article of David Burrell, "Jesus and the Qur'an: The Word of God among Us," in *Who Do You Say I Am? Confessing the Mystery of Christ,* ed. John Cavadini and Laura Holt (Notre Dame: University of Notre Dame Press, 2004), 173–85.

13. Francis J. Butler, "A Professional Code of Ethics Reflecting the Nature of a Christian Vocation and an Understanding of Leadership in the Church," in *Church Ethics and Its Organizational Context: Learning from the Sex Abuse Scandal in the Catholic Church,* ed. Jean M. Bartunek, Mary Ann Hinsdale, and James F. Keenan (New York: Rowman and Littlefield, 2006), 141.

14. Ronald Rolheiser, *The Holy Longing: The Search for a Christian Spirituality* (New York: Doubleday, 1999), 74.

15. See *Lumen Gentium,* nos. 1 and 48.

16. Ibid., no. 40.

17. *Novo Millennio Ineunte,* no. 43.

18. "Building a Church of Communion," 9.

19. George Orwell, "Politics and the English Language," in *Why I Write* (New York: Penguin Books, 2005), 102–20.

20. See Cardinal Joseph Bernardin and Archbishop Oscar Lipscomb, *Catholic Common Ground Initiative: Foundational Documents* (New York: Crossroad, 1997).

21. See Paul Griffiths, "Gen Y and the Church of Choice," *Boston College Magazine* 64, no. 4 (Fall 2004): 50–54. Also John F. Kavanaugh, *Following Christ in a Consumer Society: The Spirituality of Cultural Resistance* (Maryknoll, NY: Orbis, 1991).

Chapter 9 / The Virtues of Loyalty / William A. Gamson

I am indebted to the participants in the Boston College Media/Movement Research and Action Project (MRAP) for helpful suggestions on an earlier version of this paper and to Heidi Swarts in particular for reminding me of the relevance of the concept of "moral shock."

1. Albert O. Hirschman, *Exit, Voice, and Loyalty: Responses to Decline in Firms, Organizations, and States* (Cambridge, MA: Harvard University Press, 1970).

2. Ibid., 81.

3. Ibid., 78.

4. Ibid., 79.

5. Ibid., 80.

6. Jeff Goodwin, James M. Jasper, and Francesca Polletta, *Passionate Politics: Emotions and Social Movements* (Chicago: University of Chicago Press, 2001).

7. David A. Zizik, "Voice of the Faithful Misleads the Laity," *National Catholic Reporter*, August 29, 2003.

Chapter 10 / Fundamental Strategic Tasks for Leaders Organizing Grassroots Insurgencies / John D. McCarthy

1. Hanspeter Kriesi, "Political Context and Opportunity," in *The Blackwell Companion to Social Movements*, ed. David A. Snow, Sarah A. Soule, and Hanspeter Kriesi (Malden, MA: Blackwell Publishing, 2004), 67–90; Hanspeter Kriesi, Ruud Koopmans, Jan Willem Duyvendak, and Marco Guini, "New Social Movements and Political Opportunities in Western Europe," *European Journal of Political Research* 22 (1992): 219–44; Doug McAdam, "Conceptual Origins, Current Problems, Future Directions," in *Comparative Perspectives on Social Movements: Political Opportunities, Mobilizing Structures and Cultural Framings*, ed. Doug McAdam, John D. McCarthy, and Mayer N. Zald (New York: Cambridge University Press, 1996), 23–40; J. Craig Jenkins and Charles Perrow, "Insurgency of the Powerless: Farm Worker Movements," *American Sociological Review* 42 (1977): 248–68.

2. McAdam, "Conceptual Origins, Current Problems, Future Directions."

3. Calvin Morrill, Mayer N. Zald, and Hayagreeva Rao, "Covert Political Conflicts in Organizations: Challenges from Below," *Annual Review of Sociology* 29 (2003): 391–415; Mayer N. Zald, "The Strange Career of an Idea and Its Resurrection: Social Movements in Organizations," *Journal of Management Inquiry* 14 (2005): 157–66; Mayer N. Zald and Michael Berger, "Social Movements in Organizations: Coup d'état, Bureaucratic Insurgency, and Mass Movement," *American Journal of Sociology* 83 (1978): 823–61.

4. Margaret Keck and Katherine Sikkink, *Activists beyond Borders* (Ithaca, NY: Cornell University Press, 1998).

5. David Snow, E. Burke Rochford Jr., Steven K. Worden, and Robert D. Benford, "Frame Alignment Processes, Micromobilization, and Movement Participation," *American Sociological Review* 51 (1986): 464–81; Robert D. Benford and David A. Snow, "Framing Processes and Social Movements: An Overview and Assessment," *Annual Review of Sociology* 26 (2000): 611–39; David A. Snow, "Framing Processes, Ideology, and Discursive Fields," in *The Blackwell Companion to Social Movements,* ed. David A. Snow, Sarah A. Soule, and Hanspeter Kriesi (Malden, MA: Blackwell Publishing, 2004), 380–412.

6. Holly J. McCammon, "Stirring Up Suffrage Sentiment: The Formation of the State Woman Suffrage Organizations, 1866–1914," *Social Forces* 80 (2001): 449–80.

7. John D. McCarthy, "Pro-Life and Pro-Choice Mobilization: Infrastructural Deficits and New Technologies," *Social Movements in an Organizational Society* (New Brunswick, NJ: Transaction Books, 1987), 49–66.

8. VOTF has also assiduously avoided taking any position on "hot button" issues such as celibate clergy and sexual preference in an effort to distance itself from the divisiveness in contrast to the divisive rhetoric of its main counter-movement organization, Faithful Voice (*www.faithfulvoice.com*).

9. Charles Tilly, *Popular Contention in Great Britain, 1758–1834* (Cambridge, MA: Harvard University Press, 1995); Elisabeth Clemens, "Organizational Repertoires and Institutional Change: Women's Groups and the Transformation of U.S. Politics, 1890–1925," *American Journal of Sociology* 98 (1993): 755–98; Elisabeth Clemens, *The People's Lobby: Organizational Innovation and the Rise of Interest Group Politics in the United States, 1890–1925* (Chicago: University of Chicago Press, 1996); Verta Taylor and Nella Van Dyke, " 'Get Up, Stand Up': Tactical Repertoires of Social Movements," in *The Blackwell Companion to Social Movements,* ed. David A. Snow, Sarah A. Soule, and Hanspeter Kriesi (Malden, MA: Blackwell Publishing, 2004), 262–93.

10. John D. McCarthy and Mayer N. Zald, "Resource Mobilization and Social Movements: A Partial Theory," *American Journal of Sociology* 82 (1977): 1212–41; Theda Skocpol, *Diminished Democracy: From Membership to Management in American Civic Life* (Norman: University of Oklahoma Press, 2003); Robert D. Putnam, "Tuning In Tuning Out: The Strange Disappearance of Social Capital in America," *PS* 28 (1995): 664–83.

11. Debra Minkoff, "Producing Social Capital: National Movements and Civil Society," *American Behavioral Scientist* 40 (1997): 606–19.

12. John D. McCarthy, "Persistence and Change among Nationally Federated Social Movements," in *Social Movements and Organization Theory,* ed. Gerald F. Davis, Doug McAdam, W. Richard Scott and Mayer N. Zald (New York: Cambridge University Press, 2005): 193–225.

13. Lawrence S. Rothenberg, *Linking Citizens to Government* (New York: Cambridge University Press, 1992).

14. John D. McCarthy and Mark Wolfson, "Resource Mobilization by Local Social Movement Organizations: Agency, Strategy and Organization in the Movement Against Drinking and Driving," *American Sociological Review* 61 (1996): 1070–88.

15. David S. and Sidney Tarrow, *The Social Movement Society: Contentious Politics for a New Century* (Lanham, MD: Rowman and Littlefield, 1998).

16. While this may seem an incredibly large number of members, to put the number into some perspective, the Knights of Columbus presently report 1.7 million

members, and at their peaks MADD reported 3.2 million (mostly isolated) members, the NAACP 400,000 members, and NOW 250,000 members. (McCarthy, "Persistence and Change among Nationally Federated Social Movements").

17. David A. Snow, Louis A. Zurcher, and Sheldon Eckland-Olson, "Social Networks and Social Movements: A Microstructural Approach to Differential Recruitment," *American Sociological Review* 45 (1980): 787–801; Bert Klandermans and Dirk Omega, "Potentials, Networks, Motivations, and Barriers: Steps toward Participation in Social Movements," *American Sociological Review* 52 (1987): 519–31; Bert Klandermans, *The Social Psychology of Protest* (New York: Blackwell, 1997); Bert Klandermans, "The Demand and Supply of Participation: Social-Psychological Correlates of Participation in Social Movements," in *The Blackwell Companion to Social Movements*, ed. David A. Snow, Sarah A. Soule, and Hanspeter Kriesi (Malden, MA: Blackwell, 2004), 360–79; Mario Diani, "Networks and Participation," in *The Blackwell Companion to Social Movements*, ed. David A. Snow, Sarah A. Soule, and Hanspeter Kriesi (Malden, MA: Blackwell Publishing, 2004), 339–59.

18. McCarthy and Wolfson, "Resource Mobilization by Local Social Movement Organizations."

Chapter 11 / Conclusion

1. D'Antonio et al., National Survey of American Catholics, 2005.

2. John Allen, "Bishops Peer into Cyberspace" *National Catholic Reporter,* April 17, 1998.

3. They are the dioceses of Tucson and Spokane, and the archdiocese of Portland, Oregon.

4. Allen, "Bishops Peer into Cyberspace."

5. Philip Jenkins, *The New Anti-Catholicism: The Last Acceptable Prejudice* (Oxford and New York: Oxford University Press, 2003).

6. Mary Fainsod Katzenstein, "Discursive Activism by Catholic Feminists," in *The Social Movements Reader,* ed. Jeff Goodwin and James M. Jasper (Malden, MA: Blackwell, 2003).

7. James E. Muller and Charles Kenney, *Keep the Faith, Change the Church* (Emmaus, PA: Rodale Books, 2004), 98.

8. William A. Gamson, "Defining Movement Success," in *The Social Movements Reader,* ed. Jeff Goodwin and James M. Jasper (Malden, MA: Blackwell, 2003).

9. James M. Jasper, "The Emotions of Protest," in *The Social Movements Reader,* ed. Jeff Goodwin and James M. Jasper (Malden, MA: Blackwell, 2003).

10. Randall Collins, "Stratification, Emotional Energy, and the Transient Emotions," in *Research Agendas in the Sociology of Emotions,* ed. Theodore D. Kemper (Albany: SUNY Press, 1990), 28.

11. Jasper, "The Emotions of Protest."

Coauthors and Contributors

Dr. William D'Antonio, after serving in the U.S. Navy in World War II, received his B.A. from Yale University, his Master's from the University of Wisconsin, and his Ph.D. from Michigan State University. He has taught at Michigan State, Notre Dame, and the University of Connecticut. From 1982 to 1991 he was Executive Officer of the American Sociological Association in Washington, DC. He is currently a Fellow at the Life Cycle Institute of Catholic University. With three colleagues he recently published *American Catholics Today: New Realities of Their Faith and Their Church*. He was a Fulbright Senior Scholar to Italy in 2004, and received an Honorary Doctor of Humane Letters from St. Michael's College in 2003.

Rev. Dr. Anthony Pogorelc is a Sulpician priest on the faculty of the Theological College of Catholic University. He also teaches in the Department of Sociology and is a Fellow in the Life Cycle Institute. He has an M.Div. from St. Michael's College of the Toronto School of Theology and an M.S. and a Ph.D. from Purdue University. His specialization is the sociology of religion, with special focus on social movements and professional ministers.

Dr. Nancy Ammerman is Professor of Sociology of Religion at Boston University, with a joint appointment between the School of Theology and the Department of Sociology. She earned her Ph.D. degree from Yale University and has also taught at Hartford Seminary in the Institute for Religion Research, and at Emory University. Her most recent book, *Pillars of Faith: American Congregations and Their Partners,* describes the common patterns that shape the work of Americans' diverse communities of faith. It was awarded the 2005 Distinguished Book Award by the Religion Section of the American Sociological Association.

Dr. Michele Dillon received her undergraduate education in Ireland (B. Soc. Sc., M. Soc. Sc., University College Dublin) and her Ph.D. in sociology from the University of California at Berkeley. Her research interests are in the sociology of religion broadly interpreted to engage important questions in sociological theory and the sociology of culture. Among her publications is *Catholic Identity: Balancing Reason, Faith, and Power.* Dr. Dillon's current research uses longitudinal life course data spanning adolescence and late adulthood to examine the socio-biographical antecedents, life course trajectories, and social implications of religion and spirituality in a sample of American men and women born in the 1920s.

Dr. William Gamson is interested in the efforts of social movements to change society. His earlier work focused on what kinds of organizational and influence strategies are most likely to succeed under what circumstances. Since coming to Boston College in 1982 he has focused on the role of the mass media in the process of change, working with graduate and post-doctoral students on the Media Research and Action Project (MRAP). His most recent book, *Shaping Abortion Discourse* (2002), coauthored with Myra Ferree, Juergen Gerhards, and Dieter Rucht, compares the success of different types of groups in Germany and the United States in influencing abortion discussions in the mass media.

Dr. Mary Hines is Professor of Theology and Chair of the Departments of Religious Studies and Philosophy at Emmanuel College. In addition to her teaching, her research interests include contemporary theologies of the church, feminist theologies, theology of Mary, and ecumenism. She is a long-term appointee of the U.S. Catholic bishops to the Anglican-Roman Catholic Consultation in the United States. She is the author of *The Transformation of Dogma* and *What Ever Happened to Mary?* She is also co-editor of the *Cambridge Companion to Karl Rahner* and has published numerous articles in ecclesiology, theology of Mary, and feminist theology.

Rev. Dr. Robert P. Imbelli, a priest of the Archdiocese of New York, studied in Rome during the years of the Second Vatican Council and was ordained there in 1965. After parish ministry in New York, he obtained his Ph.D. in Systematic Theology from Yale University. He has taught theology at the New York Archdiocesan Seminary and at the Maryknoll School of Theology, and has been visiting lecturer at Princeton Theological Seminary and Fordham University. From 1986 to 1993, Fr. Imbelli was Director of the Institute of Religious Education and Pastoral Ministry at Boston College and is currently Associate Professor of Theology at Boston College. He has been a member of the Steering Committee of the Common Ground Initiative since its founding by Cardinal Bernardin. He is also a member of the Catholic-Anglican Dialogue in the United States.

Dr. John McCarthy is Professor of Sociology and Chair of the Department at the Pennsylvania State University. He was on the faculty of the Catholic University of America for twenty-five years. His research interests include social movements and collective action, the sociology of protest, the policing of protest, and the sociology of social movement organizations. Currently he is at work with Andrew Martin and Clark McPhail on a study of campus community public order disturbances.

Index

Of Related Interest

Patrick Fleming, Sue Lauber-Fleming, Mark Matousek
BROKEN TRUST
*Stories of Pain, Hope, and Healing
from Clerical Abuse Survivors and Abusers*

This hopeful book is being hailed as the one book everyone must read on the clerical sexual abuse scandals. First-person stories from priest abusers and abuse survivors, with insights for personal healing and church renewal.

"Everyone should read *Broken Trust!*"
— **Fr. Ronald Rolheiser, O.F.M.,**
author of *The Holy Longing*

"This insightful work, *Broken Trust*, reintroduces the theme of forgiveness and reconciliation as a way forward for the Church in responding to the sexual abuse crisis. The stories stir in us the ancient memories of the Church about redemption, not only for individuals, but for the Church as a community of faith. By tapping into these deep sources of our tradition, we find the possibility of a hope which is totally undeserved because it is total grace." — **Bishop Blase J. Cupich,**
Diocese of Rapid City, South Dakota

0-8245-2410-1, 240pp, paperback

crossroad

Of Related Interest

Robert McClory
AS IT WAS IN THE BEGINNING
The Coming Democratization of the Catholic Church

"With courage and conviction, intelligence and wit, Robert McClory delivers a fascinating study of the church's past and present in order to divine its future. McClory is honest with himself, charitable to those who would disagree, but uncompromising in his argument for hope and, yes, even optimism. This is a model for the kind of debate the church needs, but too often avoids."
        — **David Gibson,** author of *The Coming Catholic Church*

Lay participation has a strong precedent in Catholic Tradition! In this well-researched book, Robert McClory dispels the myth that the Catholic Church has functioned in a purely top-down leadership model. He shows there have been many periods in Catholic history when laypeople were consulted frequently and had strong, leading voices. McClory argues that a more democratic, decentralized church is nearly inevitable and helps to interpret the signs of the times for the world's longest-running corporation.

0-8245-2419-15, 192pp, paperback

Check your local bookstore for availability.
To order directly from the publisher,
please call 1-800-707-0670 for Customer Service
or visit our Web site at *www.cpcbooks.com.*
For catalog orders, please send your request to the address below.

THE CROSSROAD PUBLISHING COMPANY
16 Penn Plaza, Suite 1550
New York, NY 10001

All prices subject to change.

crossroad